New Directions in Policy History

Issues in Policy History
General Editor: Donald Critchlow

NEW DIRECTIONS IN POLICY HISTORY

Edited by
Julian E. Zelizer

The Pennsylvania State University Press
University Park, Pennsylvania

This work was originally published as a special issue of *Journal of Policy History* (vol. 17, no. 1, 2005). This is its first separate paperback publication.

Library of Congress Cataloging-in-Publication Data

New directions in policy history edited by Julian E. Zelizer.

      p. cm. — (Issues in policy history)
  "Originally published as a special issue of Journal of policy history (vol. 17, no. 1, 2005)" — T.p. verso.
    Includes bibliographical references.
    ISBN 0-271-02719-3 (alk. paper)
    1. Policy sciences—History. I. Zelizer, Julian E. II. Journal of policy history. III. Series.
H97.N489 2005
320. 6—dc22

                                 2005051486

The Pennsylvania State University Press is a member of the Assoc-iation of American University Presses.

It is the policy of The Pennsylvania State University Press to use acid-free paper. Publications on uncoated stock satisfy the minimum requirements of American National Standard for Information Sciences—Permanence of Paper for Printed Library Materials, ANSI Z39.48-1992.

Contents

Editor's Preface

Nearly twenty years ago, in the fall of 1985, the University of Notre Dame sponsored a conference on federal social policy in historical perspective. Leading scholars in the Social Sciences and History were invited to discuss the place of historical analysis in public policy. At this conference it was decided to launch a scholarly journal to provide a voice to scholars interested in understanding public policies and their development through historical inquiry and interpretation. Through funding from the University of Notre Dame and the support of Penn State University Press, the *Journal of Policy History* (*JPH*) was launched.

Those involved in the conference and the founding of the *JPH* believed that we were establishing not only a new subfield in History and the Social Sciences but also a new approach to historical scholarship. Through the study of policy history, those of us involved in the project believed, scholars would be able to integrate social history, political history, and intellectual history into the study of state development. We saw this as the next step in the development of policy history as a field.

From the outset, there were divisions among those who saw policy history as a means of informing policymakers and those historicists who saw the field primarily as a scholarly field without necessarily direct application to contemporary public policy. Ernest May, Richard Neustadt, Robert Kelley, Hugh Graham, and Otis Graham represented this view that policy history should be linked to public policy. Differences between the two approaches were only of degree and perspective. There was a shared belief that policy history was set to take off as an established field.

This optimism about the field was belied by the decline of American political and institutional history and the dominance of social and later cultural history in the 1980s and 1990s. Within a general context of a deteriorating job market for historians in general, policy history appeared marginalized, even while the *Journal of Policy History* continued to prosper in terms of the number of manuscripts submitted and the quality of essays published. Moreover, the subfield of American political development continued to grow within the American Political Science Association. Still, there was an emotional letdown for many who had entertained such high hopes for the new field of public history. The late Hugh Davis Graham captured this in his controversial essay "The Stunted Career of Policy History: A Critique and Agenda" published in *The Public Historian* (Spring 1993). In this essay, Graham lamented that policy history had experienced a checkered career within the academy and in policy circles. "Instead of emerging from the 1960s as a strengthened component of political history," he wrote, "its analytical power reinforced by the interdisciplinary ferment of the public history movement, policy history has wandered in unfocused directions." He added that "in the expanding professional world of policy analysts who advise decision-makers, historians have remained marginal. During the 1960s and 1970s graduate schools of public policy were created at many of the nation's leading institutions. . . . History courses, however, remained invisible in the curricula of the policy schools and historians were rarely found on their faculties or on the staffs of the policy institutes and think tanks."[1]

Although his concerns were not unfounded, Graham was too precipitous in declaring policy history a marginalized field. While often giving the appearance of operating under the radar of academic fashionability, policy history made steady progress in attracting younger scholars who undertook research in the field. Dissertations, articles, and books appeared on a wide-range of topics involving policy history. The *Journal of Policy History* and *Studies in American Political Development* became major outlets for historians and social scientists working in the field. As policy history entered into the twenty-first century, it appeared to have come into its own. Academic openings were announced in the field of policy history. Graham had lamented that historians were not in the major schools of public policy, and while this is often the case still, the John F. Kennedy School of Government recently appointed Alexander Keyssar to a distinguished chair in history and social policy. Another indication of the growth of the field came at the third annual meeting of Policy History in May 2004, when a group of younger and older scholars, including Edward Berkowitz, John Skrentny, Thomas Sugrue, and Dianne Pinderhughes appeared on a panel to evaluate the scholarship and legacy of Hugh Graham. At the conference, Julian Zelizer, the editor of this volume, announced a campaign to establish the Hugh Davis Graham Research Award to provide research support for archival research projects in political and policy history. Less than six months later, he announced that the endowment for this award had been established through the contributions from more than sixty donors.

As the field of policy history enters the twenty-first century, scholars are exploring new directions in the field. Policy history has moved beyond the narrow confines of social welfare history into women's history, fiscal policy, foreign relations, comparative politics, legal and administrative history, and health policy. These new directions are explored in this volume, which will be of benefit to established scholars, younger scholars just beginning their careers, and students who understand the importance of government in shaping social and cultural life in contemporary America.

Donald T. Critchlow
General Editor

---

[1] Hugh Davis Graham, "The Stunted Career of Policy History: A Critique and Agenda, *The Public Historian* 15:2 (Spring 1993). See in response, Donald T. Critchlow, "A Prognosis of Policy History: Stunted—or Deceivingly Vital?" *The Public Historian* 15:4 (Fall 1993).

JULIAN E. ZELIZER

Introduction:
New Directions in Policy History

The state of policy history is good. This is a dramatic change from only four years ago, when I started an article in this very journal about the evolution of policy history by asserting: "The future of policy history remains unclear."[1] At the time, my statement reflected the sentiment shared by many fellow policy historians who did not feel that professional opportunities had fully caught up with the intellectual vitality of the subfield.

But by the year 2004, the quality and the volume of scholarship have reached unprecedented levels. *The Journal of Policy History* and *Studies in American Political Development* offer innovative articles on a large variety of periods, issues, and actors. The lists of prestigious university presses that are publishing work on the evolution of domestic and foreign policy continues to expand at a brisk pace. Since it was founded in 1999, the Policy History Conference has become a routine trip for those in the subfield as it has been jam packed with exciting interdisciplinary panels.[2] Top graduate programs are filled with students interested in the relationship between state and society. Many scholars in sub-fields that were born out of the social history revolution have now turned their attention back to the public-political realm. As a result of this interest, there has even been a notable spike in the number of departments hiring political—often defined as policy—historians.

The road to success has not been easy. Policy history emerged in the 1970s through a group of maverick historians who sought to produce scholarship that would influence the decisions of government officials, the training of policy experts, as well as the historical profession. The founding generation included academic historians who were disenchanted with the move of their profession away from the study of government and formal politics. The founders likewise consisted of public historians who were seeking to write scholarship that appealed to those outside the academy. Many of these scholars came together at a conference at the Harvard Busi-

THE JOURNAL OF POLICY HISTORY, Vol. 17, No. 1, 2005.

ness School in 1978, convened by Professors Tom McGraw and Morton Keller. This landmark conference was the first time that practitioners came to see themselves as part of a distinct sub-field. Since then, policy historians have written about such issues as the institutional and cultural patterns that effected policy over time, the soundness of conventional assumptions about the past, the influence of political culture on public policy, and the evolution of the policymaking process.[3]

There have been many landmark moments since the 1970s. In 1984, for instance, Tom McGraw won the Pulitzer Prize for his book on the history of economic regulation in the twentieth century.[4] Professors Ernest May and Richard Neustadt taught one of the most popular classes at Harvard University's prestigious Kennedy School of Government that focused on the applied uses of historical policy analysis. Based on their class, their book entitled *Thinking In Time* inspired many students and teachers to appreciate how historical analysis had practical value to public officials.[5] In 1987, Donald Critchlow announced the formation of *The Journal of Policy History*, which became the premier outlet for this research. By the early-1990s, there were numerous scholars whose work made policy central to their study.[6]

Despite these accomplishments, members of the sub-field confronted obstacle after obstacle. During their first two decades as a sub-field, policy historians were unable to secure a foothold in the mainstream of any profession. Most policy schools did not employ historians in the 1980s and early-1990s, because their programs generally privileged economics and organizational studies. Policy historians did not help matters by abandoning the applied spirit that animated their founders.

The historical profession, moreover, maintained its emphasis on studying social life and popular culture from "the bottom up." Government elites, institutions, and public policies were of marginal concern. In this atmosphere, the major historical publishing outlets such as *The American Historical Review* and *Journal of American History* only accepted a minimal number of works related to policy. Attendees at the Organization of American Historians or American Historical Association Conferences were more likely to see panels on the formation of working-class communities, gender roles, or the struggles of marginalized groups than discussions about the history of health care, tax, and public housing policies.

These changes were not unwelcome. The field of American history diversified significantly as it started to include a much richer canvass of subjects and issues being studied. Without any doubt, the field was much stronger and inclusive by the 1990s than it had been in the 1950s. The pluralization of historical studies is a change that will not be reversed. But there was a cost for the study of the political past, since the initial decades of the social and cultural history revolution were treated as a zero-sum game: the sub-field of political history was downplayed in order to make room for the new areas of intellectual growth.[7]

The sub-field of policy history only survived because there were historians willing to specialize on these subjects despite the professional costs they incurred. The sub-field also benefited from scholars in other disciplines, such as political science and sociology, who were stimulated by the new historical institutionalism to explore how institutions structured, and restructured, policies over long periods of time. Historical institutionalism gained an organizational base within the American Political Science Association following the formation of the History and Politics section of the association in 1988.

Recently, however, conditions have improved as the professional opportunities are slowly catching up to the intellectual advances of policy history. As previously mentioned, the history profession has begun to open its doors to the study of public policy, political elites, and government institutions, at the same time that the publishing world has been offering multiple outlets for this work. Although policy historians have not been able to break into the realm of think tanks or government staff (and there are scholars who would prefer to avoid these venues altogether), more historians have gained national reputations in media venues that discuss public affairs. There are also a handful of policy historians who are currently employed in public affairs programs at institutions such as Harvard, UCLA, and Duke.

Policy history holds tremendous intellectual promise because it offers numerous ways for the new generation of political historians to chart a fresh intellectual path for their field. As political historians wrestle with the challenges of reconstituting their subject matter without recreating the problems or weaknesses of previous scholarship, many are finding that policy constitutes an ideal focal point. One of the biggest advantages of policy history is that it can result in the formulation of fresh chronological frameworks for understanding political development. In recent years, younger political historians have been struggling to break free from the traditional time frames used in political history, ranging from presidential centered accounts, to the cycles of liberalism, and conservatism, to the modernization schema that claimed the turn-of-the twentieth century to be *the* central watershed moment in America's political evolution.[8] While those older time frames have much to offer, political historians are eager to experiment with different approaches to organizing political time—a central goal of the historical profession—and testing to see whether the existing scholarship has missed watershed turning points or historical patterns. Importantly, policy does not fit into most existing chronological

structures. Indeed, different public policies have different timelines, something that makes the subject enormously challenging. As policy historians delve into different policy sectors, they are starting to perceive more
complex chronological structures of political history than previous historians had suggested. For instance, a recent history of tax subsidies that
provide social welfare has revealed that the period of greatest state expansion took place between the 1970s and 1990s, decades that are usually
characterized as being dominated by the anti-government conservative
movement.[9]

Policy history also allows historians to incorporate a broader range of
actors into narratives than previous generations of historians have been
able to do. The tension between scholars who study elite politics and grass
roots politics quickly dissipates when policy is made the center of inquiry.
After all, public policies are crafted by government officials in alliance
with, and in response to, other social and political actors. Federal, state,
and local policies influence—and are reshaped by—all types of social actors and institutions. A history of diplomatic policy during World War II,
for instance, can encompass everyone from the White House officials who
made the final decisions to go to war to the citizens whose lives were
forever altered as a result of combat. A history of social welfare, moreover, must span from the committee rooms on Capitol Hill where legislators hammered out compromises about who should or should not be
included in federal provisions to the poverty-stricken homes of northern
urban families where individuals were deeply affected by the government
monies they received. Social and cultural historians have looked at how
race and gender has influenced the formation of public policy, and how in
turn, policies structure social relationships throughout the country.[10]

Recent work in policy history has thus started to accomplish what
many scholars have been talking about in abstract theory for years: breaking down the once-rigid barriers between state and society through the
use of policy as the object of study and not locating scholarship in any
single social realm. Policy likewise encourages historians to examine institutions that are often overlooked by historians, such as the mass news
media, local government, and the non-profit sector.

Comparative and internationalist scholars can also rejoice over the
focus on policy history. Regardless of the unique institutional and cultural configurations that exist in different countries around the globe,
every nation deals with a common set of policy problems. As Peter Baldwin
reminds us, different nation-states handle common problems—poverty,
war, health care, urban decay, taxation, and more—in different ways.
Unlike many subjects in political history (such as the presidency, for example), public policy provides scholars with an opportunity to see how

countries deal differently or similarly with common problems and how policy challenges have been handled through international networks.

Finally, policy continues to offer historians an excellent opportunity to contribute to contemporary public debates—an animating motive of the founders of the sub-field. This vision has remained unfulfilled. Since the 1970s, policy historians have tended to write for an audience of fellow scholars while policy analysts have not enthusiastically embraced historical research. But the promise of this sub-field—to break out of academia and influence the public realm—remains alive and historians who often clamor to make their scholarship more relevant beyond the classroom have an opportunity to provide advice and insights about problems that nation's currently face. Historical debates, for example, have been raging at the front and center of public discourse throughout the war with Iraq in 2003 as well as during the post-war reconstruction.

Despite all of its promise and potential, however, policy history still has a long way to go before the sub-field realizes its full potential. Having reached a critical point when the intellectual vitality of the sub-field is thriving and the professional opportunities are expanding, policy historians must re-think the types of questions that we ask, improve our analytic and methodological strategies, and broaden the range of issues that we consider. In the words of the popular television chef Emeril Lagasse, it is time to "kick it up a notch." In doing so, it is essential that we connect our discoveries to larger historical narratives and political science debates. More importantly, we need to reexamine our basic analytic assumptions and move beyond artificial sub-field boundaries that have inhibited us from expanding the horizons of our research.

The contributors to this volume tackle these challenges by anticipating new directions that policy history is likely to take in the coming years. As the second generation of policy historians launch their careers, the time is right to reflect on the foundations of the sub-field. Since policy history has always been inter-disciplinary, the contributors include political scientists, historians, and sociologists. Each contributor looks at policy history through a distinct disciplinary lens to discuss how the sub-field should evolve.

Two of the authors, Peter Baldwin (History) and Paul Pierson (Political Science), focus on some the biggest overriding questions confronting the sub-field by re-examining the analytic and methodological foundations that have guided policy historians since the 1970s. Baldwin challenges the basic comparative assumptions that have been used when analyzing policy history. Embracing an ideal model of the state, most scholars have explicitly or implicitly accepted a hierarchy that separates "strong" from "weak" states (usually, with the United States as a model of the weak state and countries in Northern Europe as shining examples of strong states). This hierarchy has served as the focal point for historical narratives as they have sought to explain how the policies of countries fall at a particular point in this continuum. Surveying recent research, Baldwin reveals that the hierarchy masks more than it reveals. Research has made it abundantly clear that each nation-state handles different kinds of policies in different ways. Some nation-states that look non-interventionist, for example, have a very strong influence on civil society when one opens up discussion to include a broader range of government interventions. While direct social welfare spending has been relatively low in the United States, when compared with other industrialized western democracies, the federal government spends a vast amount of money indirectly by offering tax incentives and tax breaks to select groups of citizens. The U.S. has also developed a vibrant system of private sector welfare that is often subsidized—and works in tandem with—government programs.[11] These are just some examples of how characterizations of "weak" states fall apart when historians take a more nuanced look at what constitutes policy. At the same time, allegedly "strong" states have refused to intervene in certain areas. Sweden, for example, has maintained a regressive tax system.[12] Britain, Germany, and France, moreover, have adopted a laissez-faire approach toward public health issues such as smoking and alcohol consumption. European countries lagged behind the United States, rather than vice versa, with regard to the protection of individual privacy or the rights of the disabled.

In the end, Baldwin urges policy historians to retain a comparative framework while avoiding the hierarchy that is based on ideal notions of the state. Baldwin posits that we should understand historically how and why states handle similar problems in multiple ways and how conceptions of the state vary throughout the world. Most important, Baldwin argues that the "multiplicity of policy styles" should itself be the focus of scholarly inquiry.

Whereas Baldwin encourages us to think in new ways about the analytic assumptions that we use to understand policies in different nations, Paul Pierson embraces a complicated challenge that few historians have been willing to tackle: explaining why studying policy historically matters at all. Most historians would tend to answer this question by simply asserting that the past is crucial. But for policy historians to seriously engage other disciplines in the social sciences, we need to think more self-consciously about what they are doing and why it is important analytically. Pierson offers several rationales for why policy history is significant in contrast to other social scientific approaches. Pierson argues, for example, that policy must be understood as an unfolding process. Scholars who develop a "snapshot" portrait of public policy, which focuses just on the moment of enactment, frequently develop inaccurate hypotheses. When looking moments of policy reform, for instance, it is essential to follow reforms after they have passed Congress to understand which reforms stick and which implode. Another contribution of policy history, Pierson argues, is to reveal the effects of policy over time. The greatest impact of policies can be to reshape political interests or reconstitute institutional configurations, effects that are hard to glean without temporal analysis. Furthermore, the pressure behind policy change is usually the culmination of a long period of incremental developments. "'Snapshot' views of major policy events often focus on the immediate sources of change—the catalysts," Pierson explains. "They will often have a hard time identifying the role of structural factors. These, by their very nature, will typically show little variation within a limited period." Scholars who focus on a limited time-period when developing their explanations about public policy are thus likely to miss the broader forces pushing policy change that take decades, if not centuries, to accumulate such as demography or technology. Historical studies of policy likewise move beyond the functionalist explanation of politics that has been so prevalent in the social sciences for decades. Pierson shows that the long-term effects that policies have are often the result of broad historical social and political processes rather than the result of individual choices.

Policy historians also need to rethink some core assumptions that have been used when explaining the trajectory of American policy history. For example, Jill Quadagno (Sociology) and Debra Street (Sociology) challenge the common use of "anti-statism" to explain America's allegedly laggard welfare state. The argument about a laggard state in America, they say, has been a "staple across all historical eras." While acknowledging that anti-statism is one ideology that some Americans believe and that in some areas of policy America has trailed behind other nations, Quadagno and Street offer the outlines of a very different story. Looking at several policy domains, they argue that the causal link between anti-statism and public policy is tenuous. Moreover, in many areas of government, the American state resembles—rather than differs from—comparable countries. Quadagno and Street show how Americans have often been willing to allow the state to expand in its power, as has been the case with pensions and health care since World War II. Writing about health care for the elderly, for instance, the authors argue that "provider payment policies in Medicare to control costs have empowered the federal government in ways remarkably similar to policies adopted by other countries." Rather than a rigid ideological consensus, Quadagno and Street say that anti-statism has been a rhetorical tool that is tactically employed by interest groups in their battles against the federal government.

Eileen Boris (History) analyzes how historical scholarship on race and gender has significantly challenged—and frequently undermined—conventional narratives about policy history. The literature has accomplished several objectives. First, following the "policy turn" which pushed these scholars to look at public-political power, the work on race and gender in the 1980s and 1990s has revealed how marginalized groups played a significant role in the expansion and character of the federal government. Moreover, post-modern analysis in the 1990s opened up the categories of race and gender, revealing how they were not fixed or timeless. Indeed, government policies influenced how these social relationships were experienced and how they fit within the parameters of citizenship at any given point in history. Historians have also found how conceptions of race and gender were imbedded in public policies and the language used to define those programs. Boris concludes by stating that the evolving categories of race and gender—and, more importantly, the relationship between them, racialized gender—must be incorporated into public policy history.

Another finding of this volume is that policy historians, particularly those who study the United States, must broaden the range of issues and subjects that they focus on. Policy history has been in an "internalist" phase, common to most fields and sub-fields when they start, in that scholars focused on their own subject matter and did not do as much as possible to connect their findings to other literatures. With all the advances of policy history, the sub-field has remained isolated from several other critical areas of historical study where there are important connections that must be addressed. For example, Robert McMahon (History) examines why diplomacy has remained so marginal to policy history since both sub-fields shared such a common set of interests and professional challenges. Ironically, diplomatic and policy history both took form as independent sub-fields, just as the profession lost interest in those subject matters. Rather than uniting into a common front, policy and diplomatic history—despite a similar focus and shared methodologies—kept their distance by trying to build individual, autonomous base or to link up with more sub-fields that had a better potential to broaden their popularity. The result was unfortunate since each sub-field developed insights that would be useful to the other, and each tackled an area of policy (with policy historians generally focusing on domestic policy) that was closely linked to the other. In recent years, both sub-fields have been enjoying a renaissance and McMahon argues that this is the time the sub-fields should consider joining forces and building on their collective strengths. "Scholars of the domestic and foreign dimensions of policy . . . have far more in common than most of them recognize." His essay points to ways that schol-ars of diplomacy and war could benefit from the work being produced on domestic policy. For example, the increased attention by diplomatic his-torians to internationalist history (breaking free of the nation-state as a defining parameter for studying policy) can help policy historians jettison the bias toward American Exceptionalism. McMahon also argues that this partnership will push historians to look more closely at the interconnec-tions between domestic and diplomatic policy rather than treating them as separate entities.

While McMahon suggests points of convergence with diplomatic his-tory, Reuel Schiller (Law and History) reminds readers that the law is an integral component to public policy that has been overlooked by most policy historians. As a result, legal and policy history have been moving in two very related directions, but they have rarely communicated. In his essay, Schiller takes aim at some major works in the social sciences, such as Dan Carpenter's book on agency autonomy, to argue that ignoring the law leaves major holes in causal explanations about why institutions and policies take the form that they do.[13] Schiller offers several examples of how to forge a better relationship. In particular, he stresses the relation-ship between the courts and federal agencies. Schiller argues that we can learn from how the courts have constrained agency autonomy. According to Schiller, the law has been a powerful force in twentieth century state-building, and not just an obstacle as it has been portrayed by many schol-ars since the progressive era. Courts have inscribed their values into the modern government by imposing certain rules and ideals on agencies. Understanding the role of administrative law in policy history, helps an-swer big questions about why the government took the form that it did and the boundaries of action that have faced policymakers. This course of study, according to Schiller, also helps us see the evolution of legal values and to understand how those values are informed by broader social and cultural norms.

In other areas, the task is to start bringing together vast amounts of scholarship that have already been written on specific topics: the goal is no longer knowledge accumulation, but rather, to develop greater ana-lytic rigor, synthetic interpretation, and to raise new types of questions. Since the 1990s, scholars have written an extensive body of work on the growth of the welfare state, with particular emphasis on issues such as race, gender, business power, and hidden government benefits. Jacob Hacker (Political Science) argues that "while work on the American wel-fare state has dramatically improved our understanding of U.S. social policy development, there is a real risk that the stories that emerge will read like 'one damn thing after another'—study piled upon study, fact upon fact, without adequate integration, explanation, or advancement." Moving through each body of literature, Hacker points out key advances and persistent analytic flaws, such as the tendency to conflate the effect of policies with the intention of those who create the policies. After providing an insightful critique of each group, Hacker points out specific questions that should be central to all works on policy history, regardless of the policy domain or country they are studying. For example, Hacker urges policy historians to better understand the relationship between intensions and effects by focusing on social policy development, rather than any particular stage of the policymaking process: "scholars should trace the unfolding historical development of specific policies across long periods of attention and inattention, action and inaction." He also calls for a more systematic analysis of the historical evaluation power in social welfare policymaking and politics by thinking more clearly about how we gauge and define power in this realm. Echoing Paul Pierson, Hacker urges policy historians to do a better job of historicizing history in making a stronger and more explicit case about why history matters.

Therefore, this is a volume that points to the promise and potential of policy history. While the sub-field faces many challenges in the future, one of the primary objectives of policy historians from all disciplines must be to intensify the flow of intellectual blood throughout the sub-field so that the new generation of policy historians, who are entering the profession with the foundation having been established, can move in new directions with this subject matter and so that the sub-field continues to evolve. The essays are also aimed at all students of history who want to know want to know where this sub-field came from, where it has gone in recent years, and in what directions it is now moving.

Boston University

Notes

1. Julian E. Zelizer, "Clio's Lost Tribe: Public Policy History Since 1978," *Journal of Policy History*, 12 (2000): 369.

2. In this essay, and other work, I define policy history as a sub-field of political history rather than a separate field.

3. For a history of policy history, see Zelizer, "Clio's Lost Tribe"; Hugh Davis Graham, "The Stunted Career of Policy History: A Critique and an Agenda," *The Public Historian* 15 (1993): 15–37.

4. Thomas McGraw, *Prophets of Regulation: Charles Francis Adams, Louis D. Brandeis, James M. Landis, Alfred E. Kahn* (Cambridge, Mass., 1984).

5. Richard E. Neustadt and Ernest R. May, *Thinking in Time: The Uses of History for Decision Makers* (New York, 1986).

6. See, for examples, Michael Katz, *The Undeserving Poor: From Poverty to the War on Welfare* (New York, 1989); Brian Balogh, *Chain Reaction: Expert Debate and Public Participation in American Commercial Nuclear Power, 1945–1975* (Cambridge, 1991); Linda Gordon, *Pitied But Not Entitled: Single Mothers and the History of Welfare* (New York, 1994).

7. There is no shortage of articles tracing the professional difficulties policy historians encountered within the history profession. See, for example, Steven M. Gillon, "The Future of Political History," *Journal of Policy History* 9 (1997): 240–55; Joel H. Silbey, "The State of American Political History at the Millennium: The Nineteenth Century as a Test Case," *Journal of Policy History* 11 (1999): 1–30; Brian Balogh, "The State of the State among Historians," *Social Science History* 27 (Fall 2003): 455–63.

8. Julian E. Zelizer, "Beyond the Presidential Synthesis: Reordering Political Time," in *A Companion to Post-1945 America*, ed. Jean-Christopher Agnew and Roy Rosinweed (Oxford, 2002), 345–70.

9. Christopher Howard, *The Hidden Welfare State: Tax Expenditures and Social Policy in the United States* (Princeton, 1997).

10. See, for examples, Linda Gordon, *Pitied But Not Entitled: Single Mothers and the History of Welfare* (New York, 1994), and Alice Kessler-Harris, *In Pursuit of Equity: Women, Men, and the Quest for Economic Citizenship in 20th-Century America* (New York, 2003).

11. Jacob S. Hacker, *The Divided Welfare State: The Battle over Public and Private Social Benefits in the United States* (Cambridge, 2002); Jennifer Klein, *For All These Rights: Business, Labor, and the Shaping of America's Public-Private Welfare State* (Princeton, 2003).

12. Sven Steinmo, *Taxation and Democracy: Sweden, British, and American Approaches to Financing the Modern State* (New Haven, 1993).

13. Daniel P. Carpenter, *The Forging of Bureaucratic Autonomy: Reputations, Networks, and Policy Innovation in Executive Branch Agencies, 1862–1928* (Princeton, 2001).

PETER BALDWIN

Beyond Weak and Strong: Rethinking the State in Comparative Policy History

Most public problems can be approached in many ways.[1] Urban noise, the honking of car horns, for example, could be tackled by building effective mass transit and discouraging automobile use, by forbidding the use of horns within city limits and fining violators, by encouraging harmonious social circumstances, or at least stress-reduction education programs, to make drivers less aggressive, by developing horns that target sound waves only at offending motorists, or by encouraging everyone to wear noise-reduction earphones. The problem of sexually transmitted diseases can be solved by encouraging chastity and fidelity as virtues, by strictly criminalizing transmission, or by prescribing antibiotics after the fact. Such varying approaches are qualitatively different. They do not just reflect distinct degrees of statutory intervention. States that adopt divergent solutions may, in a similar fashion, be fundamentally different from one another, not just stronger or weaker versions of an abstract ideal of public authority.

Some solutions involve massive investment in infrastructure or extensive social reform. Some involve punctilious enforcement of legal strictures; others, nothing more than a relatively minor technical breakthrough. Which approach wins favor is a political choice. Build a perfect society, says the utopian social reformer or the revolutionary, and the citizens will follow suit. Forbid what is unwanted and it will not happen, claims the autocrat. Even in the midst of inevitably bad circumstances, hopes the moralist, the ethical person will fare well. Name the problem and eventually we will find a solution, insists the technocrat.

Not every problem has the same palette of possible solutions. Some can best be tackled collectively. We could all wear respirators, but clean air laws are probably the better approach. Sometimes, a technical fix spares us heroic interventions. We could exhort children never to go near the

THE JOURNAL OF POLICY HISTORY, Vol. 17, No. 1, 2005.

medicine cabinet, but childproof bottle caps are much simpler. Still other problems require an individual solution. Municipal bike paths, however desirable, will probably never tackle obesity as effectively as individual eating habits.

Yet many problems can be solved equally well in an array of different ways. Does one allow a heroin addict maintenance doses of his accustomed poison, switch him to legal methadone, as in Britain, or insist that he abstain altogether, as in France? Is prostitution rendered yet another profession—taxable and insurable—among others, as in Germany and the Netherlands, or regarded as a crime to be punished, as in Sweden. Are criminals locked up and harshly punished, or rehabilitated?[2] Are the disabled given pensions or do quotas require employers to hire them? Is culture subsidized, directly through government grants, as in most of Europe, or indirectly via tax deductions, as in the United States? Is safety encouraged by direct regulation, as in Europe, or via courts holding manufacturers liable for damages, as in the United States?[3] Does one have informal social trust to encourage and cement economic relations, as in the United States, Germany, and Japan, or does the state need to intervene in cultures where such social capital is lacking?[4] Is air pollution tackled by encouraging mass transit, as in most of Europe, or strict emissions controls, as in the United States? Is redistribution achieved through the tax (U.S.) or the welfare (Sweden) system?[5]

States are often thought to differ mainly in having stronger or weaker abilities and desires to intervene. They all do much the same thing, in other words, but do it more or less. Recent comparative scholarship across a variety of public policies has demonstrated, however, that such a simple two-dimensional view of what states do fails to account for the full range of their activities. In fact, states make choices among a variety of solutions that are not merely more or less interventionist but are simply different. Comparative policy history has helped uncover the extent to which similar problems are dealt with among nations via different statutory tools. The time has come to modify our overall conception of the state in accord with this ever more nuanced historical understanding of what public authorities actually do at the coalface. States are, in this sense, qualitatively different, not merely stronger or weaker than one another.

A Thousand Flowers Blooming

Allowing for a multiplicity of policy styles has not been the usual way to approach political history. But slowly, the development of comparative approaches to policy history has encouraged a focus on the variety of statutory responses to similar problems, both historically and among nations. Take, as an example, the historiography of the welfare state.

In its earliest formulations, all nations were seen to become welfare states, much as all nations were thought to industrialize in similar ways. Social policy was simply an appurtenance of industrialization; increasing wealth allowed resources to be redistributed to the dependent and the disadvantaged. Subsequent generations of analysis, which examined the details of national social policy histories, distinguished, in contrast, among various forms of welfare state development. While there might be a common residual element of statutory social policy, and while levels of government spending increased in all industrialized nations, not every country tackled problems in the same way or with the same generosity. Typologies were elaborated that distinguished between developed welfare states and the merely residual. High-spending nations included Scandinavia and northern Europe. The rest of the world fell short of such exalted standards. An even later cohort of interpretations, further informed by closer examinations of national histories, recognized, however, that differences existed even among generous welfare states. They developed a more nuanced typology that distinguished between liberal states, with less-developed social policy, and then again between social democratic and corporatist welfare states, each high spenders, but with divergent ways of employing their resources.[6]

It was in this historiographical context that Richard Rose threw down a memorable provocation.[7] Rather than assume that the social democratic welfare states of Scandinavia were the norm, to which social policy elsewhere should be compared, Rose argued that, taking into account geopolitical and demographic significance, the American-Pacific model of the welfare state should set the standard. More of the world's citizens lived in such welfare states, ones that were residual and privatized, than under the Scandinavian model. If one sought to explain the development of the welfare state as it was, not necessarily as it should be, then the focus had to shift away from northern Europe. Rose's challenge has now, in the intervening decade, begun to be met. A school of social policy history has arisen that, though not always comparative in its execution, is so in the framing of its questions. Some of these works were prompted by scholars from Australia, who were insulted that the inherited typologies had relegated their nation to the same liberal category as the United States. They argued that Australia tackled similar problems as the Scandinavian welfare states, but did so differently.[8]

The can now opened, such arguments have increasingly been trained also on the homeland of an exceptionalist view of the welfare state in the United States. Where America was once regarded as the most irremediably residual of welfare states, in recent studies it has come to seem more different than merely backward.[9] Such work explains the U.S. welfare state not solely as a hobbled or underdeveloped variant of the social democratic ones. Instead, it is portrayed as different from those of northern Europe without necessarily being less extensive.

First and simplest, the percentage of GNP devoted to social policy, broadly understood, is much higher than that which is channeled only through the state. In its totality, the amount of money spent through direct and indirect social policies (statutory, local, and private) bears comparison with most European nations. American policies are, however, marshaled and employed differently. Assistance is distributed more through tax expenditures (credits, exemptions, loopholes) than elsewhere, and it is more reliant on private and voluntary measures. These are not issues only for trans-Atlantic comparisons. Recent work on the French welfare state, for example, highlights the interplay of public and private efforts while debunking the claim that French social policy is closer to the Scandinavian than the American model.[10] Similar is the work on social policy inspired by parties to the right of center.[11] If anyone ever bothered to write an account of the Swiss welfare state in comparative perspective, the presence of a very Americanized, and certainly very privatized, system on European soil would be one of the conclusions.

The main insight won by such comparative work is the divergence of approaches taken by states to common problems. The question in studying American social policy becomes not, why is it so weak in comparison to some European equivalents, but why is so much of it arranged outside the state? The tendency of recent welfare state studies to adopt more individualized categorizations and to increase the number of alleged "models" of welfare statism to the point where almost each nation has its own, has thus been extended across the Atlantic to include also the United States. Social science has succumbed to the historian's particularization and it has done so as comparisons were extended ever outward.

Despite such sea changes in particular areas of policy, a larger reconceptualization of the state still awaits us. Ever more sophisticated monographs on specific policy fields have appeared, as well as empirically-based works ruminating more broadly on the state.[12] And yet, comparative conceptions of the state remain surprisingly underdeveloped. When theorized, the state is an often lamentably provincial concept, reflecting the national experiences and prejudices of its formulator. When comparing states to one another, the distinguishing concepts tend to be simple binary categorizations: bureaucratic versus patrimonial, centralized versus federal, and, above all, laissez-faire versus interventionist.

Americans distrust the state and limit its growth, it is said, while Europeans are more favorably inclined.[13] Much the same is claimed for the British vis à vis their Continental neighbors.[14] When it comes to comparisons among the Continental nations, the concepts are vague and inconsistently applied. France has a more centralized and, on paper, stronger state than federalized Germany. Yet, gut instinct holds the German state to be more interventionist, one way or another, than the French. Throwing Scandinavia into the mix confuses matters further. If anything, one would expect these nations to be more teutonic than the Germans: strong centralized states, homogenous civil societies, long traditions of Lutheran acceptance of worldly rulers' prerogatives.

Had we posed the question in the nineteenth century, the Scandinavians would probably have accepted, possibly even welcomed, such a comparison. But things look different in the post-Nazi era. Few Scandinavians care to make the obvious comparison across the Eider any longer, except to distinguish themselves. One heroic act of conceptual quarantine was the insistence by scholars of social policy that a radical distinction separated the Swedish from the German welfare states, the one social democratic, the other corporatist.[15] Except for Hitler, such an intuitively uncompelling distinction would unlikely have been drawn so firmly. In other respects, there are surprisingly few comparisons.[16] Most are debunking attempts to puncture the myths of Swedish ideological virginity. They seek to show, for example, that political ideology here, and even some aspects of practice, such as eugenics and sterilization policies during the interwar period, shared more teutonic assumptions than most Swedes care to acknowledge.[17]

We are, in other words, far from being able to develop an empirically grounded account of the state that will span from Reykjavik to Rome, much less from Berlin to Washington. How, then, can we begin to write a better comparative history of the state—which is, after all, what the history of policy ultimately does? Most rudimentarily, we need good empirical studies informed by an implicitly comparative framing of their questions. Too often, regardless of what the data show, the results are neatly pressed into already established conceptual categories. If framed comparatively, however, such new empirically informed studies should be able to change the very concept of the state. To take the case of the American welfare state, we need a new understanding of social policy that accounts for total efforts, not just those channeled directly through the state. Of course, differences remain between privatized and statutory social policy. The latter may be more robustly armored against retrenchment, for example. But to dismiss the former as somehow not pertinent is to employ a

concept of the welfare state that chokes off further conceptual development rather than encourages it.

Imagine a similar conceptual broadening applied to the state as a
whole. Would this not burst the old, rough-and-ready categories of laissez-
faire and interventionist? Significant comparative work has already been
done to modify traditional couplets between authoritarian and bureaucratic states, on the one hand, and liberal and patrimonial or decentralized ones, on the other.[18] Much has been done to question the inherited
concept of strong and weak states when applied to the comparative couplets of England and Prussia, or England and France, or France and
Prussia.[19] Take, as examples, two fields in which the supposedly laissez-
faire British state of the nineteenth century appears to have been stronger than its Continental counterparts: taxation and public health.[20]
Despite its flexible and, in some sense, amateurish tax collection system,
the British state was able to extract a far higher percentage of GNP than
the French.[21] It also implemented direct income taxation earlier and more
thoroughly than France or Germany—a form of extraction involving great
knowledge of the individual citizen and intense meddling in his business.
The British state was also able to extract more resources via voluntary
loans from its citizens than other nations.[22] It thus had greater fiscally
penetrative power than the Continental states, which were forced to rely
on ineffective, but administratively less demanding, indirect taxes.[23]

Similarly counterintuitive contrasts held for public health. The
Prussians joked that their police could do whatever they wanted in such
respects.[24] But, compared to the British, both the Germans and the French
were ineffectual interveners. True, they rattled their prophylactic sabers
at the borders, imposing inspections, disinfections, and quarantines on
arriving passengers and goods from abroad. But they did so largely because they distrusted their governmental machinery to undertake the sorts
of domestic interventions employed by the British to tame and control
epidemic disease. Most obviously, the British invested greater sums in sanitary infrastructure during the nineteenth century than the Continentals,
cleaning up the urban environment and rendering it less noxious. But
even in more specific senses, the British state's machinery of preventive
intervention was impressive. During the cholera epidemics of the late nineteenth century, for example, the French insisted on detaining at the border suspected travelers from abroad until it was clear that they were not
infected. The British, in contrast, were willing to allow them entry, on
the condition that they report their whereabouts and submit to periodic
medical examination. They were confident in their ability to police visi-
tors after their arrival, just as they had the machinery to impose house-to-

house visitations in search of premonitory cholera symptoms on a scale unknown on the Continent.[25]

If we broaden our scope from the comparison between England and the Continent to extend also across the Atlantic, similar contrasts arise. Recent studies of the nineteenth-century American state have challenged the assumption that it was inherently limited. They have argued, for example, that in the regulation of public health and safety, interventions were much more extensive than previously thought.[26] Early railways were publicly financed and regulated to a degree unexpected in a laissez-faire system.[27] But what if one pushes beyond such topics to others? Was the American state as residual as the myth of its resolutely laissez-faire character insists?

In the micromanagement of certain bad habits through prohibitive legislation, whether alcohol or tobacco, the U.S. state should be compared to Sweden rather than to the more hands-off British, German, or French.[28] On the testing and regulation of medicines, the United States has long been more stringent than many other developed nations. Courts meet out harsh punishments to producers and providers of services, holding them to strict standards of liability. American consumer protection laws are often regarded by Europeans as exaggerated and evidence of— surprisingly—a nanny state. In environmental legislation, the United States was an early and strict intervener.[29] In protections for the disabled, the United States has set the pace, mandating more drastic interventions to assure handicap access to public facilities than in most of Europe. The 1990 Americans with Disabilities Act remains the standard against which attempts at emulation abroad are measured. In Europe, quaintly corporatist measures sometimes remain in place, like those reserving certain professions for the handicapped: elevator and car park attendants positions are kept for the disabled in the U.K. and the blind are preferred for vacant telephonists' jobs in Greece and as masseurs in Italy.[30]

Styles of Statism

To notice that there were areas in which the British state was in fact more interventionist than the Continental is not to argue that it was stronger or more active across the board. Nor is the point of new work on the American state just to reconsider its administrative prowess, rating it higher on the inherited scale of statism. If such implicitly comparative studies are to bear fruit worth the effort, then a reconceptualization of states and statism altogether should be the result.

First and simplest: Should we expect states to be uniformly one thing or the other? States are lumpy. They may focus their energies and attention on certain matters while ignoring others. They may not be consistently laissez-faire or interventionist, but be so in one respect and the opposite in another. Why do those easygoing, anarchistic Germans allow their citizens to drive as fast as they please on the Autobahnen, take their clothes off and drink alcohol in public, and set off fireworks on a practically military scale at New Year? While the *kadavergehorsam* Americans enforce the pokiest speed limits in the Western world, prohibit public drinking, keep their citizens in sartorial purdah, and mandate boring, bangless New Year's Eves? Why do the French, whose police boast of an ability to get their man within twenty-four hours and who parade about with armaments otherwise reserved for the military in full combat readiness, regard American antismoking laws as health totalitarianism? The interesting question, from a comparative point of view, is why a given state is preoccupied with certain matters while ignoring others.

Beyond this, there is a broader question of whether different states tackle common problems differently. If so, a better set of conceptual tools is required to understand what it is they do. We need to abandon the idea that all states can be positioned on a single scale of behavior defined at its respective endpoints by laissez-faire and interventionism. A two-dimensional axis of social policy endeavor between active and residual welfare states is now, after two decades of empirical comparative work, inadequate. So, too, must the palette of statutory activities be understood as encompassing a wider range of possibilities. Some scholars have proposed studying national differences in policy styles.[31] Yet, more is required. We need, as a starting point, a typology, or at least a grasp of the possibility, of various kinds of states.

In the late nineteenth century, two of the great British public health reformers, Edwin Chadwick and Richard Thorne Thorne, sought to contrast the British approach to public health, broadly speaking, with that of the Continental nations. They distinguished between the preventive approach of the British with the curative approach taken across the Channel.[32] A number of matters were their concern. First, the emphasis in England on measures to prevent industrial accidents that concentrated the costs of risk on employers, who were best positioned to prevent them. Though interventionist in the daily management of production, this solution was better than downplaying safety concerns and giving workers disability pensions after the fact. To this came the massive investment in sanitary infrastructure that Britain undertook half a century before the Continent. This meant both that the nation could snap its fingers at disease and was spared reliance on the massive and intrusive governmental machinery of keeping transmissible illness out of the country—the quarantinist interventions still prevalent across the Channel. Chadwick and Thorne Thorne traced back the curative system of the Continent to the still undeveloped nature of these nations' economies, with long working hours, low wages, and inefficient production. From this sorry economic base, the authorities were forced to take what actions they could, which were less decisive and effective than the Victorian state's.

Whatever we may think of the details of the contrast drawn here, Chadwick and Thorne Thorne sought to formulate a concept of different forms of statutory activity going beyond simply more or less intervention. In a similar way, recent work on the American state has argued that it has tackled problems faced by every industrialized polity in ways that differed from European solutions. The point of liability legislation, often remarked on as an unusual feature of the American regulatory landscape, has been similar to the logic of contributory accident insurance: positioning the costs of risk on those actors best able to mitigate them.[33] It allots the burden of risk preemptively via regulation, rather than distributing it post facto through a statutory welfare system. The American state in this sense sought to bypass the state while still dealing with the problem of managing risk. It established what one observer has called statism for antistatists. It passed worker compensation laws rather than providing public medical care, introduced deposit insurance rather than setting up state banks. Product liability and medical malpractice laws were more stringent than elsewhere, managing risks without involving the state directly.[34]

The distinction between preventive and curative approaches to risk is suggestive. Risk can be dealt with by avoiding it, preventing it, shifting it, or redistributing it.[35] Perhaps such various strategies lie at the heart of the different kinds of statutory responses possible to otherwise commonly shared problems. Whether a society seeks to prevent or cure, to tackle problems before or after the fact, is a political decision. One can seek to avoid calamity or redistribute its effects post facto: require lightning rods on houses or engage in barn raisings after the fires; insist on vaccination or isolate the sick; allow contraception or abortions; fluoridate the water or foot the dentist's bills; eat healthily or install defibrillators in public places; pasteurize milk or treat consumptives; provide night schools or spend money on the dole; enhance workplace safety or distribute disability pensions; circumcise or treat cervical cancer; place condoms in all hotel rooms or give penicillin post-coitally. Stimulating and otherwise managing the economy may cut the need for unemployment insurance, promoting health and safety may lessen the need for disability pensions.[36]

Of course, not all decisions are clearly one way or the other. Substitution therapy for narcotics addiction, for example, may be curative from the point of view of preventing drug use (whether by criminalizing such behavior, cutting off the supply of drugs, or providing good social circumstances to discourage drug use in the first place), but it may be preventive from that of lowering crime by addicts in search of a fix. Generally speaking, as a million samplers attest, prevention is better than cure. But matters are not quite that simple. Prevention often involves greater investments than otherwise would be necessary. It was a political decision to foot the costs of making air travel safer than the risks we are willing to accept for automobiles. Prevention also frequently means unwanted control over personal lifestyles. Banning smoking in public places, stoically accepted by most Americans as a victory for health, is rejected as an unwarranted incursion in the individual's right to tar and feather his own lungs by the same European pedestrians who happily wait in the driving rain on an empty night for the crossing light to turn green. "Health fascism" is the accusation leveled by those who wish to see less preventive control on personal behavior.[37] A preventive approach can also lead to outcomes that turn out to be politically undesirable. Eugenics, enthusiastically promoted not only in fascist Germany but also in social democratic Sweden and liberal America, enjoyed favor before being tainted by the Nazis precisely because of its commonsensically preventive approach: Why let unnecessary problems appear in the first place?[38]

Which issues a state and its nation approaches preventively and which, instead, it prefers to mop up after the fact would be very interesting to pursue broadly and comparatively. During the first decade of the AIDS epidemic, for example, the U.S. government financed the lion's share of basic research into a biomedical solution. The other developed nations, with the exception—at a far remove in terms of spending—of France, freeloaded.[39] The bulk of American federal spending on AIDS went to basic biomedical research, vaccine development, clinical trials, and epidemiological surveillance, rather than to public health education and prevention programs.[40] Most European nations, in contrast, spent their monies on care of the ill.[41] In the 1980s, American research spending was a hundredfold that of the British and ten times per inhabitant of the Swedes.[42] In 1993, French spending was only 3 percent (2 percent in 1997) of the American, but even this modest sum was a third more than the British, its nearest competitor, and thrice that of Germany. The United States provided some 90 percent of global governmental AIDS research funding.[43] The equivalent French budget, one critic calculated, would have paid for constructing four kilometers of mountainous highway.[44]

Why was this the case? Of course, a vaccine or other biomedical solution would have been the best outcome, providing a universal public good of use to all humanity. But the question remains, Why did some nations feel prompted to pursue this, while others remained unmoved? To some extent, of course, the disease had afflicted the United States earlier and harder than any European nation. But such simple functionalism does not get us far, since problems rarely produce their own solutions in any straight-forward sense. American culture was imbued with a faith in biomedicine that may have nudged it in this direction, but whether enough more than other nations to make a difference is unclear.[45] More pertinent is the ob-servation that the United States had interests in a form of prevention because the epidemic tested the limits of its haphazard, complicated, in-efficient, and profoundly inegalitarian health system. It was precisely groups often excluded from the system—poor minorities and gays (who raised the issue of family-based coverage in a system where membership was heavily contingent on the work contract)—who suffered the most early in the epidemic. Pouring greater resources into medical research than other nations had been an American tradition since the 1930s. Besides the universalist goal of pursuing public goods, there were political pay-offs. Voting for research funding allowed American politicians to demon-strate their support for health, since other avenues of largesse, such as health insurance for all, were blocked. "Medical research," as Congress-man Melvin Laird put it in 1960, "is the best kind of health insurance" the American people could have.[46]

For countries with universal and effective health-care systems, in contrast, the epidemic posed less of a political problem. So long as citi-zens were entitled to reasonable standards of care and so long as the prob-lem did not mushroom out of hand, a new illness was just another blip on the political radar. For these nations there was little political advantage to funding biomedical research rather than, say, building hospices to en-sure comfortable terminal care for the stricken. (Even in France, the an-nual budget for indemnifying infected hemophiliacs was many times that for research; in America the proportions were reversed.)[47] For the United States, in contrast, a new epidemic was much less digestible. It suffered the perennial problem of insurance coverage and the disease struck pre-cisely groups that were least cared for (as well as articulate and politically surprisingly adroit sexual minorities).

More generally, the Americans found a biomedical approach consis-tent with the values of pluralistic democracy. It appealed especially to a polity fraught with multiculturalism—its social, cultural, and sexual balkanization—and unable to rely either on the cohesion of traditional European ethnic and cultural homogeneity or even on the classic assimilationist ethos of Americanization.[48] In a heterogeneous nation, with multiple moral and religious standards, even the act of disseminating con-sistent information was fraught with delicate issues of what could be said to whom. Informal behavioral control was even less something to rely on.[49] Seeking biomedically to cure or avoid a stigmatized disease, one spread via behaviors and lifestyles widely regarded as immoral, was the socially and politically most liberal approach. It involved the least tinkering with civil society and its mutually antagonistic proclivities. A biomedical approach promised to spare the United States vexing political choices. By intervening in nature, social interventions could be sidestepped. The behavioral change that was unlikely to arise through informal social influence, and whose strict enforcement via rules and laws was difficult, could thus be avoided altogether. The biomedically proactive approach sought to head off political issues that were most conveniently left alone.[50]

Distinguishing between preventive and curative approaches might help make sense of the American proclivity to spend monies on education rather than welfare in the more traditional sense. It has long been known, and the results have become increasingly clear as European higher education settles into underfinanced mediocrity, that American society pours more resources into education of all sorts than most others. Equality of opportunity rather than of outcome is the goal and education rather than welfare is the way chosen to achieve it.[51]

Such a distinction might also shed light on a fundamental statist conundrum: whether a strong state can intervene to reduce its own role. Similar in its logic to the classic theological dilemma of whether an omnipotent God can create a problem he cannot solve, this question might be more easily resolved if one allowed for different styles of statutory intervention. Antitrust and monopoly laws, which in the United States went further to rule out conglomerates than in many other nations, intervened in the economy in order to keep the state at bay in other respects.[52] This might be taken as evidence of a strong, or at least confident, state. But on the other hand, it might also prompt the need for further intervention in other respects. If banks are prevented from organizing supra-regionally and condemned to remain small and fragmented, hence more liable to fail, and therefore in need of government insurance: Is this evidence of strong or weak statism?

Or take the similar case of privacy legislation. Although starting from a shared common-law background with the U.K., the United States nonetheless developed privacy protection and legislation throughout the first half of the twentieth century, while Britain did not. The U.S. government was an early participant in such activities, even though it could be argued that, as in England, Anglo-American culture does not put as much value on citizens' privacy as does the Continental.[53] Is it a strong state that, as until quite recently in the U.K., guaranteed its citizens few protections against intrusion, especially by the media, upheld freedoms of speech and the press as primary goods, and reserved for itself wide-ranging powers of information gathering and storage?[54] Or is a strong state one that pries open its own archives and databases, allowing itself no particular advantage, and sets clear limits as to what can be known by whom about its citizens, as in the United States and, nowadays even more so, on the Continent?

This raises, in turn, the question of how to measure and evaluate state strength or weakness. Too often, what government authorities do is accepted at face value. Huffing and puffing is taken as the equivalent of action. Does the inordinate complexity of the U.S. tax system, with its labyrinthine legislation and lengthy and detailed returns, indicate a strong fiscal apparatus? Or does it betray the weaknesses, even amid much churning, of a system that has made so many concessions to interest groups that its structure threatens to dissolve in intricacy, leaving its overall effect almost impossible to gauge?[55] After a morning spent filling out the forms required of him as a newly appointed visiting professor at an American state university, Göran Therborn, theorist of a large, powerful, and redistributive state, once remarked, "I can see what they mean about cutting back the state." What he was referring to, of course, were not the excesses of a powerful state, but precisely the last-ditch, desperate measures of a weak one, unable to track its citizens adequately, constantly needing to repeat information for a fragmented social insurance system.

Similarly, in public health, the quarantinist nations of the Continent may have seemed as though they were doing more than the British to keep disease at bay in the nineteenth century. In fact, seen from another angle, the British were much more interventionist. Their sanitationist agenda involved statutory incursions into civil society and presupposed a wealth and willingness to act on the part of the authorities, both central and local, that put Continental efforts to shame. Quarantinist public health was, from this vantage, not the tactic of strong states but precisely that of weak administrations able to enforce their power only at particular bottlenecks, but otherwise unconvinced of their ability to penetrate civil society very far.[56] A strong state, one might be tempted to conclude, is not seen, while a weak one flails about noisily.

States may thus adopt quite different approaches to similar problems. Such divergent solutions can often not be compared with each other merely in terms of being more or less interventionist. Often they are equally, but differently, interventionist. Indeed, it may be true that the most thoroughgoing interventions are also the least noticeable. Still interventions run deep.

The Pas de Deux of State and Civil Society

So far, I have focused on the state by itself. But the state is, of course, only half of the classic binary division in political theory that opposes it to civil society. One of the main reasons states differ from one another in their approaches is that they interact variously with civil society. The controls and regulations that shape behavior can be imposed by authorities from outside on civil society. But they can also come from within civil society, regulating itself and thus obviating the need for formal impositions. Whence, precisely, control and regulation emanate is crucial to understanding what states do or need to do. Not all authorities have the same work cut out for them. It is time to remove the state from its splendid Hegelian isolation and soften up the hard binary edges of the dichotomy between state and civil society.

Norbert Elias's work points in this direction. He shows the extent to which social controls were not just imposed from the outside by authorities on their subject population, but internalized during the course of historical development, so that citizens became in large measure self-policing. Michel Foucault continued similar themes, not always in ways that historians could reproduce, much less operationalize. But at least power was not seen as flowing in just one direction but was shared across the divide that once separated the state from civil society. Nikolas Rose has pursued such themes very interestingly, showing how democratic social and political systems rest on the ever-greater self-policing of civil society.[57] The work of communitarian social thinkers—Amitai Etzioni, Robert Putnam, and others—suggests that certain forms of civil society do not require the same kind of statutory intervention as others.[58]

Useful in tandem with such work is the distinction drawn by Michael Mann between despotic and infrastructural power.[59] On the one hand is the official, formal, and evident power of the state to constrain and coerce its citizens' behavior. On the other is the administrative and organizational ability actually to implement such powers. Also elaborating the interplay between the public and private exercise of power is the work of John Hobson on taxes. He argues that, in examining the respective abilities of governments to extract resources from their societies, more than just the brute power of the state must be considered. States have had to negotiate with their civil societies. Where a consensual agreement developed between the two actors, greater resources were freed up with less effort than where coercion was required.[60]

Considering the interplay between state and society, one can imagine two ends of a theoretical spectrum: on the one hand, a garrison state

with omnipotent authority and an abjectly subject population; on the
other, a withering away of any formal control imposed from the outside as
citizens learn and internalize what is expected of them and social sham-
ing accomplishes what police functions used to. Social theorists like Elias
and Rose have argued that there is an overall progression in the development from one toward the other. In the process of modernizing and civilizing, societies become ever more informally controlled and autocratic
interventions become decreasingly necessary. Elias located a caesura some-
time in the early modern period, after which humans began to control
their baser instincts, becoming civilized in the modern sense. He has been
attacked, both on historical and anthropological grounds, for the temporal and cultural provincialism of his belief in a unique transition characteristic of Western culture at a particular moment.[61]

Similarly, one may question Rose's Whiggish conviction that the
course of historical development proceeds in only one direction. Yes, in
many ways we govern ourselves via internal controls that have made external impositions less necessary. Our thresholds of sexual arousal, to take
an obvious example, are much higher than in the past, with public all-but
nudity provoking no apparent reactions. And yet, at the same time, external controls are becoming more prevalent than they were just a few
decades ago. Citizens are no longer obliged to dress according to their
social station, but official sartorial prescriptions are increasingly common,
whether regulating Muslim headdress among women in France or outlaw-
ing gang insignia on high school students in Los Angeles. Sexual relations in the workplace are more highly regulated now than just a decade
ago. Relations between adults—even parents—and children are more for-
malized than earlier, down to the explicit prohibition of corporeal punishment in many nations. Our consumption of inebriants is more controlled
by law than used to be true. Indeed, the very heterogeneity of modern
society, its multiculturalism, may be leading to a renaissance of formal
controls, as the informal behavioral standards we used to learn with our
mother's milk can no longer be taken for granted.[62]

Historians always find exceptions to, and therefore correct and nu-
ance, the overarching trends discovered by the harder social sciences. That
is part of their job. They will therefore be more impressed by the differences among nations in terms of where they locate control—formally or
informally—and the unsimultaneity of such developments than they will
be by their alleged grand uniformity. Nonetheless, the attention drawn by
theorists like Elias and Rose to the multiple sources and interplay of forms
of social control is stimulating. For one thing, it means that historians
other than those interested in politics or the machinery of government
must be drawn into a discussion of the state. If we see the informal shap-

ing of behavior also as part of the history of the state, new topics appear on the horizon.

A few examples: American historians have paid much attention recently to the way the United States, with its heterogeneous population, had to work to develop and nourish the informal behavioral control that in more homogeneous European societies could be taken for granted.[63] Understanding why only some nations took drastic sanctions against alcohol requires consideration of the differences in drinking habits between the beer and spirits nations, with their binge consumption, and the everyday imbibition of the wine-based Mediterranean, and these in turn are connected to theological distinctions between Protestant and Catholic.[64] Grasping the extent to which privacy is protected, or not, requires plumbing cultural attitudes about celebrity, exposure, and shame.[65]

All nations had to deal with the problems of turning country dwellers into city folk, encouraging them to act with consideration for their newfound olfactory, auditory, and epidemiological proximity to others. But the United States was confronted with another dimension of this problem since many of those being metropolitanized were also immigrants from abroad. Out of this sprang two contradictory aspects of American public health development: (1) the interventions that officials invoked against immigrants who were considered unable or unwilling to follow behavioral prescriptions, which were often much harsher than equivalents in Europe;[66] and (2) the hopes invested in the educational system of encouraging appropriately hygienic behavior, the endless attempts to create by official persuasion what in other cultures could be taken as given.[67]

Cultural historians could be enlisted to make sense of policies on drug addiction. Conventionally, when comparisons of measures against narcotics are written, they are framed as a contrast between the U.S. and the U.K., with occasional attention paid to the Netherlands. In this dichotomy, the U.S., for reasons that are often summed up as some variant on Puritan traditions, has taken a harsh line, seeking to block supplies rather than worrying about demand and how to diminish or deflect it. The U.K., in contrast, followed a liberal line of maintaining some drug users on minimal doses of their poison and widely administering substitution drugs. In fact, if one casts the comparative net wider, the contrasts look quite different. Including Germany, France, and Sweden forces a reframing of the entire issue. The implicit assumption, based on a fleeting knowledge of Dutch and sometimes Swiss or Spanish policies, that Continental attitudes toward drug use were, if anything, even more liberal than the British, is revealed as misleading. The major (northern) Continental nations, in fact, took an even more moralistic approach, at least to hard drugs. The United States may have been the main power behind attempts to block international traffic in narcotics, the supply-side approach.[68] In terms of demand, however, the main distinction has run between the Anglo-American nations and those of the Continent. The tendency among the latter has been to reject anything short of absolute abstinence. While both the British and Americans—the former more than the latter—accepted substitution therapy, whereby heroin addicts were shifted to methadone or other drugs, the Continentals resisted, at least until the AIDS epidemic made a new approach imperative.

From their vantage (and this attitude was especially strong in France), addiction was addiction, regardless of the drug in question. Only by foregoing narcotics altogether could the citizen be reclaimed for the community. The view, implicit in substitution therapy, that the user remain addicted and that the goal be simply to shift him to drugs that (because easily and legally available) rendered him less harmful to society—this was regarded from the Continental vantage as immoral social triage. It elevated society's merely practical interests in reducing harm above the individual's claims to whatever treatment promised to render him fit again for full citizenship.[69] The French ideology of universalist republicanism decreed that all must be citizens and no one might be a member of the nation except by belonging fully and uniformly. What might otherwise seem like a technical aspect of public policy is thus, in comparative perspective, revealed as the outcome of a fundamental ideological worldview. French conceptions of citizenship were crucial to the nation's approach to addiction. Just as the foreigner had to assimilate, just as politics based on gayness, or any other multicultural subgrouping, were regarded as impermissible balkanization, so too addicts had to toe the line of republican universalist citizenship.[70]

Different Kinds of States?

Seeing states as either laissez-faire or interventionist implies a single standard according to which they are active or not. More plausible, but still largely unconceptualized—much less worked out in its empirical glory— is the possibility that similar problems may be tackled quite differently. States may be blind to certain issues, fixated on others. Problems may be universally, but not uniformly, tackled. States, in a word, may simply be different.

There may be overarching trends of statutory activity among modern, democratic, industrialized societies. Yet, it is hard to say precisely what they are. The belief that behavior can be regulated by edict and law, possibly characteristic of absolutist regimes, may no longer hold as firmly in democratic systems. While an effective autocracy can mandate public health, as observers have noted, democratic regimes can do little more than educate their citizens.[71] And yet, in some areas this is not the case. The world's arguably most liberalist societies—America's granola belt: Madison, Berkeley, Santa Monica, Cambridge—now treat tobacco smoking as it was in absolutist Prussia, with prohibitions in public and sometimes private.

Democratic regimes may rest on internalized behavioral limitations that eliminate the need for formal controls imposed externally, an ethos of what has been called "prudentialism."[72] If theorists like Rose are correct, with the internalization of informal controls, the state might well wither away. Other than for a few inherently public goods, such as defense, that require collective action, the need for external behavioral constraints would fade. We would all act appropriately, live healthily, indulge only in moderation, raise our children well, ensure against unavoidable risks on the open market. The result would be a kind of genteel middle-class anarchy: the world as a Santa Monica PTA meeting.

And on our octopus's third hand, it is plausible that a liberal, democratic, multicultural society with no single dominant standard of morality and few possibilities of enforcing or even encouraging a common ethos would favor the least incursive, quickest technical fix: build ever more foolproofly safe cars rather than teach good driving techniques, much less rely on automotive politeness; encourage universal condom use rather than insist on sexual parsimony; put locks on firearms rather than ban them outright; employ cyphers and codes rather than enforce confidentiality of communication or rely on discretion, and so forth.

Which sort of solution a given political culture opts for is hard to predict. Industrialized democratic nations may tend to favor one sort of solution over another, and they may make consistent choices among different options. On the other hand, it is equally possible that they are lumpy in their preoccupation with certain problems and issues, as well as in their vacillating decision for one type of solution in some instances and another elsewhere. This is an empirical, not a theoretical, question. Before we can answer it, much more groundwork on what states actually do is needed, much more history of public policy must be written. Indeed, a moratorium on further theorizing of the state should be called until the empirical basis of our claims has been brought up to speed.

University of California, Los Angeles

Notes

1. One of the themes of Joseph R. Gusfield, *The Culture of Public Problems: Drinking-Driving and the Symbolic Order* (Chicago, 1981).

2. James Q. Whitman, *Harsh Justice: Criminal Policy and the Widening Divide Between America and Europe* (New York, 2003).

3. Lawrence M. Friedman, *The Republic of Choice: Law, Authority, and Culture* (Cambridge, Mass., 1990), 191; Christian Ruby and Kévin Nouvel, "Le révélateur sida," *Regards sur l'actualité* 194–95 (1993): 86. From a European point of view, there is something distinctly nutty about American efforts to limit gunshot harm by holding manufacturers liable rather than regulating firearms. *Tagesspiegel*, 27 July 1998.

4. Francis Fukuyama, *Trust: The Social Virtues and the Creation of Prosperity* (New York, 1995), 17.

5. Enrique Rodriguez and Sven Steinmo, "The Development of the American and Swedish Tax System: A Comparison," *Intertax* 3 (1986).

6. Peter Baldwin, "Welfare State and Citizenship in the Age of Globalization," in Andreas Føllesdal and Peter Koslowski, eds., *Restructuring the Welfare State: Ethical Issues of Social Security in an International Perspective* (Berlin, 1997); idem, "Can We Define a European Welfare State Model?" in Bent Greve, ed., *Comparative Welfare Systems: The Scandinavian Model in a Period of Change* (London, 1996); idem, "The Welfare State for Historians," *Comparative Studies in Society and History* 34, no. 4 (October 1992).

7. Richard Rose, "Is American Public Policy Exceptional?" in Byron E. Shafer, ed., *Is America Different? A New Look at American Exceptionalism* (Oxford, 1991).

8. Francis G. Castles, ed., *The Comparative History of Public Policy* (Oxford, 1989).

9. Theda Skocpol, *Protecting Soldiers and Mothers: The Political Origins of Social Policy in the United States* (Cambridge, Mass., 1992); Neil Gilbert, *Transformation of the Welfare State: The Silent Surrender of Public Responsibility* (New York, 2002); Christopher Howard, *The Hidden Welfare State: Tax Expenditures and Social Policy in the United States* (Princeton, 1997); Jacob S. Hacker, *The Divided Welfare State: The Battle over Public and Private Social Benefits in the United States* (Cambridge, 2002); Laura S. Jensen, *Patriots, Settlers, and the Origins of American Social Policy* (Cambridge, 2003); Marc Allen Eisner, *From Warfare State to Welfare State: World War I, Compensatory State-Building, and the Limits of the Modern Order* (University Park, Pa., 2000); Julian E. Zelizer, *Taxing America: Wilbur D. Mills, Congress, and the State, 1945–1975* (Cambridge, 1998); Lee J. Alston and Joseph P. Ferrie, *Southern Paternalism and the Rise of the American Welfare State: Economics, Politics, and Institutions, 1865–1965* (Cambridge, 1999).

10. Paul V. Dutton, *Origins of the French Welfare State: The Struggle for Social Reform in France, 1914–1947* (Cambridge, 2002); Timothy B. Smith, *France in Crisis: The Welfare State, Inequality and Globalization since 1980* (Cambridge, 2004).

11. Kees van Kersbergen, *Social Capitalism: A Study of Christian Democracy and the Welfare State* (London, 1995).

12. Examples of the latter: Abram de Swaan, *In Care of the State: Health Care, Education, and Welfare in Europe and the USA in the Modern Era* (New York, 1988), François Ewald, *L'état providence* (Paris, 1986), James C. Scott, *Seeing Like a State: How Certain Schemes to Improve the Human Condition Have Failed* (New Haven, 1998).

13. Garry Wills, *A Necessary Evil: A History of American Distrust of Government* (New York, 1999); David DeLeon, *The American as Anarchist: Reflections on Indigenous Radicalism* (Baltimore, 1978).

14. José Harris, "Society and the State in Twentieth-Century Britain," in F. M. L. Thompson, *The Cambridge Social History of Britain, 1750–1950*, vol. 3 (Cambridge, 1990), 68.

15. Gøsta Esping-Andersen, *The Three Worlds of Welfare Capitalism* (Oxford, 1990).

16. One of the few: Madeleine Hurd, *Public Spheres, Public Mores, and Democracy: Hamburg and Stockholm, 1870–1914* (Ann Arbor, 2000).

17. Norbert Götz, *Ungleiche Geschwister: Die Konstruktionen von nationalsozialistischer Volksgemeinschaft und schwedischem Volksheim* (Baden-Baden, 2001); Gunnar Broberg and

Mattias Tydén, *Oönskade i folkhemmet: Rashygien och sterilisering i Sverige* (Stockholm, 1991); Maija Runcis, *Steriliseringar i folkhemmet* (Stockholm, 1998); Maciej Zaremba, *De rena och de andra: Om tvångssteriliseringar, rashygien och arvsynd* (n.p., 1999); Gunnar Broberg and Nils Roll-Hansen, eds., *Eugenics and the Welfare State* (East Lansing, 1996); Patrick Zylberman, "Les damnés de la démocratie puritaine: Stérilisations en Scandinavie, 1929–1977," *Le Mouvement Social* 187 (1999): 99–125.

18. Thomas Ertman, *Birth of the Leviathan: Building States and Regimes in Medieval and Early Modern Europe* (Cambridge, 1997).

19. John Brewer and Eckhart Hellmuth, "Introduction: Rethinking Leviathan," in John Brewer and Eckhart Hellmuth, eds., *Rethinking Leviathan: The Eighteenth-Century State in Britain and Germany* (Oxford, 1999); C. B. A. Behrens, *Society, Government, and the Enlightenment: The Experiences of Eighteenth-Century France and Prussia* (New York, 1985).

20. Peter Baldwin, "Preemption vs. Reaction: Civil Society and the State in the Victorian World," in Peter Mandler, ed., *Liberty and Authority in Victorian England* (Oxford, forthcoming).

21. Pat Thane, "Government and Society in England and Wales, 1750–1914," in Thompson, *Cambridge Social History of Britain*, 3:3–4; Margaret Levi, *Of Rule and Revenue* (Berkeley and Los Angeles, 1988), 97–109 and passim. The standard, and magisterial, work on British taxation is now Martin Daunton, *Trusting Leviathan: The Politics of Taxation in Britain, 1799–1914* (Cambridge, 2001), and *Just Taxes: The Politics of Taxation in Britain, 1914–1979* (Cambridge, 2002).

22. Michael J. Braddick, *The Nerves of State: Taxation and the Financing of the English State, 1558–1714* (Manchester, 1996), 193–94. See also David Stasavage, *Public Debt and the Birth of the Democratic State: France and Great Britain, 1688–1789* (Cambridge, 2003).

23. John M. Hobson, *The Wealth of States: A Comparative Sociology of International Economic and Political Change* (Cambridge, 1997), 10–15.

24. Thomas, ed., *Verhandlungen der Cholera-Konferenz in Weimar am 28. und 29. April 1867* (Munich, 1867), 72–77.

25. Peter Baldwin, *Contagion and the State in Europe, 1830–1930* (Cambridge, 1999), chap. 3. In the early modern period, too, it has been observed, federalized systems, where local authorities could deal rapidly with an epidemic threat, often responded more effectively than centralized regimes, with localities awaiting orders from distant centers. Martin Dinges, "Pest und Staat: Von der Institutionengeschichte zur sozialen Konstruktion," in Martin Dinges and Thomas Schlich, eds., *Neue Wege in der Seuchengeschichte* (Stuttgart, 1995), 83.

26. William J. Novak, *The People's Welfare: Law and Regulation in Nineteenth-Century America* (Chapel Hill, 1996); William R. Brock, *Investigation and Responsibility: Public Responsibility in the United States, 1865–1900* (Cambridge, 1984); Daniel T. Rodgers, *Atlantic Crossings: Social Politics in a Progressive Age* (Cambridge, Mass., 1998), 80–81.

27. Colleen A. Dunlavy, *Politics and Industrialization: Early Railroads in the United States and Prussia* (Princeton, 1994), 45–97, 98–144; Timothy Dowd and Frank Dobbin, "Origins of the Myth of Neo-Liberalism: Regulation in the First Century of U.S. Railroading," in Lars Magnusson and Jan Ottosson, eds., *The State, Regulation, and the Economy: An Historical Perspective* (Cheltenham, 2001).

28. Howard M. Leichter, *Free to Be Foolish: Politics and Health Promotion in the United States and Great Britain* (Princeton, 1991), 27.

29. Lennart J. Lundqvist, *The Hare and the Tortoise: Clean Air Policies in the United States and Sweden* (Ann Arbor, 1980).

30. Brian Doyle, *Disability, Discrimination, and Equal Opportunities: A Comparative Study of the Employment Rights of Disabled Persons* (London, 1995), 43–46, 68–69.

31. Jeremy Richardson, ed., *Policy Styles in Western Europe* (London, 1982); Laura Cram and Jeremy Richardson, eds., *Policy Styles in the European Union* (London,1998); David Vogel, *National Styles of Regulation: Environmental Policy in Great Britain and the United States* (Ithaca, 1986).

32. R. Thorne Thorne, "On Sea-Borne Cholera: British Measures of Prevention v. European Measures of Restriction," *British Medical Journal* 2 (13 August 1887): 339–40; Edwin Chadwick, "Preventive Administration, as Compared with Curative Administration, as Practised in Germany," *Sanitary Journal*, n.s., 169 (18 March 1890).
33. Peter W. Huber, *Liability: The Legal Revolution and Its Consequences* (New York, 1988).
34. David A. Moss, *When All Else Fails: Government as the Ultimate Risk Manager* (Cambridge, Mass., 2002), 17, 319–20.
35. William O. Douglas, "Vicarious Liability and Administration of Risk," *Yale Law Journal* 38 (1929): 587–88.
36. Peter Baldwin, "The Return of the Coercive State? Behavioral Control in Multicultural Society," in John A. Hall et al., eds., *The Nation-State Under Challenge: Autonomy and Capacity in a Changing World* (Princeton, 2003).
37. Stephen Davies, *The Historical Origins of Health Fascism* (London, 1991).
38. Teresa Kulawik, "The Nordic Model of the Welfare State and the Trouble with a Critical Perspective," *Netværk for Nordisk Velfærdsstatshistorie, Nyhedsbrev* 21 (December 2002): 4.
39. These are themes explored in Peter Baldwin, *Disease and Democracy: The Industrialized World Faces AIDS* (Berkeley and New York, 2005), chaps. 1, 11.
40. Philip R. Lee and Peter S. Arno, "AIDS and Health Policy," in John Griggs, ed., *AIDS: Public Policy Dimensions* (New York, 1987), 10; William Winkenwerder et al., "Federal Spending for Illness Caused by the Human Immunodeficiency Virus," *New England Journal of Medicine* 320, no. 24 (1989): 1599, 1603.
41. John Street, "British Government Policy on AIDS: Learning Not to Die of Ignorance," *Parliamentary Affairs* 41 (October 1988): 495; House of Commons, 1986–87, Social Services Committee, *Problems Associated with AIDS* (13 May 1987), vol. 2, p. 153; Barbara A. Misztal, "AIDS in Australia: Diffusion of Power and Making of Policy," in Barbara A. Misztal and David Moss, eds., *Action on AIDS: National Policies in Comparative Perspective* (New York, 1990), 190.
42. *Hansard*, 13 January 1989, vol. 144, col. 1147; *Riksdagens Protokoll*, Bihang, 1985–86, Socialutskottets betänkande 1985–86:15, p. 10.
43. Jonathan M. Mann and Daniel J. M. Tarantola, eds., *AIDS in the World II* (New York, 1996), 203; Michael Balter, "Europe: AIDS Research on a Budget," *Science* 280 (19 June 1998): 1856.
44. Christophe Martet, *Les combattants du sida* (Paris, 1993), 223.
45. Michael Bess, *The Light-Green Society: Ecology and Technological Modernity in France, 1960–2000* (Chicago, 2003), emphasizes the favor in which technological solutions are held by French political culture.
46. Stephen P. Strickland, *Politics, Science, and Dread Disease: A Short History of United States Research Policy* (Cambridge, Mass., 1972), 213; Victoria A. Harden, *Inventing the NIH: Federal Biomedical Research Policy, 1887–1937* (Baltimore, 1986), 25.
47. David Kirp, "The Politics of Blood: Hemophilia Activism in the AIDS Crisis," in Eric A. Feldman and Ronald Bayer, eds., *Blood Feuds: AIDS, Blood, and the Politics of Medical Disaster* (New York, 1999), 312.
48. Although, of course, there are debates over whether multiculturalism in fact throws up real differences or merely masks a fundamental assimilation beneath a veneer of difference. Stanley Fish, *The Trouble with Principle* (Cambridge, Mass., 1999), chap. 4; John A. Hall and Charles Lindholm, *Is America Breaking Apart?* (Princeton, 1999).
49. Matti Hayry and Heta Hayry, "AIDS and a Small North European Country: A Study in Applied Ethics," *International Journal of Applied Philosophy* 3, no. 3 (1987): 59.
50. Elizabeth Fee, "Public Health and the State: The United States," in Dorothy Porter, ed., *The History of Public Health and the Modern State* (Amsterdam, 1994), 260; Alfred Yankauer, "Sexually Transmitted Diseases: A Neglected Public Health Priority," *American Journal of Public Health* 84, no. 12 (1994): 1896.
51. Arnold J. Heidenheimer, "Education and Social Security Entitlements in Europe and America," in Peter Flora and Arnold J. Heidenheimer, eds., *The Development of Welfare States in Europe and America* (New Brunswick, N.J., 1981), 269–304.

52. Marc Allen Eisner, *Antitrust and the Triumph of Economics* (Chapel Hill, 1991).

53. Ulrich Amelung, *Der Schutz der Privatheit im Zivilrecht: Schadensersatz und Gewinnabschöpfung bei Verletzung des Rechts auf Selbstbestimmung über personenbezogene Informationen im deutschen, englischen und US-amerikanischen Recht* (Tübingen, 2002), 47; Blanca R. Ruiz, *Privacy in Telecommunications: A European and an American Approach* (The Hague, 1997), 19, 54; John D. R. Craig, *Privacy and Employment Law* (Oxford, 1999), chap. 4.

54. David Vincent, *The Culture of Secrecy: Britain, 1832–1998* (Oxford, 1998).

55. Sven Steinmo, *Taxation and Democracy: Swedish, British, and American Approaches to Financing the Modern State* (New Haven, 1993), 8–9, 38.

56. Baldwin, *Contagion and the State*, 530–36.

57. Colin Jones and Roy Porter, eds., *Reassessing Foucault: Power, Medicine, and the Body* (London, 1994); Graham Burchell et al., eds., *The Foucault Effect: Studies in Governmentality* (Chicago, 1991); Johan Goudsblom, "Zivilisation, Ansteckungsangst und Hygiene: Betrachtungen über ein Aspekt des europäischen Zivilisationsprozesses," in Peter Gleichmann et al., eds., *Materialen zu Norbert Elias' Zivilisationstheorie* (Frankfurt, 1977); Nikolas Rose, *Governing the Soul: The Shaping of the Private Self*, 2d ed. (London, 1999).

58. Amitai Etzioni, *The Third Way to a Good Society* (London, 2000); idem, *The Active Society: A Theory of Societal and Political Processes* (New York, 1968); Robert D. Putnam, *Bowling Alone: The Collapse and Revival of American Community* (New York, 2000). Edward Banfield can perhaps be considered a forerunner of such ideas, though with the advantage of not being hampered by the current communitarians' penchant for *gemeinschaftlich* nostalgia: Edward C. Banfield, *The Moral Basis of a Backward Society* (New York, 1967).

59. Michael Mann, *The Sources of Social Power*, vol. 2, (Cambridge, 1993), 58–63.

60. Hobson, *Wealth of States*; Levi, *Of Rule and Revenue*, 124.

61. Hans Peter Duerr, *Der Mythos vom Zivilisationsprozess*, 4 vols (Frankfurt, 1988); Michael Hinz, *Der Zivilisationsprozess: Mythos oder Realität? Wissenschaftssoziologische Untersuchungen zur Elias-Duerr Kontroverse* (Opladen, 2002).

62. Baldwin, "Return of the Coercive State?" and "Welfare State and Citizenship in the Age of Globalization."

63. Peter N. Stearns, *Battleground of Desire: The Struggle for Self-Control in Modern America* (New York, 1999).

64. Mariana Valverde, *Diseases of the Will: Alcohol and the Dilemmas of Freedom* (Cambridge, 1998), 144–47; Jon Elster, *Strong Feelings: Emotion, Addiction, and Human Behavior* (Cambridge, Mass., 1999), 119–22.

65. Deborah Nelson, *Pursuing Privacy in Cold War America* (New York, 2002); Charles L. Ponce de Leon, *Self-Exposure: Human-Interest Journalism and the Emergence of Celebrity in America, 1890–1940* (Chapel Hill, 2002).

66. Baldwin, *Disease and Democracy*, chap. 10.

67. Suellen Hoy, *Chasing Dirt: The American Pursuit of Cleanliness* (New York, 1995), chaps. 4, 5; Nancy Tomes, *The Gospel of Germs: Men, Women, and the Microbe in American Life* (Cambridge, Mass., 1998).

68. William B. McAllister, *Drug Diplomacy in the Twentieth Century: An International History* (London, 2000).

69. Aquilino Morelle, *La défaite de la santé publique* (Paris, 1996), 145–53.

70. Alain Ehrenberg, "Comment vivre avec les drogues?" in Alain Ehrenberg, ed., *Vivre avec les drogues: Régulations, politiques, marchés, usages* (Paris, 1996), 6–15.

71. Kenneth F. Kiple, ed., *The Cambridge World History of Human Disease* (Cambridge, 1993), 205; Jacob Rüdiger, *Krankheitsbilder und Deutungsmuster: Wissen über Krankheit und dessen Bedeutung für die Praxis* (Opladen, 1995), 37–38; Nora Kizer Bell, "Ethical Issues in AIDS Education," in Frederick G. Reamer, ed., *AIDS and Ethics* (New York, 1991), 137; Arnold J. Rosoff, "The AIDS Crisis: Constitutional Turning Point?" *Law, Medicine, and Health Care* 15, nos. 1–2 (Summer 1987): 81.

72. Nikolas Rose, "Governing 'Advanced' Liberal Democracies," in Andrew Barry et al., eds., *Foucault and Political Reason: Liberalism, Neo-Liberalism, and Rationalities of Government* (Chicago, 1996), 58.

PAUL PIERSON

The Study of Policy Development

What do we mean by the term "policy history"?[1] In conventional usage, "history" refers to one of two kinds of investigation: the study of something that happened at some point in the past, or the study of how something came to be what it is. It is this second usage—the idea of policy history as an unfolding story of *policy development*—that I want to examine in this essay. Understanding the sources of policy often requires that we pay attention to processes that play out over considerable periods of time.

Thinking systematically about how social processes unfold over time has fallen into disfavor in much of the social sciences. Contemporary social scientists are more likely to take a "snapshot" view of political life, especially in areas of inquiry where "large-N" statistical methods and the analytic tools of microeconomics and game theory have been ascendant. Although it is not inherent in the use of these techniques, in practice they lend themselves to inquiries that focus on the "moves" of particular "actors" at a moment in time.

Recent scholarship on policy development, by contrast, reveals the very high price that social science often pays when it ignores the profound temporal dimensions of real social processes. Attentiveness to issues of temporality highlights aspects of social life that are essentially invisible from an ahistorical vantage point. Placing politics in time can greatly enrich the explanations we offer for social outcomes of interest. Indeed, it can expand our vision of what is worth explaining in the first place.

Of course, the social sciences have had a rich tradition of historical research. Scholarly communities devoted to extending such traditions flourish in parts of the social sciences. Indeed, some claim to witness a "historic turn" in the human sciences as a whole.[2] Yet in spite of this activity there has actually been surprisingly limited attentiveness to the specifically temporal dimensions of social processes. In contemporary so-

THE JOURNAL OF POLICY HISTORY, Vol. 17, No. 1, 2005.

cial science, the past serves primarily as a source of empirical material rather than as the site for serious investigations of how politics happens over time.

Too often, the adoption of a historical orientation has failed to exploit its greatest potential contribution to the more systematic understanding of social processes. Especially in the field of American political development, the turn to history has been a turn to the study of what happened in the past. Here analysts study particular historical events or processes, with a focus on offering convincing explanations of specific outcomes of interest. Such investigations often greatly increase what we know about particular facets of American political history. What is less clear, however, is how particular studies fit into some broader research program. Little effort is made to suggest what, if anything, might "travel" from one investigation to another. Indeed, many historically-oriented analysts are uninterested in this question, assuming the stance of most historians—that the rich particularities of each event or process render it unique. Alternatively, these analysts seem to assume (usually implicitly) that a discussion of, say, how social movements contributed to policy outcomes in the 1930s, generates clear implications for our understanding of contemporary policymaking. Such an assumption is highly problematic. Moreover, this kind of "historical" analysis can be profoundly ahistorical in practice. Inquiry may focus on the past but nonetheless zero in too narrowly on a particular moment of time. In doing so, it risks replicating many of the limitations of social science work that ignores the past entirely.

We do, however, have another basis for connecting history to the social sciences. We can turn to an examination of history because social life unfolds over time. Real social processes have distinctly temporal dimensions. Exploring these dimensions can lead us to assess prominent areas of inquiry and conventional practices in new and fertile ways. Often we will be led to new hypotheses regarding important subjects and exciting possibilities will be opened for extending existing theoretical work in new directions. Focusing on how social processes unfold over time suggests new questions and reveals new outcomes of interest—questions and outcomes that are linked to, but distinct from, those that command attention in existing lines of inquiry.

These general comments about social analysis apply to the study of public policy. Here as well, a "snapshot" orientation has become increasingly evident in the efforts of social scientists to understand important social outcomes. In the study of public policy, ahistorical investigation takes two distinctive forms. Most obviously, it may entail a focus on *policy enactments*—the moments of policy choice. From case studies of individual policy battles to broader studies that examine how a range of factors influences legislative productivity, it is the birth of public policies that most often captures scholarly attention.[3] Alternatively, an analyst may take a snapshot of *extant* public policies. In this case, the analyst works backward from existing public policies in an attempt to understand why they take the form they do—an approach I will call functionalist. It is particularly prevalent in rational choice analyses, which have become prominent in contemporary political science. Neither concentration on enactments nor the turn to functional explanation is an unreasonable starting point for an investigation of public policy. Each, however, has serious limitations that can be laid bare and addressed by focusing on the development of policy over time.

Studying Policy as a Moment of Choice

I shall take up the study of policy enactments first. It may seem natural to direct our attention on moments of policy choice. Isn't that obviously where the action is? Martha Derthick, in her magisterial *Policymaking for Social Security*, provides the appropriate response:

> Policymaking is a compound of exciting, innovative events in which political actors mobilize and contest with one another, and not-so-exciting routines that are performed without widespread mobilization, intense conflict, or much awareness of what is going on except among the involved few. . . . The absence of conflict . . . does not signify the absence of change, and what is routine, though it may not be interesting to analysts at a given moment, is cumulatively very important.[4]

Focusing on the dramatic moments of policy choice blinds us to two broad aspects of policy development: what happens before the moment of choice and what happens after. First, let me discuss the "after" part of these unfolding processes. In a recent essay, Eric Patashnik provided a powerful critique of the way in which focusing on dramatic enactments can be highly misleading if analysts are not also attentive to aftermaths.[5] He examines several large-scale "public interest" reforms in the past twenty-five years: airline deregulation, the Tax Reform Act of 1986, and the 1996 reform of agricultural subsidies. Each of these policy enactments commanded attention because of the surprising triumph of diffuse interests over concentrated ones. Each has provided the basis for broad claims about the character of American policymaking.

Patashnik presses us not to be misled by these dramatic moments of choice. Instead, we need to see what happened after the dust settled. We need to think not only about policy enactment, but what he calls *policy sustainability*. And in fact, only one of these reforms—airline deregulation—proved to have staying power once its moment in the public eye passed. The Tax Reform Act of 1986 and the 1996 farm bill, by contrast, were undercut over time as powerful, concentrated interests reasserted themselves. Indeed, as we approach the twentieth anniversary of the heralded tax reform, one has to look closely to locate the scattered remnants of this dramatic "simplifying" initiative. Once again, the tax code sags under the ever-increasing weight of particularistic benefits.

Sustainability, Patashnik argues, depends in part on whether new policy initiatives effectively undercut the reassertion of traditional interests (e.g., by eliminating their institutional bases of support). Perhaps even more, sustainability turns on whether or not these reforms generate self-reinforcing dynamics of social adaptation, leading to the development of new supportive interests. Indeed, a core claim of recent work that has begun to focus self-consciously on policy development is the significance of "policy feedback." Once enacted, policies with specific qualities can produce social effects that reinforce their own stability.

Political scientists working on a range of empirical issues have shown growing interest in how public policies can reconfigure politics in this way.[6] Among comparativists, much of the focus has been on "policy regimes" that engender distinct patterns of interest-group formation and distinctive distributions of public opinion, thus reinforcing divergent and enduring political coalitions. In the comparative study of welfare states, Gosta Esping-Andersen's path-breaking work emphasized the distinct policy configurations generated in the "liberal," "social democratic," and "conservative" worlds of welfare capitalism.[7] Although Esping-Andersen traced these different regimes to distinct constellations of political power, he argued that the establishment of these policy regimes had enduring political effects.

Arguments about regime effects have become standard in this literature.[8] Huber and Stephens, in their remarkably comprehensive treatment of welfare state development, strongly emphasize the impact of early policy initiatives in shaping long-term courses of policy development. "As each policy is put into place," they note, "it transforms the distribution of preferences; as the regime increasingly entrenches itself, it transforms the universe of actors. The economic and political costs of moving to another regime become greater, and conversely the returns of staying on the same track become greater."[9] Here is their account of the impact of early policy initiatives on public opinion, which they term "the policy ratchet" effect:

Until the era of retrenchment, it was rare for secular conservative parties to roll back welfare state reforms instituted by social democratic or Christian democratic parties. Indeed they generally accepted each new reform after it has been instituted, and the new center of gravity of the policy agenda became defined by the innovations proposed by the progressive forces in society. The reason for the change in posture of the conservative parties was that the reforms were popular with the mass public, especially the broad-based policies in the areas of pensions, education, and health care. . . . The support for policies quickly broadened once citizens enjoyed the benefits of the new policies, and thus the mass opposition to cutbacks in the policies was much broader than the mass support for their introduction. *Thus, the new policy regime fundamentally transforms the preferences of the population.*[10]

Comparative research has also begun, at least haltingly, to assemble "micro" data, focusing on the behavior of individuals, which explores and documents the links between policies and important political variables. This is an important development because much of the previous research had simply sketched out what might be happening at the level of individuals without investigating these connections directly. Iversen and Soskice, for instance, argue that strong social insurance states promote the development of specific skills in the workforce.[11] They demonstrate, in turn, that this fact has consequences for political behavior. Countries with large groups of workers with these skills, who need social insurance to protect against risks associated with their investments in nontransferable skills, will exhibit higher levels of public support for expansive social programs.

Research in American politics has also begun to generate substantial evidence of large-scale policy effects. Not surprisingly, given its focus on processes unfolding over substantial stretches of time, this has been especially true in the field of American political development. Theda Skocpol's work on early initiatives in social policy shows that they had significant political effects.[12] Jacob Hacker's recent study breaks important new ground in demonstrating the scope of policy effects.[13] By focusing on the regulatory and tax policies that support the "private" or "hidden" welfare state, he extends an appreciation for policy effects beyond the range of previous studies. By systematically tracking the implications of early policy initiatives over roughly five decades, he provides a particularly compelling examination of the ways in which initial policy arrangements profoundly influenced interest-group structures, the preferences of key political groups, and the range of possibilities open to future policymakers.

Hacker's analysis of the interests of employers is particularly revealing. Political economists often present the policy preferences of business
actors as almost hard-wired—something innate in their status as employers. Yet Hacker shows that in the United States the same employers developed dramatically different viewpoints on the desirability of social
insurance in health care (vehemently opposed) and retirement (largely
supportive). Early divergences in policy structures were key factors, Hacker
demonstrates, in altering the developing stances of employers in these
two areas. This was not only because established policy structures changed
what employers thought they could get, but because these structures gradu-
ally changed what employers perceived as desirable.

Just as in the study of comparative politics, analyses of how these
processes operate at the individual level have recently appeared in research on American politics. Andrea Campbell's study of Social Security
policy and the elderly and Suzanne Mettler's analysis of the G.I. Bill of
Rights both offer strong evidence linking policy structures to political
behavior.[14] Campbell demonstrates that the expansion of Social Security
heightened levels of political activity among the elderly (and, most strik-
ingly, among the less affluent elderly). Mettler's survey of World War II
veterans reveals significant effects of the G.I. Bill on levels of participation
and political attitudes.

Thus we have considerable empirical research, focused on both broad
trends in policy development and more intensive examination of how
individuals respond to specific government programs, suggesting that policy
effects can be very substantial. There is now strong support for E. E.
Schattschneider's insistence that "new policies create a new politics."[15]
This suggests the considerable prospects for thinking not just about what
grand policy enactments may occur at a moment in time, but about how
those policies develop—whether they are or are not likely to become sus-
taining elements of a durable policy regime or, as with the TRA, initiatives that have a much more fleeting impact on patterns of governance.

Indeed, this research on the feedback effects of policy has another
considerable benefit. Examining the aftermath of enactments, as suggested
by Patashnik, highlights not only the checkered long-term records of much-
heralded policy initiatives. Just as an exploration of self-reinforcing features of legislation may reveal that policy enactment does not ensure policy
sustainability, it also suggests that we must be attentive to the possibility
that policy initiatives may start small but grow substantially over time.
For instance, recent research on what Christopher Howard has aptly
termed the "hidden welfare state" of tax expenditures, as well as regulation of private social welfare activities, reveals a story of small or at least
unheralded initiatives whose true significance only becomes apparent over

an extended period.[16] These key programs developed in a pattern quite different from the grand legislative dramas that capture the attention of "snapshot" analysts. As a result, explanations for many of the programs that give the American welfare state its highly distinctive mix of private and public social welfare initiatives were simply missing prior to recent work on policy development.

Thus Patashnik and others have rightly emphasized that we should not see policy enactment as the end of the story. Approaching public policy as a matter of policy development suggests, moreover, that we should not necessarily treat enactments as the beginning of the story either. If it is crucial to consider what happens after enactments, it is also important to think carefully about what happens *before*.

Here again, the snapshot orientation of much social science creates big problems. Too often, it leads social scientists seeking explanations of policy outcomes to focus their inquiries on aspects of causal processes that unfold very rapidly and immediately prior to the outcome of interest. Yet many things in the social world take a long time to happen. The fact that something happens slowly does not make it unimportant. A wide range of processes cannot be understood unless analysts remain attentive to extended periods of time. Snapshot analyses of moments of choice will often miss important elements of the real story, or even make drastically inaccurate interpretations of the parts of the story that do attract their attention.

"Snapshot" views of major policy events typically focus on the immediate sources of change—the catalysts. They will often have a hard time identifying the role of structural factors. These, by their very nature, will typically show little variation within a limited period.[17] Studies of enactments, unless carefully designed, are unlikely to highlight structural factors that influence outcomes only with substantial lags, or by restricting the range of possible outcomes. In many contexts, however, a long, slow erosion of the status quo may be a crucial factor in generating policy change. What may seem like a relatively rapid process of reform is in fact only the final stage of a process that has in fact been under way for an extended period.

Doug McAdam's *Political Process and the Development of Black Insurgency, 1930–1970* (1982) presents a powerful example. McAdam places great weight on the role of big but slow-moving processes that established the preconditions for successful black mobilization and the onset of the "Rights Revolution" in the United States:

> The Montgomery bus boycott of 1955–56 . . . [and] the 1954 Supreme Court decision in the Brown case . . . were landmark events.

Nonetheless, to single them out serves . . . to obscure the less dramatic but ultimately more significant historical trends that shaped the prospects for later insurgency. Especially critical . . . were several broad historical processes in the period from 1933 to 1954 that rendered the political establishment more vulnerable to black protest activity while also affording blacks the institutional strength to launch such a challenge. Later events such as the 1954 decision and the Montgomery bus boycott merely served as dramatic (though hardly insignificant) capstones to these processes.[18]

At the heart of McAdam's analysis is the decline of the cotton economy in the quarter-century after 1925. This decline simultaneously diminished the strength of forces opposed to black insurgency and generated patterns of migration that boosted the organizational capacities (e.g., massive expansion of black churches, colleges, and southern chapters of the National Association for the Advancement of Colored People [NAACP]) of a long-oppressed minority. It was these gradual interconnected social processes that created conditions ripe for a set of triggering events.

In part because studies of policy enactment make it possible to examine moments of change in fine detail, the role of particular actors in initiating such movements is likely to be highlighted. Yet these studies have greater difficulty in identifying those features that facilitate, impede, or channel entrepreneurial activity. Broad, structural features, as well as long, slow-moving processes, which may be crucial preconditions for policy change, recede from view.

To see these features, we will typically need to examine a greater stretch of time in advance of a particular enactment.[19] Some causal processes occur slowly because they are incremental—demographic shifts, for instance, simply take a long time to add up to anything. In others, the critical factor is the presence of "threshold effects": some social processes may have little significance until they attain a critical mass, which may then trigger major change. Other social processes involve considerable time lags between the appearance of a key causal factor and the occurrence of the outcome of interest. This may be true because the outcome depends on a "causal chain" that takes some time to work itself out (a causes b, which causes c . . .). Alternatively, causal processes may turn on "structural" features that involve transformations that are probabilistic during any particular period, which means that several periods may be necessary before the transformation occurs. Under conditions such as these, the social outcome of interest may not actually take place until well after the appearance of key causal factors.

Analysts who fail to be attentive to these slow-moving dimensions of social life are prone to a number of serious mistakes. They may ignore potentially powerful hypotheses. They are particularly likely to miss the role of many "sociological" variables, like demography, literacy, or technology. Their explanations may focus on triggering or precipitating factors rather than more fundamental structural causes.

It can get worse. By truncating an analysis of processes unfolding over an extended period of time, analysts can easily end up *inverting* causal relationships. Daniel Carpenter's *The Forging of Bureaucratic Autonomy* presents a striking demonstration of how attention to a long-term sequence of causes can turn our understandings of policy outcomes on their heads.[20] He criticizes the large and influential literature on relations between legislatures and bureaucrats grounded in Principal-Agent theory.[21] The literature argues that policy outcomes will typically reflect the preferences of congressional "principals," because they have substantial political resources to assure the acquiescence of their bureaucratic "agents."

Carpenter transforms the question from one about policy selection to one about policy *development*. By doing so, he flips this analysis upside down. He persuasively demonstrates how conventional analyses substantially underestimate the potential for bureaucratic autonomy because they adopt a cross-sectional approach to studying what should be understood as a long-term historical process. Working under favorable conditions and over extended periods of time, ambitious and entrepreneurial bureaucrats were able to enhance their reputations for innovativeness and competence and develop strong networks of support among a range of social actors. These achievements created a context in which Congress, facing pressure from below and deferring to the expertise of leading bureaucrats, essentially asked for what the bureaucrats wanted. Viewed as a moment in time, one sees what looks like congressional dominance; viewed as a process unfolding over time, *the same cross-sectional evidence* provides indications of substantial bureaucratic autonomy.

All of these examples suggest some of the ways in which analysts can gain insights from studying policy development as an unfolding historical process. The shaping of public policy is more than a matter of "policy choice" at a particular moment in time. That moment of choice is framed by prior and later events and processes that we exclude from our analyses at considerable cost.

Functionalist Explanations of Public Policy

There is a second strand of work on policy that also takes a "snapshot" approach. Indeed, a focus on the rational selection of policy designs by strategic actors has, in various guises, become perhaps the dominant approach to explaining policy outcomes in the social sciences. I want to explore this approach in more detail, both because it has become so prevalent and because it usefully demonstrates some additional advantages of thinking more systematically about policy development.

When social scientists have sought to explain policy outcomes, they have had a strong tendency to employ "functionalist" interpretations—outcomes are to be explained by their consequences. In particular, what I term "actor-based functionalism" typically rests on the claim that policies take the form they do because powerful actors engaged in rational, strategic behavior are seeking to produce the outcomes observed. Analysts focus on the choices of individual and collective actors who select public policies, and fashion explanations through reference to the benefits those actors expect to derive from particular policy designs. In fact, in most cases they work *backwards* from extant policy arrangements to develop an account of how they were (or might have been) rationally chosen.

Taken alone, however, these arguments are at best incomplete and at worst seriously misleading. Again, in reducing a moving picture to a snapshot, we run the risk of missing crucial aspects of the processes through which public policies take shape, as well as the ways in which they either endure or change in constantly shifting social environments. This is not to say that functional explanations of policy arrangements are not often plausible. They may be, but the adoption of an extended time frame reveals numerous problems for such accounts. Functional interpretations of politics are often suspect because of the sizable time lag between actors' actions and the long-term consequences of those actions. Political actors, facing the pressures of the immediate or skeptical about their capacity to engineer long-term effects, may pay limited attention to the long term. Thus the long-term effects of policy choices, which are frequently the most profound and interesting ones, should often be seen as the *by-products* of social processes rather than embodying the goals of social actors.

A second issue is that of unintended consequences. Even where actors may be greatly concerned about the future in their efforts to design public policies, they operate in settings of great complexity and high uncertainty. As a result, unanticipated consequences are likely to be widespread. Of all the limitations of the rational design argument, this is perhaps the most significant. Anyone engaged in empirical research in the social sciences knows that even the canniest of actors cannot hope to adequately anticipate all the consequences of their actions. Policies may not be functional because designers make mistakes.[22]

Those who study the evolution of public policy are typically struck by the difficulty political actors have of exercising effective control in an increasingly complex world. The profound implications of the high and increasing social complexity that typifies modern polities need to be underlined. As the number of decisions made and the number of actors involved proliferate, relations of interdependence—among actors, organizations, and institutions—expand geometrically. This growing complexity has two distinct consequences. First, more prevalent and complex political activity places growing demands on decision makers, generating problems of overload. Time constraints, scarcities of information, and the need to delegate decisions may promote unanticipated effects.[23] At the same time, increasing social complexity leads to growing interaction effects. Initiatives often will have important consequences for realms outside those originally intended. We should expect that social processes involving large numbers of actors in densely institutionalized societies routinely generate elaborate feedback loops and significant interaction effects. In such settings, decision makers cannot hope to fully anticipate all of the major implications of their actions.[24]

Nor is it just that social contexts are extremely complex; the difficulties are exacerbated by the fact that the abilities of individuals to draw inferences and judgments from their experiences have systematic biases. Levitt and March provide an excellent summary:

> [I]ndividual human beings are not perfect statisticians. . . . They make systematic errors in recording the events of history and in making inferences from them. They overestimate the probability of events that actually occur and of events that are available to attention because of their recency or saliency. They are insensitive to sample size. They tend to overattribute events to the intentional actions of individuals. They use simple linear and functional rules, associate causality with spatial and temporal contiguity, and assume that big effects must have big causes. These attributes of individuals as historians all lead to systematic biases in interpretation.[25]

For all these reasons, social activity—even when undertaken by highly knowledgeable and instrumentally motivated actors—should typically give rise to significant unintended effects.[26]

Here we can see a definite limitation of the "cross-sectional" or snapshot view of public policies typical in actor-centered functionalism. Depending on whether the analyst's starting point is the moment of policy selection or the examination of some extant policy, either the long-term development of public policy or the original factors generating the choice of policy in the first place will be outside the scope of the analysis. So, of course, will be any recognition of disjunctures between the two. Focusing *either* on policy origins or on the eventual outcome—that is, on a snapshot of a policy removed from time—the issue of unintended consequences simply vanishes from view.

As Jacob Hacker emphasizes in his contribution to the current issue, this is just one way in which functionalist analyses succumb to the "temptation to conflate intentions with effects." Operating from the premise that policies reflect the preferences of powerful actors, these approaches too easily impute a comfortable "fit" between policy outcomes and structures of political interests. In fact, there is room for dramatic slippage between the desires of powerful actors and the actual policy structures that develop over time.

Moreover, even where we do see a "fit," in which currently powerful actors endorse current structures of public policy, it is entirely possible that a functionalist interpretation will be seriously off the mark. Indeed, the emphasis I have placed on the downstream social and political consequences of policy arrangements—the effects of policy feedback—contains a double irony for functionalist accounts. First, it suggests that functionalism will often have the causal arrow backwards. Rather than actors necessarily selecting policies that fit their needs, policies, once in place, may "select" actors. This would occur through two processes, familiar to those interested in evolutionary arguments.[27] First, actors adapt to policy environments, by adopting new agendas, strategies, and mobilizing techniques. In the long run, policy arrangements can powerfully shape actors' very identities. Second, individual and collective actors who do not adapt will often be less likely to survive. Through processes of adaptation and selection, actors whose strategies do not "fit" well in a particular policy context may become less common over the long haul.[28]

The second and broader irony is that a snapshot view of such a process will mistakenly be viewed as a confirmation of actor-based functionalism. When an analyst cuts into a process of policy development at any moment in time, he or she may indeed see a relatively nice "fit" between the preferences of powerful actors and the functioning of policies. This might seem to suggest that we are in the realm of functionalist policy design, but in fact such an assertion would get the causality exactly backward. Rather than these powerful actors generating the policy, the policy arrangements may have played a substantial role in generating the properties of the actors.

Functionalist arguments that start from the benefits particular actors derive from institutions and infer that their power accounted for those arrangements typically ignore important feedback processes that may generate the same observed outcome in a completely different way.[29] As just emphasized, an understanding of policy-generated, self-reinforcing dynamics may suggest alternative explanations for policy arrangements that are *too easily* attributed to power relations.

At the same, we also need to consider the possibility that self-reinforcing processes may magnify power imbalances over time, while simultaneously rendering those imbalances less visible.[30] In the famous community power debate of the 1960s and 1970s, Bachrach and Baratz and Lukes argued persuasively that power asymmetries are often hidden from view; where power is most unequal, it often does not need to be employed openly.[31] Pluralist critics essentially countered that it was impossible to systematically evaluate such claims.[32] Although he did not frame the issue quite this way, Gaventa demonstrated that such power asymmetries can reflect positive feedback processes operating over substantial periods of time.[33] Processes of positive feedback can transform a situation of relatively balanced conflict into one of great inequality. Political settings where one set of actors must initially impose their preferences on another set through open conflict ("the first face of power") may change over time into settings where power relations are so uneven that anticipated reactions ("the second face of power") and ideological manipulation ("the third face") make open political conflict unnecessary. Thus positive feedback over time may simultaneously increase asymmetries of power and, paradoxically, render power relations less visible.

Where certain actors are in a position to impose rules on others, the employment of power may be self-reinforcing. Actors may use political authority to change the rules of the game (both formal institutions and various public policies) to enhance their power. These changes may not only shift the rules in their favor, but may increase their own capacities for political action while diminishing those of their rivals. And these changes may result in adaptations that reinforce these trends, as undecided, weakly committed, or vulnerable actors join the winners or desert the losers. Many political conflicts, from the Nazi seizure of power to the gradual process through which the Labour Party supplanted the Liberals in Great Britain in the early twentieth century, reveal this sort of dynamic. Disparities in political resources among contending groups may widen dramatically over time as positive feedback sets in. In the process, political conflict and imbalances of power may become less visible, not more.

The disenfranchisement of African Americans in the post-reconstruction American South provides a clear and poignant example of how shifts in political power can be self-reinforcing. In Alexander Keyssar's marvelous study of the history of suffrage in the United States, the end of Reconstruction precipitated a dynamic process of shifting power relations that played out over a considerable period of time.[34] In 1876, a contested presidential election led to the removal of federal troops from the South. In 1878, Democrats won control of both houses of Congress for the first time in twenty years. "The upshot of these events," Keyssar writes, "was to entrust the administration of voting laws in the South to state and local governments."[35]

These breakthroughs, it must be stressed, did not result in immediate victory for Democratic "Redeemers" in the South. Instead, they ushered in a "period of limbo and contestation, of participation coexisting with efforts at exclusion." In many parts of the South, the Republican Party "hung on, and large, if declining, numbers of blacks continued to exercise the franchise":

> Periodically they were able to form alliances with poor and upcountry whites and even with some newly emerging industrial interests sympathetic to the probusiness policies of the Republicans. Opposition to the conservative, planter-dominated Redeemer Democrats, therefore, did not disappear: elections were contested by Republicans, by factions within the Democratic Party, and eventually by the Farmers' alliance and the Populists. Consequently, the Redeemers, who controlled most state legislatures, continued to try to shrink the black (and opposition white) electorate through gerrymandering, registration systems, complicated ballot configurations, and the secret ballot (which served as a de facto literacy test). When necessary, they also resorted to violence and fraudulent vote counts.[36]

Social and political power was used over time to reinforce and consolidate political advantage. By the early 1890s, major challenges to the Redeemers began to dissipate, giving way to a durable system of planter hegemony. As late as 1964, only 10 percent of African Americans in Mississippi would be registered to vote.

These observations point to deep-rooted difficulties in the treatment of power in contemporary social science: sometimes analysts see power when it is not there, and sometimes they do not see it when it is. "Snapshot" views will often miss important elements of power relations. In short, shifting to the study of policy development provides the basis for a revitalized effort to investigate issues of power in political life.

The Study of the Past and the Study of the Present

One final implication of this focus on issues of policy development deserves emphasis. Students of policy history should vigorously contest the tendency to separate the study of the past from the study of the present, to draw sharp distinctions between students of "policy history" and those who study contemporary politics. There are many reasons to study policy history, and scholars can do so very profitably even if their research has no particular implications for the present. But good work on policy development will often have crucial implications for contemporary issues. Even more important, it is often extremely useful to treat the present itself as but a specific moment within a larger dynamic process. As I have argued, central to the notion of development is the recognition that the social world is marked by processes that unfold over time. Studying the present as a "snapshot" of a moment of time can distort what we see and how we understand it in profound ways. Shifting to a developmental perspective presses us, even when we are focusing on the present, to pay more attention to the long-term sources of policy change, to address the central issue of policy sustainability, to consider the possibilities that in the long run "small" outcomes may end up being very big, while "big" ones end up being small, and to adapt our analyses to the reality of ubiquitous unintended consequences.

Thinking systematically about how policies develop through time can also refine our expectations about the possibilities and constraints of contemporary politics. I have argued that a sensitivity to processes of policy development allows us to identify the factors that provide the "glue" for a particular policy arrangement. This in turn can be extremely helpful for identifying likely paths of policy reform. If we know, for example, which elements of policy arrangements have generated important adaptations for which sets of actors, we are more likely to be able to identify which kinds of revisions they would regard as acceptable and which they would view as problematic.

Consider the following example: the deeply institutionalized arrangements of public pension systems in mature welfare states.[37] Most of these pension systems became well institutionalized by 1980. Yet a series of profound social, economic, and political changes have generated a climate of austerity in which virtually all national pension systems are undergoing substantial revisions. Because different national systems are starting from different points of departure, with greatly differing degrees of institutionalization, the menu of options available to reformers varies dramatically. Where generous, earnings-related pay-as-you-go pension systems have been in place for a substantial stretch of time, established precommitments make a shift to a funded, individualized system of retirement accounts virtually impossible. Instead, policymakers have pursued reforms designed to control costs and link contributions more closely to benefits. In systems without mature pay-as-you-go plans, more radical reform options remain on the table, and have in fact been implemented in some cases (e.g., the United Kingdom). In short, a clear understanding of where countries are in a course of policy development give us a much sharper sense of what kinds of reform are most plausible.

There are enormous benefits to be gained from bringing the orientations and insights of work on policy development to bear on issues central to contemporary polities—a step that will help us to identify new questions and contribute to the understanding of old ones. On this score there are encouraging signs. For example, recent years have seen a number of impressive works that directly address the contemporary American polity, but approach it through the study of policy development over time. Jonathan Skrentny's analysis of the minority rights revolution, Suzanne Mettler's research on the long-term political effects of the G.I. Bill, and Jacob Hacker's investigation of the divided welfare state are telling examples.[38] These works all rest on the explicit assertion that historical investigation focusing on unfolding processes can greatly illuminate our understanding of the present. If work in this vein continues, it will mark the end of a strict separation between our efforts to comprehend "the historical" and "the contemporary" in public policy. This will be good news for the study of policy history, and even better news for the social sciences.

University of California, Berkeley

Notes

1. This essay presents an introduction to issues explored in much more depth in Paul Pierson, *Politics in Time: History, Institutions, and Social Analysis* (Princeton, 2004). I would like to thank Julian Zelizer for very helpful comments on an earlier draft.

2. Terrance J. McDonald, ed., *The Historic Turn in the Human Sciences* (Ann Arbor, 1994); Robert Bates et al., *Analytic Narratives* (Cambridge, 1998).

3. See, for example, Sarah Binder, *Stalemate: Causes and Consequences of Legislative Gridlock* (Washington, D.C., 2003), and David Mayhew, *Divided We Govern* (New Haven, 1991).

4. Martha Derthick, *Policymaking for Social Security* (Washington, D.C., 1979), 9.

5. Eric Patashnik, "After the Public Interest Prevails: The Political Sustain-ability of Policy Reform," *Governance* 16 (2003): 203–34.

6. Arguments about what is now often termed "policy feedback" are usually traced back to sources such as Theodore Lowi's classic article, "American Business, Public Policy, Case Studies, and Political Theory," *World Politics* 16 (1964): 677–715. Lowi's argument, however, is really about the structure of *issues* and the associated (diffuse or concentrated)

winners and losers. It is not an argument about how specific structures of public policy can influence politics. Recent strands of work on this topic stem largely, in my view, from lines of argument set down by Theda Skocpol and her collaborators in the 1980s. See especially Margaret Weir and Theda Skocpol, "State Structures and the Possibilities for 'Keynesian' Responses to the Great Depression in Sweden, Britain, and the United States," in Peter B. Evans, Dietrich Rueschemeyer, and Theda Skocpol, eds., *Bringing the State Back In* (Cambridge, 1985), 107–62.

7. Gosta Esping-Andersen, *The Three Worlds of Welfare Capitalism* (Princeton, 1990).

8. Duane Swank, *Global Capital, Political Institutions, and Policy Change in Developed Welfare States* (Cambridge, 2002); Evelyn Huber and John Stephens, *Development and Crisis of the Welfare State: Parties and Policies in Global Markets* (Chicago, 2001); and Paul Pierson, ed., *The New Politics of the Welfare State* (Oxford, 2001).

9. Huber and Stephens, *Development and Crisis of the Welfare State*, 32.

10. Ibid, 28–29, emphasis added.

11. Torben Iversen and David Soskice, "An Asset Theory of Social Policy Preferences," *American Political Science Review* 95 (2001): 875–94.

12. Theda Skocpol, *Protecting Soldiers and Mothers* (Cambridge, Mass., 1992).

13. Jacob Hacker, *The Divided Welfare State: The Battle over Public and Private Social Benefits in the United States* (Cambridge, 2002).

14. Andrea Louise Campbell, *How Policies Make Citizens: Senior Political Activism and the American Welfare State* (Princeton, 2003); Suzanne Mettler, "Bringing the State Back In to Civic Engagement: Policy Feedback Effects of the G.I. Bill for World War II Veterans," *American Political Science Review* 96 (2002): 367–80.

15. E. E. Schattschneider, *Politics, Presures, and the Tariff* (New York, 1935).

16. Christopher Howard, *The Hidden Welfare State* (Princeton, 1997); Hacker, *The Divided Welfare State*.

17. Dietrich Reuschemeyer, Evelyn Huber Stephens, and John Stephens, *Capitalist Development and Democracy* (Chicago, 1992), 32–34.

18. Douglas McAdam, *Political Process and the Development of Black Insurgency, 1930–1970* (Chicago, 1982), 3

19. For a detailed discussion, see Paul Pierson, "Big, Slow-Moving, and . . . Invisible: Macrosocial Processes in the Study of Comparative Politics," in James Mahoney and Dietrich Rueschemeyer, eds., *Comparative Historical Analysis in the Social Sciences* (Princeton, 2003), 177–207.

20. Daniel P. Carpenter, *The Forging of Bureaucratic Autonomy: Reputations, Networks, and Policy Innovation in Executive Agencies, 1862–1928* (Princeton, 2001).

21. Matthew D. McCubbins, Roger G. Noll, and Barry R. Weingast, "Administrative Procedures as Instruments of Political Control," *Journal of Law, Economics and Organization* 3 (1987): 243–77; Matthew D. McCubbins and Thomas Schwartz, "Congressional Oversight Overlooked: Police Patrols versus Fire Alarms," *American Journal of Political Science* 28 (1984): 165–79.

22. Of course, this was a standard conclusion of implementation research, which of course was well placed to examine unintended consequences precisely because it examined what happened *after* policies were enacted—although typically considering only a limited stretch of time. The classic in this genre is Jeffrey L. Pressman and Aaron Wildavsky, *Implementation* (Berkeley and Los Angeles, 1973).

23. James March and Johan Olsen, *Rediscovering Institutions: The Organizational Basis of Politics* (New York, 1989); Herbert A. Simon, *Models of Man* (New York, 1957).

24. Robert Jervis, *System Effects: Complexity in Political and Social Life* (Princeton, 1997).

25. Barbara Levitt and James G. March, "Organizational Learning," *Annual Review of Sociology* 14 (1988): 323

26. Friedrich Hayek, *Law, Legislation, and Liberty: Rules and Order* (London, 1973); Fred Hirsch, *The Social Limits to Growth* (Cambridge, Mass., 1977); Thomas Schelling,

Micromotives and Macrobehavior (New York, 1978); Charles Perrow, *Normal Accidents* (New York, 1984); Jervis, *System Effects*.

27. Miles Kahler, "Evolution, Choice, and International Change," in David A. Lake and Robert Powell, eds., *Strategic Choice and International Relations* (Princeton, 1999), 165–96.

28. Huber and Stephens, *Development and Crisis of the Welfare State;* Jacob Hacker and Paul Pierson, "Business Power and Social Policy: Employers and the Formation of the American Welfare State," *Politics and Society* 30 (2002): 227–325.

29. Hacker and Pierson, "Business Power and Social Policy."

30. Terry Moe, "Power and Political Institutions," paper presented at the Conference on Crafting and Operating Institutions, Yale University, New Haven, 2003; Kathleen Thelen, "Historical Institutionalism and Comparative Politics," *Annual Review of Political Science* 2 (1999): 369–404.

31. Peter Bachrach and Morton S. Baratz, "The Two Faces of Power," *American Political Science Review* 56 (1962): 947–52; Stephen Lukes, *Power: A Radical View* (London, 1974).

32. Nelson W. Polsby, *Community Power and Social Theory* (New Haven, 1963); Raymond A. Wolfinger, "Nondecisions and the Study of Local Politics," *American Political Science Review* 65 (1971): 1063–80.

33. John Gaventa, *Power and Powerlessness: Quiescence and Rebellion in an Appalachian Valley* (Urbana, Ill., 1980).

34. Alexander Keyssar, *The Right to Vote: The Contested History of Democracy in the United States* (New York, 2000), 107–16

35. Ibid, 107.

36. Ibid.

37. John Myles and Paul Pierson, "The Comparative Political Economy of Pension Reform," in Pierson, ed., *New Politics of the Welfare State*, 305–33.

38. John D. Skrentny, *The Minority Rights Revolution* (Cambridge, Mass., 2003); Mettler, "Feedback Effects of the G.I. Bill"; Hacker, *The Divided Welfare State*.

JILL QUADAGNO AND DEBRA STREET

Ideology and Public Policy:
Antistatism in American Welfare State
Transformation

Henry David Thoreau's influential essay "Civil Disobedience," published in 1849, began with a ringing declaration of opposition to government: "I heartily accept the motto, 'That government is best which governs least'; and I should like to see it acted up to more rapidly and systematically. Carried out, it finally amounts to this, which also I believe—'That government is best which governs not at all.'. . . the character of the American people has done all that has been accomplished; and it would have done somewhat more, if the government had not sometimes got in its way."[1] Thoreau's statement summarizes a central thesis in political theory, what has become a historical constant in the minds of researchers seeking to explain the development and parameters of the American welfare state. This thesis is that any power given to the government is subtracted from the liberty of the governed, a concept best captured by the term "antistatism."[2] Thus, Lipset contends that the United States is dominated by an encompassing liberal culture that honors private property, distrusts state authority, and holds individual rights sacred.[3] Similarly, according to Huntington, Americans live by a creed that views government as the most dangerous embodiment of power.[4] For Morone, American government is a "polity suspicious of its own state."[5] Hartz, too, asserts that the master assumption is that "the power of the state must be limited."[6]

The idea of antistatism as a driving political force was first asserted by socialist theorists at the turn of the twentieth century to explain the seeming absence of working-class radicalism and the lack of a socialist movement or labor party in the United States. Then as the welfare state became the primary site of the civil functions of governments, antistatism

We thank Julian Zelizer for helpful comments on a previous draft of this manuscript.

became the preferred explanation of many historians and social scientists for why the American welfare state was slow to develop, why its array of programs was incomplete (no national health insurance or family allowances), and why the benefits granted were less generous than those of other countries.[7] This argument has been a staple across all historical eras. In the Progressive Era, Lubove contends, proposals for state welfare programs failed because an entrenched ethos that "enabled groups of all kinds to exert an influence and seek their distinctive goals without resorting to the coercive powers of government."[8] Then Jacobs argues, "When Medicare was formulated in the early 1960s, politicians and policy specialists responded both to the public's support for expanding health care and its uneasiness with direct and visible government regulation of the associated costs."[9] In the 1990s, according to Skocpol, President Bill Clinton's plan for national health insurance was defeated by opponents who were able to convince middle-class citizens that Health Security was "a misconceived big government effort that might threaten the quality of U.S. health care."[10]

Although welfare state theorists imply that social programs are constructed around specific core values, they largely ignore how values get integrated into social policy outcomes. In this essay we first describe in a general way how ideology is embedded in conceptions of various welfare-state regime types and describe the particular portrayal of the United States as an archetypal "liberal" welfare state. We next consider various causal explanations regarding the proposed relationship between values and social policies. Finally, we compare the programmatic manifestations of ideology in the United States with two other "liberal" welfare states, Great Britain and Canada, to assess whether the American welfare state is more distinctively antistatist.

Our review of the historical record suggests that the American welfare state has never been as "exceptional" as is often suggested. Further, recent trends in welfare state restructuring toward what Gilbert has termed the "enabling state" (that is, one based on a market-oriented approach that seeks to promote labor force participation and encourage individual responsibility) have shifted social policy in the United States closer to other nations in character.[11] We conclude that, although antistatism frequently appears as a theme in political discourse, it does not represent an ideological consensus. Public opinion rarely reflects a clear antistatist consensus, and policy decisions frequently contradict antistatist values. An analysis of changes in U.S. government policy from the 1950s to the 1980s indicates little correspondence between public sentiment for more versus less government and the decisions made by politicians. Although antistatism is often drawn upon to justify particular conservative policy positions, it cannot be considered a determining political force in and of itself. Rather, we suggest that the concept of antistatism captures distinctive features of American political development, the structure of the state, the character of the labor movement, the racial underpinning of public policy decisions, and the content (but not the outcome) of public policy debates.

Ideology in Welfare State Regimes

The argument that antistatist values have impeded American welfare state development is most explicit in theories of welfare state regimes. The concept of "regime" types is derived from observations of common patterns across nations in the allocation of responsibility for social welfare between the state, the market, and private households.[12] These patterns were established during the period of welfare state formation by various configurations of class politics. In most classification orders, the regime type is determined by the system of stratification the welfare state produces (that is, the extent to which workers are "decommodified" or inequalities are abated).[13] Thus, the key dimension is the redistribution of resources. Yet a persistent, if often implicit, underlying argument running through each classification scheme is a presumed association between a particular welfare state structure and ideology.[14] In some cases, the structure of the welfare state is assumed to produce certain values. For example, Edlund asserts that "different types of welfare state regimes generate different attitude patterns."[15] In other instances, the causal order is reversed: ideologically-based conflicts and preferences produce different welfare state structures. Thus, Esping-Anderson contends that the institutional characteristics of the welfare state shape public attitudes toward social welfare programs, but also that variations across nations in the configuration of social programs are a product of some characteristic ideological base.[16] The relationships between particular sets of values and welfare state structures are illuminated by examining how each regime type is defined.

Social Democratic Regimes

Social democratic regimes are generally synonymous with the Nordic countries. They are seen as distinctive in their efforts to minimize market dependency and promote status equality. They are predicated on an egalitarian ideology that "*believes* that only public provision would ensure that all citizens have equal access to benefits of equal value,"[17] but that also seeks to use welfare state policies to promote cross-class alliances and enhance feelings of social solidarity. Because their objective is to endow all citizens with equal rights, regardless of social class or occupation, they fuse universalism with generous benefits and comprehensive socialization of risks.[18]

Corporatist Regimes

The second regime type is termed "corporatist." The corporate regime model was favored by conservative ruling elites in continental Europe who perceived social programs as a way to uphold traditional society. Corporatist welfare became the dogma of the modern Roman Catholic Church and was espoused in two papal encyclicals. In countries where Christian Democrats ascended to power, they became a notable force in the construction of welfare states that incorporated "a philosophy of respect for all classes and transcendence of class conflict in the interest of society as a whole," although this respect did not necessarily mean all classes were to be treated identically.[19] Rather, corporatism emphasizes responsibility for the less fortunate, which as Kersbergen notes, derives from the Catholic interpretation of justice that it is "the duty of the secure to help the poor."[20]

Programmatically, corporatist welfare states have been infused with an ideology that blends status segmentation and familism. Status segmentation occurs in programs that differentiate entitlements according to class and status groups. For example, Bismarck's pension program in nineteenth-century Germany included myriad social insurance schemes, each with its particular rules, finances, and benefit structures. This legacy is perpetuated in the current organization of Germany's health-care system around employment-based sickness funds.[21] Familism is manifested in the corporatist principle of subsidiarity, which asserts that the state should intervene only when the family or voluntary organizations (particularly churches and church-related organizations) cannot meet a social welfare function.[22] In keeping with those values, corporatist states are more likely than others to provide direct cash transfers to individuals and families but are less likely to provide public services—such as day care—that might promote the labor-force participation of women.[23]

Liberal Regimes

The third welfare regime type is the liberal welfare state. Liberalism, in this classic usage of the term, is egalitarian, universalistic, and meliorist. It involves a valorization of the individual, the preservation of individuals' natural rights to freedom and property, and "a central role for the market and voluntary efforts in social provision."[24] Liberal welfare states are constructed around a set of values that reflect this commitment to individualize risks and maintain voluntarism.[25] The state is assigned limited scope to enforce "those rules necessary to reconcile conflicts among the rights of individuals."[26] Programmatically, this means that liberal states discourage welfare dependency by relying on social programs with complex eligibility rules such as means testing, residency requirements, and family responsibility clauses. These programs foster competitive individualism and promote private-sector enterprise.

In most welfare-state regime typologies, the United States is seen as the archetypical example of a liberal welfare state, one where social policy plays a residual role that only comes into play when the market and the family fail. It is a nation where "the progress of social reform has been severely circumscribed by traditional, liberal work-ethic norms" and where the state "encourages the market, either passively by guaranteeing only a minimum—or actively—by subsidizing private welfare schemes."[27] Comparative empirical analyses using measures such as the timing of welfare policy adoption or the level of welfare spending generally confirm this depiction of the United States as an outlier. The question, however, is whether American exceptionalism can be attributed to antistatist values. After all, at key junctures, Americans have transcended their distrust of government and supported policies that expanded state authority.[28] An individualistic ethos did not prevent the United States from developing a massive, universal public education system, deter passage of a comprehensive social security system, or block compulsory health insurance for the aged. Further, the pervasiveness of antistatist sentiments in political debates over the U.S. welfare state does not mean they are a causal force. Values cannot simply be presumed to have some kind of unexplained effect on the policy-making process. As Skocpol argues, "Many scholars who talk about national values are vague about the processes through which they influence policymaking . . . we can surmise that inherited values are thought to influence the actions that political leaders choose to take as well as the ease with which reformers outside government build popular support for proposed new policies."[29] How, then, do antistatist values shape policy outcomes? In the section that follows, we examine the specific causal processes that are hypothesized to link antistatism to American welfare state development.

Causal Mechanisms

Antistatism Within State Structures

According to one argument, the American state was constructed around an "ideology of statelessness."[30] In the founding of the nation, debates about what the Constitution should include centered around fears of a tyrannical government controlled from the center. The result was a docu-ment that diffused political authority to a degree unmatched in Europe. The Constitution created a weak federal government that gave the sover-eign states the right to nullify federal legislation. At the national level, authority was further divided among three branches of government, each with its own independent authority, responsibilities, and bases of support. At the legislative level, authority was split between the House and the Senate as well as numerous committees and subcommittees.[31] The Bill of Rights inserted additional protections against the potential abuse of gov-ernment power.[32]

The decentralized structure of American government impedes policy innovation by increasing the number of "veto" points (i.e., the courts, the legislative process, the states) where even small numbers of oppo-nents can effectively block policy initiatives and by allowing special in-terests to exert a unique influence on policy outcomes.[33] Instead of working programmatically through parties, interest groups can lobby individual legislators to support their preferred policies, oppose those that obstruct their agendas or define the issues that legislators interpret to be impor-tant in the first place.

There is ample historical evidence of special interests being able to penetrate the state to subvert progressive welfare state reform. In some instances, powerful stakeholders succeeded in blocking proposals for new programs entirely. For example, for the entire twentieth century, coali-tions of special interests mustered episodic campaigns to defeat national health insurance, lobbying legislators, cultivating sympathetic candidates through large campaign contributions, and developing new "products" whenever government action seemed imminent.[34] In other instances, pro-grams were shaped in ways that preserved private markets. Examples in-clude Workmens' Compensation and Medicare, where private insurance companies were authorized to administer the programs.[35]

To the extent that antistatism helped to shape the fragmented, mul-tilayered institutional framework of the American political arena, it is one distant "cause," manifested through the multiple veto points and op-portunities for special-interest intrusion into the political process. In terms of proximate explanations for particular policy failures, however, one would need to consider whether it is antistatism per se or its symbolic use by elites promoting their particular interests.

Antistatism and Working-Class Mobilization

A second theory asserts that antistatism impeded American welfare state development by shaping the agenda of the working class in different directions than in Europe. According to T. H. Marshall, democratization has proceeded in three stages through a struggle for civil, political, and finally social rights.[36] In Europe, the struggle for civil rights emerged out of a feudal heritage and the experience of serfdom. The transition from servile to free labor introduced the notion of citizenship as the right to pursue the occupation of one's choice without compulsion. By the beginning of the nineteenth century, the principle of individual economic freedom was accepted as axiomatic. The struggle for political rights was not won for nearly another century. Until nearly the twentieth century, in most European nations only monarchs, bureaucrats, aristocrats, and some men of property could vote. Political democratization in the form of universal suffrage advanced through the dismantling of restrictions on voting based on property rights or literacy and the displacement of constitutional monarchies with representative governments and popular sovereignty.[37] In this process, the modern European state was not viewed as a threat to autonomy but rather as an instrument in the destruction of the ancient social order. In the third stage of democratization, a mobilized working class sought to win social rights in the form of national programs that would provide workers with some immunity from market forces. In the ideal typical case, workers organized into trade unions, formed labor-based political parties, and then used their "power resources" to forge cross-class alliances to expand the welfare state.[38]

The working class in the United States confronted a different problematic than its European counterparts. Even as colonists under British rule when the franchise was based on property ownership, 50 percent to 80 percent of white males were qualified to vote. As property restrictions were liberalized, by the 1880s voting rights for adult white males were nearly universal. Thus, the emancipatory project of gaining citizenship rights in Europe (by necessity, a collective effort) was not a part of the class struggle in the United States. While the European working class regarded the modern state as a key to gaining autonomy, in the United States the state was an instrument of coercion that was used to break strikes and prevent unionization. Suspicion of state power made American trade unions wary of mobilizing for government programs, preferring instead union-controlled benefits negotiated through collective bargain-ing.[39] That meant the American labor movement in some instances op-posed national legislation and instead sought to build a "private" welfare state that protected union members and reinforced union autonomy. The American Federation of Labor, which represented four-fifths of organized workers by 1904, opposed model bills for state health insurance in the Progressive Era. During the New Deal, the single most important social welfare legislation of the century, the Social Security Act of 1935, was enacted without strong labor backing. Instead, many unions established funds for pensions and health care and a few set up their own health cen-ters through the mid-1940s.[40] After World War II, some unions did sup-port the drive for national health insurance, but for the most part they focused their energies on gaining and then preserving the right to bargain for fringe benefits in their own employment contracts.[41] As Stevens notes, "The political pressure exerted by the American labor movement was a demand for a private alternative to state-run welfare programs."[42] In the 1990s, the AFL-CIO failed to mobilize on behalf of President Bill Clinton's Health Security plan and instead devoted its energies and resources to fighting the North American Free Trade Agreement (NAFTA), which the unions viewed as an effort to shift production to low-wage countries with more lax environmental and labor standards.[43]

The preference of union leaders in the United States for political action through an autonomous workers' politics does not mean that the entire labor movement embraced free-market principles entirely or that it abhorred all state intervention. In the Progressive Era, some state and local labor federations defied the national union leadership and took an active role in supporting social welfare legislation. AFL affiliates in some states joined with the United Mine Workers to press for state old-age pen-sion legislation.[44] In the 1950s and 1960s, the AFL-CIO worked for Dis-ability Insurance and Medicare.[45] In the 1970s, the United Auto Workers resurrected the fight for national health insurance. While it is true that workers' demands for universalist policies in the United States were nei-ther as early nor as sustained and widespread as their European counter-parts, it would be an oversimplification to conclude that antistatism was the primary determinant of labor action.

Racism and States' Rights

American antistatism is also bound up in racial issues and manifested in the doctrine of states' rights. The reactionary element in American po-litical thought stems not from feudalism but from slavery. While the North was formally a democracy, in the South black slaves were not considered whole persons. A more historically-based interpretation of the Constitution recognizes that it preserved states' rights as much to protect the institution of slavery as to protect citizens from government tyranny. Following the abolition of slavery in 1865, the principles of states' rights remained a primary force for preserving white privilege and for maintaining a fixed southern minority and a fixed northern majority in Congress. Until well into the twentieth century, African Americans were denied basic democratic rights—the right to vote, the right to work without coercion, and the right to economic security. The grand movement for civil rights in the United States was not based on class but on race. It occurred in the twentieth century, not the eighteenth, and the revolutionaries were African Americans, not the working class.[46]

The antistatist, states' rights agenda of the South impeded the development of the welfare state for the first two-thirds of the twentieth century. This agenda was derived from an agricultural economy dependent on tenant labor—not entirely unlike European feudalism—that was sustained by a sometimes paternalistic system of labor management in which planters would provide tenants various benefits, such as old-age assistance, unemployment insurance of a sort, and medical care, in exchange for loyal service. Because national welfare programs could undermine paternalism and threaten practices that maintained the racial order, southern politicians resisted these threatened intrusions into local practices. For two-thirds of the twentieth century, southern politicians used their power either to bottle up legislation entirely or to demand that new social welfare programs be locally administered.[47] At the insistence of southern Democrats, the Social Security Act of 1935 excluded agricultural and domestic workers entirely from the social insurance programs (Social Security, Unemployment Insurance) and allowed local welfare authorities to administer the means-tested programs for the poor (Aid to Dependent Children, Old Age Assistance) through a joint federal-state formula. This association between antistatism and racism was finally disentangled when the civil rights movement successfully challenged the constitutionality of the states' rights principle.

The question of the American welfare state's exceptionalism rests, in part, on putative differences between the United States and everyone else. Liberal welfare states clearly differ in structure and intent from social democratic and corporatist states. But the United States is regarded as an outlier—exceptional—even among nations in the "least generous" liberal welfare state regime. That presumption raises two questions. How exceptional is the United States, that is, are its social welfare programs fundamentally different than those of other similar nations? If so, can these differences be plausibly attributed to antistatism? These questions can best

be answered by comparing the United States with two other liberal welfare states, Canada and Great Britain, in terms of the timing, scope, and
generosity of social welfare programs. For illustrative purposes, we use
public pensions and national health programs to assess the relevance of
antistatism in explaining American exceptionalism or indeed to determine the extent to which exceptionalism actually exists.

Is Antistatism More Prominent in the United States?

Modern welfare states originated with the "liberal break" of the late eighteenth century, when paternalistic forms of poor relief were replaced with
benefits infused with the concept of the free individual and an emphasis
on self-help. By the nineteenth century, liberalism was understood as an
ideology of free-market capitalism that supported restraints on the role of
the state. Its tangible expression varied but was characterized by a preference for meager, means-tested benefits that promoted the work ethnic
and self-help.

The Pre–World War II Era

Great Britain was the first among the three "liberal" nations to enact a
public national old-age pension. The Old Age Pensions Act (1908) provided pensions for every British resident at age seventy. Excluded were
those whose income exceeded a certain amount, those who had "habitu-
ally failed to work," and recipients of poor relief.[48] In 1925 the Widows,
Orphans' and Old Age Contributory Pensions Act created flat-rate, means-
tested contributory pensions for workers and survivors payable at age sixty-
five. Canada created its first national pension program with the Old Age
Pensions Act of 1927 (a joint federal-provincial program), which provided flat-rate, means-tested pensions to individuals over the age of seventy. In the United States, a relatively extensive public pension system
for Civil War veterans and widows predated both the British and Canadian programs. Although these pensions did not constitute a formal national pension program, they were fairly widespread, at least throughout
the North, dampening demand for benefits based on other criteria.[49] During the Progressive Era, some states enacted old-age pension laws, but
they were poorly funded and unevenly available. Not until 1935 did the
Social Security Act establish a national old-age pension for industrial workers
coupled with a federal/state program of old-age assistance for the elderly poor.
  On the surface, the earlier enactment of national pensions in Canada
and Great Britain compared to the later enactment of Social Security in

the United States lends credence to the definition of the United States as a welfare state "laggard." Yet this commonly-drawn conclusion ignores variations among the three pension systems. What is notable, first, is that unlike the means-tested benefits in Canada and Great Britain, the Social Security Act (and amendments to it in 1939) established a comprehensive, social insurance entitlement for retired workers sixty-five and older and their dependents. Although later in timing, the American public pension system was broader in scope, somewhat more generous, and covered a much wider swath of the population than the pre–World War II pension programs of either Canada or Great Britain. If means-testing is a core indicator of antistatism, then early pension policies of Canada and Great Britain appear to be significantly more so than the U.S. Social Security system.[50] What is also significant is that the Social Security Act included means-tested benefits as well as a social insurance scheme, thus creating a two-tier system that would remain an enduring characteristic of the American welfare state.

In the arena of health care, the American Association for Labor Legislation (AALL) waged an effort during the Progressive Era to enact state legislation for compulsory health insurance, but the campaign was thoroughly defeated. Lubove attributes the failure to an entrenched ethos that "enabled groups of all kinds to exert an influence and seek their distinctive goals without resorting to the coercive powers of government."[51] One might agree that antistatism was the causal force, except that neither Canada nor England, which were both presumably less antistatist, enacted compulsory health insurance during that period. Further, the evidence suggests that the most salient factor in the defeat of the AALL plan was the opposition of physicians, insurance companies, business groups, and labor leaders, who employed antistatist rhetoric but, more important, mobilized their resources to assert their economic interests.[52] Not only is antistatism insufficient to explain the "underdevelopment" of American social welfare during the pre–World War II era, but it not clear that the United States actually was a laggard.

The Post–World War II Era

The ideological foundations of the national welfare states that developed in European countries after World War II represented a break with classical liberal ideology. They were based on a synthesis of individual and collectivist values that retained a concern with individual freedom, but they also recognized the constraints on social conditions that limited choice. In particular, the new liberalism recognized that old-age poverty was less an individual failing than an effect of social and economic conditions. It

viewed contributory social insurance as a mechanism to reduce dependence and reward thrift and hard work and was coupled with a Keynesian
commitment to government action to ameliorate inequality and maintain full employment.[53] Both Canada and Britain, but not the United
States, expressed this new liberalism in arrangements for national health-
care programs that covered their entire populations. It is in the area of
health care that the United States presents the most stark exception to
this spirit.

Of the three countries, the British National Health Service (NHS) is
the most "statist." It was established under the National Health Service
Act of 1946, which created a system of publicly funded, free health-care
services that would be run by a central authority.[54] Specialists became
employees of the NHS but were allowed to maintain private practices.
General practitioners remained independent contractors but derived nearly
all of their income from NHS payments.[55]

Canadian arrangements for financing health care were created in two
phases. The first public hospital insurance plan was established in 1946
by the province of Saskatchewan; other provinces developed similar plans
over the next several years.[56] In 1957 federal legislation provided a framework for federal subsidies to the provinces to establish universal coverage
for hospital care, and by 1961 all ten provinces had entered the plan.[57]
Government financing of medical services was a more contentious issue
because of opposition from Canadian physicians. Although parts of some
provinces included physician's services in their health programs, it was
not until 1962 that the first province-wide plan was established. In 1964
a government commission recommended that all ten Canadian provinces
adopt similar plans, and two years later a new federal program for medical
services was created. By 1971 all provinces had established programs for
physician services that met the federal criteria.[58] Legislation that prevented private insurance companies from covering the majority of hospital and physician services, except for supplemental items such as private
hospital rooms or prescription drugs, strengthened the public programs.[59]

During the period when Canada and Great Britain were installing
universal health coverage, the United States developed an employment-
based health insurance system. Private insurance was embedded first, leaving public programs to cover only the high-risk groups—the aged and the
disabled (Medicare) and the poor (Medicaid). Private insurers are allowed
to use sophisticated forms of medical "underwriting" or using "risk-rat-
ing" to set premiums and to skim off the more desirable employee groups
and individuals, abandoning the rest, either by refusing to issue policies
or by pricing coverage beyond their means.[60] An important caveat is that
employment-based health coverage is not inherently antistatist, since other

countries also have used employment as the vehicle for providing health coverage. In these cases, however, coverage is typically mandated and alternative public mechanisms exist to protect people who are detached from the labor force.[61] Private insurance elsewhere is also heavily regulated to prevent insurers from rejecting clients based on health status.

Yet, if health policy in the United States is driven by an antistatist political culture, then it should provide an inhospitable environment for centralized control of health-care spending. Over time, however, provider payment policies in Medicare to control costs have empowered the federal government in ways remarkably similar to policies adopted by other countries. The creation of Professional Standards Review Organizations in 1972 to monitor Medicare hospital admissions, while largely ineffectual, nonetheless established a precedent for government oversight of health-care services. The 1983 amendments to the Social Security Act replaced Medicare's cost-plus reimbursement formula with a prospective payment system (PPS) that reimbursed hospitals according to fixed-payment schedules for various diagnosis-related groups (DRGs). In 1989 a resource-based relative-value scale (RBRVS) with standardized fee schedules was adopted for Medicare reimbursements to physicians.[62] These payment systems have given the U.S. government control over the flow of most income to providers and ended market pricing of services, hardly an antistatist trend.

Canada employs a variant of a prospective payment system that operates through periodic provincial/hospital contract negotiations over hospital fees. Legislation in 1984 eliminated the small amount of discretion Canadian physicians had over fees by ending the extra billing option that had been used to "top up" public insurance payments for services. In the 1990s, the budgets of provincial governments for physicians' services were capped.[63] Although the provincial insurance programs operate with a relative degree of autonomy, the Canadian federal government does set a global budget for annual health expenditures, the one mechanism of control that is anathema in the United States.[64]

The expansion of pension rights and health insurance coverage between the postwar years and the early 1970s represented the "golden age" of welfare states, as all nations expanded public programs and extended social welfare protections more generously and for more citizens.[65] Their relative standing gave rise to the classification scheme according to regime types. What is less clear is whether these regime types are still useful for characterizing trends in various countries. Although the United States remained an outlier insofar as health insurance is concerned, Medicare and Medicaid were broadened to include new beneficiary groups. During the same period, the populations covered in both Great Britain and Canada (with nearly universal coverage of residents in both places) has remained intact, but some previously covered services have been "de-insured." Further, when both direct and indirect public expenditures are taken into account (total public spending, including tax relief for private pension and health insurance premiums), over time the United States has come to resemble more closely its counterpart nations.[66] The regulatory framework that has been constructed around Medicare, Medicaid, private insurance, and pensions has also moved the United States in similar directions to other national social welfare systems, not only Canada and Great Britain, but other European countries as well.[67] This convergence among the three welfare states is not only inconsistent with an antistatist explanation but also challenges the validity of the regime categories for understanding processes of welfare state restructuring.

Neo-liberalism in Great Britain, Canada, and the United States

In the international context, social welfare spending peaked as a percentage of GDP in the early 1990s. Since then, observers have been struggling to capture the essence of the changes that have been occurring. A consensus seems to be building that the trends of the last decades of the twentieth century represent a neo-liberal restatement of classic liberalism. Neo-liberalism has been oriented toward restraining the growth of the state and restoring market forces through privatization of public benefits and services.[68]

This process of restructuring is best captured by what Gilbert has termed the "enabling state." The enabling state involves a rejection of the central premises of social insurance with its emphasis on universal access to publicly provided benefits to which workers have an earned right. Rather, it is based on a market-oriented approach that targets benefits to the most needy and seeks to promote labor-force participation and individual responsibility. Programmatically, the transformation has been manifested in an increase in work-oriented policies, a privatization of social welfare, increased targeting of benefits, and a shift away from an emphasis on the social rights of citizenship to individualizing risk.[69] In Sweden, once viewed as the classic social-democratic exemplar, this shift has involved pension reform that reallocates 2.5 percent of the payroll tax contribution from the public system to private individual investment accounts.[70]

Among leaders in liberal welfare states, the antistatist rhetoric and actions of the governments of Prime Minister Margaret Thatcher in Great Britain and President Ronald Reagan in the United States began the transition toward a neo-liberal agenda. In Great Britain, neo-liberalism was

the credo of successive Conservative governments, which launched a series of assaults on universalist programs. Thatcher made retrenching the
"nanny state" a core principle of her domestic agenda. Marketlike compe-
tition would be injected into NHS practices, the "workshy" (the unem-
ployed, lone mothers) would be encouraged to "make work pay" through
reductions in unemployment and antipoverty benefits, and the elderly of
the future would be increasingly reliant on private pensions. In the 1980s,
tax incentives were introduced to encourage people to purchase private
health insurance, but the incentives never caught on and were rescinded
in 1997. In Canada, despite some lukewarm attempts to retrench public
services and transfers, pensions and national health insurance emerged
from the attentions of successive Progressive Conservative governments
relatively unscathed, although the generosity and scope of unemployment
and antipoverty programs was reduced there, too.[71]

While historically the rhetoric of the enabling state has been a persistent theme in the United States, policies reinforced this ideology in
the 1990s.[72] In 1995, Congress funded four experiments in state Medicaid
programs for public/private partnerships that gave people who purchased
an approved long-term-care insurance policy easier access to Medicaid.
These experiments in effect turned Medicaid into a backup reinsurance
plan that protected the assets of the elderly and allowed insurance companies to pay a set, predictable cost for care.[73] In 1996, Congress also
enacted the Personal Responsibility and Work Opportunity Act, which
replaced traditional Aid to Families with Dependent Children (AFDC)
benefits with Temporary Assistance to Needy Families (TANF). TANF
set time limits for receipt of benefits and placed an increased emphasis on
transitions to work.[74]

In 1996, Congress also enacted the Health Insurance Portability and
Accountability Act (HIPAA), which contained several provisions to make
health insurance more portable for workers changing jobs and to eliminate some of the more egregious practices of the small group insurance
market.[75] HIPAA spurred the development of the long-term-care insurance market by allowing people who itemize their income taxes to deduct
a portion of long-term-care expenses, including long-term-care insurance
premiums, and by making employer contributions toward the cost of group
long-term-care insurance a tax-deductible business expense. Finally, a prescription drug benefit added to Medicare in 2003 included a measure to
encourage the more affluent elderly to buy lower-cost, higher-deductible
health insurance policies and then shelter income from taxes in health
savings accounts. This legislation was coupled with $12 billion in subsi-
dies to encourage private insurance companies to offer seniors' policies
that compete with Medicare. Thus, the 1990s was characterized by programs that encouraged the purchase of private health insurance and in-

creased regulation to protect the insurance industry from its own excesses. By 2004 the only Social Security reforms under consideration were privatization bills that would allow workers to invest a portion of payroll taxes in the stock market.

Conclusion

In the timing, scope, and generosity of its national pension program, the United States is not appreciably different from other "liberal" countries. Further, opinion surveys indicate that the public can simultaneously hold contradictory views. While there is strong support for Social Security and Medicare and some variant of national health insurance, surveys also find an "extreme emphasis on individualism" and a "mistrust of central authority."[76] It is simply implausible that public pensions, public education, and other social welfare programs could surmount the ideological barrier, while health care was trumped by antistatist preferences. As the implementation of Medicare has moved the United States in similar directions to other countries, even those considered "social democratic," the United States remains exceptional in its lack of universal health insurance for the working aged population. Although antistatist arguments have been employed to explain this pattern, it is more logical to presume that the ideology supports powerful economic interests in health insurance markets.

The historical record suggests that antistatism is not a timeless national essence, a "unitary culture of consensus as embodied in the idea of a single national political culture."[77] Rather, it has provided enduring symbols and meanings that have been "available" in political debates over the U.S. welfare state. An antistatist ideology and the symbols constructed around it have served several purposes in these political struggles.[78] They have allowed supporters and opponents of a policy initiative to gain control over definitions, terms, and symbols; they have helped to dramatize the issues and identify the source of problems and the desirability of certain outcomes; and they have has been used to mobilize alliances and create solidarity between groups and individuals.[79] Alternative values have just as often been invoked to justify the expansion of the welfare state. The apparent success of elected officials and stakeholder opponents in employing antistatist rhetoric to rationalize policy positions can create the erroneous impression that the values are a causal force in and of themselves, rather than a strategic weapon to justify inaction.[80]

Florida State University
State University of New York–Buffalo

Notes

1. Henry David Thoreau, *The Portable Thoreau*, ed. Carl Bode (New York, 1947), 109–10.

2. Garry Wills, *A Necessary Evil: A History of American Distrust of Government* (New York, 1999), 21.

3. Seymour M. Lipset, *American Exceptionalism* (New York, 1996); Seymour M. Lipset and Gary Marks, *It Didn't Happen Here* (New York, 1999).

4. Samuel Huntington, *American Politics: The Promise of Disharmony* (Cambridge, Mass., 1981), 33.

5. James Morone, *The Democratic Wish* (New York, 1990), 323.

6. Louis Hartz, *The Liberal Tradition in America* (New York, 1955), 62.

7. Jill Quadagno, "Creating a Capital Investment Welfare State: The New American Exceptionalism," *American Sociological Review* 64 (February 1999): 22.

8. Roy Lubove, *The Struggle for Social Security, 1900–1935* (Pittsburgh, 1986), 2.

9. Lawrence R. Jacobs, "Health Reform Impasse: The Politics of American Ambivalence Toward Government," *Journal of Health Politics, Policy, and Law* 18, no. 3 (1993): 630.

10. Theda Skocpol, *Boomerang: Health Care Reform and the Turn Against Government* (New York, 1996), 163–64, 71.

11. Neil Gilbert, *Transformation of the Welfare State: The Silent Surrender of Public Responsibility* (New York, 2002), 13; see also Debra Street and Jay Ginn, "The Demographic Debate: The Gendered Political Economy of Pensions," in *Women, Work, and Pensions*, ed. Jay Ginn, Debra Street, and Sara Arber (Buckingham, 2001).

12. Gosta Esping-Andersen, *The Three Worlds of Welfare Capitalism* (Cambridge, 1990), 47.

13. Richard Titmuss, *Essays on the Welfare State* (London, 1958), and *Social Policy* (London, 1974); Harold L. Wilensky and C. N. Lebeaux, *Industrial Society and Social Welfare* (New York, 1958); Walter Korpi, *The Democratic Class Struggle* (London, 1983); Esping-Andersen, *The Three Worlds of Welfare Capitalism*, 49.

14. But see Robert Goodin, Bruce Headey, Ruud Muffels, and Henk-Jan Dirven, *The Real Worlds of Welfare Capitalism* (Cambridge, 1999).

15. Jon Edlund, "Trust in Government and Welfare Regimes: Attitudes to Redistribution and Financial Cheating in the USA and Norway," *European Journal of Political Research* 35–33 (1999): 342.

16. Morten Blekesaune and Jill Quadagno, "Public Attitudes Toward Welfare State Policies: A Comparative Analysis of 24 Nations," *European Sociological Review* 19, no. 5 (December 2003): 415–27.

17. Evelyne Huber and John D. Stephens, "Partisan Governance, Women's Employment, and the Social Democratic Service State," *American Sociological Review* 65 (2000): 326.

18. Gosta Esping-Andersen, *The Social Foundations of Postindustrial Economies* (Oxford, 1999), 106.

19. Alexander Hicks, *Social Democracy and Welfare Capitalism* (Ithaca, 1999), 139.

20. K. Kersbergen, *Social Capitalism* (London, 1995), 111.

21. Donald Light, "Comparative Models of Health Care Systems," in *The Sociology of Health and Illness*, ed. P. Conrad and R. Kern (New York, 1994), 465.

22. Hans Maarse and Aggie Paulus, "Has Solidarity Survived? A Comparative Analysis of the Effect of Social Health Insurance Reform in Four European Countries," *Journal of Health Politics, Policy, and Law* 28, no. 4 (2003): 585–614; Esping-Andersen, *The Three Worlds of Welfare Capitalism*, 27.

23. Huber and Stephens, "Partisan Governance," 326.

24. Julia S. O'Connor, Ann Shola Orloff, and Sheila Shaver, *States, Markets, Families* (Cambridge, 1999), 44.

25. Esping-Andersen, *The Social Foundations of Postindustrial Economies*, 75.
26. O'Connor, Orloff, and Shaver, *States, Markets, Families*, 44.
27. Esping-Andersen, *The Three Worlds of Welfare Capitalism*, 26; Theodore Marmor, Jerry Mashaw, and Philip Harvey, *America's Misunderstood Welfare State* (New York, 1990), 5; Stephanie Gould and John L. Palmer, "Outcomes, Interpretations, and Policy Implications," in *The Vulnerable*, ed. John Palmer, Timothy Smeeding, and Barbara Torrey (Washington, D.C., 1988), 428–47.
28. Sven Steinmo and Jon Watts, "It's the Institutions, Stupid! Why Comprehensive National Health Insurance Always Fails in America," *Journal of Health Policy, Politics and Law* 20, no. 2 (1995): 330.
29. Theda Skocpol, *Protecting Soldiers and Mothers: The Political Origins of Social Policy in the United States* (Cambridge, Mass., 1992).
30. David Wilsford, *Doctors and the State* (Durham, 1991), 56.
31. Jacob Hacker, "The Historical Logic of National Health Insurance: Structure and Sequence in the Development of British, Canadian, and U.S. Medical Policy," *Studies in American Political Development* 12 (1998): 57–130; Lipset, *American Exceptionalism*, 6; Lipset and Marks, *It Didn't Happen Here*, 13.
32. Hartz, *The Liberal Tradition in America*, 147.
33. Hacker, "The Historical Logic of National Health Insurance, 59.
34. Jill Quadagno, "Why the United States Has No National Health Insurance: Stakeholder Mobilization Against the Welfare State, 1945–1996," *Journal of Health and Social Behavior* 4/5 (2004): 815–34; Colin Gordon, *Dead on Arrival* (Princeton, 2003), 2.
35. Lubove, *The Struggle for Social Security*, 2; Jill Quadagno, *One Nation, Uninsured: Why the U.S. Has No National Health Insurance* (New York, 2005).
36. T. H. Marshall, *Class, Citizenship, and Social Development* (Chicago, 1964), 82–87.
37. Hartz, *The Liberal Tradition in America*, 147.
38. Walter Korpi, "Power, Politics, and State Autonomy in the Development of Social Citizenship: Social Rights During Sickness in Eighteen OECD Countries Since 1930," *American Sociological Review* 54 (1989): 309–28; John D. Stephens, *The Transition from Capitalism to Socialism* (London, 1979), 2.
39. Werner Sombart, *Why Is There No Socialism in America?* (White Plains, N.Y., [1906]1976), 22.
40. Jennifer Klein, *For All These Rights* (Princeton, 2003), 76.
41. Alan Derickson, "Health Security for All?" *Journal of American History* 80 (March 1994): 1345.
42. Beth Stevens, "Blurring the Boundaries: How the Federal Government Has Influenced Welfare Benefits in the Private Sector," in *The Politics of Social Policy in the United States*, ed. Margaret Weir, Ann Shola Orloff, and Theda Skocpol (Princeton, 1988), 125; see also Marie Gottschalk, *The Shadow Welfare State* (Ithaca, 2000).
43. Theda Skocpol, *Boomerang* (New York, 1996), 78.
44. Jill Quadagno, *The Transformation of Old Age Security* (Chicago, 1988), chap. 3.
45. Quadagno, "Why the United States Has No National Health Insurance."
46. Jill Quadagno, *The Color of Welfare* (New York, 1994), 8.
47. Lee J. Alston and Joseph Ferrie, *Southern Paternalism and the American Welfare State* (New York, 1999); Robert C. Lieberman, *Shifting the Color Line* (Cambridge, Mass., 1998).
48. Quoted in Jill Quadagno, *Aging in Early Industrial Society* (London, 1982), 115.
49. Skocpol, *Protecting Soldiers and Mothers*, 265.
50. Debra Street, "The Politics of Pensions in Canada, Great Britain, and the United States: 1975–1995" (Ph.D. diss., Florida State University, 1996).
51. Lubove, *The Struggle for Social Security*, 2.
52. Beatrix Hoffman, *The Wages of Sickness: The Politics of Health Insurance in Progressive America* (Chapel Hill, 2001), 26.
53. O'Connor, Orloff, and Shaver, *States, Markets, Families*, 50.

54. Quoted in Timothy Jost, *Disentitlement?* (New York, 2003), 208.

55. Carolyn Tuohy, *Accidental Logics: The Dynamics of Change in the Health Care Arena in the United States, Britain, and Canada* (New York, 1999), 26.

56. Malcolm Taylor, *Insuring National Health Care: The Canadian Experience* (Chapel Hill, 1991), 67–75.

57. Taylor, *Insuring National Health Care*, 161–234.

58. Tuohy, *Accidental Logics,* 55.

59. Antonia Maioni, *Parting at the Crossroads: The Emergence of Health Insurance in the United States and Canada* (Princeton, 1998).

60. Justin Keen, Donald Light, and Nicholas May, *Public-Private Relations in Health Care* London: King's Fund Publishing, 2001), 115–16; Donald Light, "The Practice and Ethics of Risk-Related Health Insurance," *Journal of the American Medical Association* 267 (13 May 1992): 2507; see also Thomas Bodenheimer, "Should We Abolish the Private Health Insurance Industry?" *International Journal of Health Services* 20, no. 2 (1990): 213.

61. Light, "Comparative Models of Health Care Systems," 465.

62. Jonathan Oberlander, *The Political Life of Medicare* (Chicago, 2003), 119–22.

63. Tuohy, *Accidental Logics*, 213.

64. Howard Waitzkin, *At the Front Lines of Medicine: How the Health Care System Alienates Doctors and Mistreats Patients . . . and What We Can Do About It* (Oxford, 2001), 156.

65. Street, *The Politics of Pensions*.

66. Ibid.; Gilbert, *Transformation of the Welfare State*.

67. Oberlander, *The Political Life of Medicare*, 108.

68. O'Connor, Orloff, and Shaver, *States, Markets, Families*, 53; Ginn, Street, and Arber, eds., *Women, Work, and Pensions*, chaps. 1 and 13; John Myles and Jill Quadagno, "Political Theories of the Welfare State," *Social Service Review* (March 2002): 34–35.

69. Ginn, Street, and Arber, *Women, Work, and Pensions*.

70. Gilbert, *Transformation of the Welfare State*, 13.

71. Thatcher observed that Progressive Conservative Canadian Prime Minister Brian Mulroney was both too progressive and insufficiently conservative.

72. O'Connor, Orloff, and Shaver, *States, Markets, Families*, 53.

73. Jennifer Mellor, "Filling in the Gaps in Long-Term Care Insurance," in *Care Work: Gender, Labor, and the Welfare State*, ed. Madonna Harrington Meyer (New York, 2000), 210; Joshua Wiener, "Financing Reform for Long-Term Care: Strategies for Public and Private Long-Term Care Insurance," in *From Nursing Homes to Home Care*, ed. Marie Cowart and Jill Quadagno (New York, 1996), 116.

74. Bowen Garrett and John Holahan, "Welfare Leavers, Medicaid Coverage, and Private Health Insurance," National Survey of America's Families, series B, no. B-13 (Washington, D.C., 2000), 3.

75. Katherine Swartz and Betsey Stevenson, "Health Insurance Coverage of People in the Ten Years Before Medicare Eligibility," in *Ensuring Health and Income Security for an Aging Workforce*, ed. Peter B. Budetti, Richard V. Burkhauser, Janice M. Gregory, and H. Allan Hunt (Kalamazoo, Mich., 2001), 16.

76. Stephanie Gould and John L. Palmer, "Outcomes, Interpretations, and Policy Implications," in *The Vulnerable*, ed. John Palmer, Timothy Smeeding, and Barbara Torrey (Washington, D.C., 1988), 428–47; Fay Lomax Cook and Edith J. Barrett, *Support for the American Welfare State* (New York, 1992), 102; Mark Schlesinger, "Reprivatizing the Public Household? Medical Care in the Context of American Public Values," *Journal of Health Politics, Policy, and Law* (2004).

77. Margaret R. Somers, "What's Political or Cultural About Political Culture and the Public Sphere? Toward an Historical Sociology of Concept Formation," *Sociological Theory* 13, no. 2 (1995): 123.

78. Murray Edelman, *Constructing the Political Spectacle* (Chicago, 1995); Anne E. Kane, "Theorizing Meaning Construction in Social Movements: Symbolic Structures and Inter-

pretation During the Irish Land War, 1879–1882," *Sociological Theory* 15, no. 3 (1997): 249–76.

79. Lawrence R. Jacobs and Robert Shapiro, *Politicians Don't Pander: Political Manipulation and the Loss of Democratic Responsiveness* (Chicago, 2000), 4.

80. Nicholas Pedriana and Robin Stryker, "Political Culture Wars 1960s Style: Equal Employment Opportunity—Affirmative Action Law and the Philadelphia Plan," *American Journal of Sociology* 10 (1997): 323–91; Kane, "Theorizing Meaning Construction in Social Movements," 249–76; Paul Burstein, "Policy Domains: Organization, Culture, and Policy Outcomes," *Annual Review of Sociology* 17 (1991): 327–50.

EILEEN BORIS

On the Importance of Naming:
Gender, Race, and the Writing of
Policy History

Twenty years ago, just as the study of policy was emerging out of the mo-
rass of political history,[1] historians of women rediscovered the state. What
I will name the policy turn challenged a kind of intellectual separate sphere
in which women's history addressed home, family, and intimate life and
left to other historians everything else. The policy turn shifted attention
from Carroll Smith Rosenberg's "Female World of Love and Ritual" without losing the self-activity and focus on female difference that investigations of women on their own terms had supplied.[2] It answered the "Politics
and Culture" debate of 1980,[3] which revolved around the efficacy of domesticity as an arena for power with a resounding move toward the public, political realm—namely, to social politics. The Reaganite assault on
the New Deal order and accompanying New Right attack on women's
rights[4] intensified investigation into the origins and growth of a welfare
state whose strength seemed precarious and whose history was up for
grabs—a welfare state that blurred the separation of private and public
and constructed, even as it reinforced, unequal social locations.[5]

The resulting narratives expanded policy history to include women
as policymakers and policies directed toward women as wives, mothers,
daughters, consumers, workers, and citizens.[6] But this shift occurred amid
changes in the theoretical underpinnings of women's history. The mid-
1980s marked the ascendancy of difference as the central problematic
within feminist thought. Scholars challenged conventional notions of
gender, promoting social constructionist understandings of womanhood
and manhood. Rejecting universal categories, the new scholarship emphasized differences among women on the basis of sexuality, race, ethnicity,
and nationality. Gender, we learned, provided a language through which
other social relations of power and authority became articulated.[7]

THE JOURNAL OF POLICY HISTORY, Vol. 17, No. 1, 2005.

Joan Scott set the terms for research when she declared that "political [or, we might add, policy] history has . . . been enacted on the field of gender." In her classic essay, "Gender: A Useful Category of Historical Analysis," she asked, "What is the relationship between laws about women and the power of the state?" "What is the relationship between state politics and the discovery of the crime of homosexuality? How have social institutions incorporated gender into their assumptions and organizations?"[8] Policies that on the surface were not about women, sexuality, or gender became subject to analysis of their gender silences and the gendered assumptions they expressed.[9]

Indeed, discourses, which policy presents and embodies, not merely express gender but also construct men and women through the very act of naming.[10] Judith Butler's understanding of "performative power" particularly illuminated this process of categorization through discourse. "The heterosexualization of the social bond is the paradigmatic form for those speech acts which bring about what they name. 'I pronounce you' . . . puts into effect the relation that it names," she explained. That is, "forms of authoritative speech," which include laws and state documents like marriage certificates, occupational licenses, and applications for social assistance, turn discourse into action or expressions of power.[11] By classifying the homosexual by sex acts performed, for example, the state created an identity.[12] Similarly, exclusion from the labor law meant denying recognition as workers to the majority of men and women of color and white women who labored at home, in the fields, or without a wage.[13]

The substitution of gender for women, and gender relations for women's experiences, still privileged gender over other social identities and structures of power and authority. A second challenge in the 1980s came from scholars of race who introduced the idea of intersectionality (the notion that identity derives from multiple factors like race, gender, and class) and promoted the concept of racialized gender.[14] As I have claimed elsewhere, despite attempts to disaggregate the workings of race from gender, individuals and groups embody both in ways that the mere addition of race to gender cannot signify. Manhood, womanhood, and sexualities probably never exist apart from race; not only is race gendered, but the policing of the boundaries of race significantly takes place through rules on who can marry or have sex with whom, that is, through gendered definitions.[15]

In some respects, policy history's encounter with race paralleled its recognition of gender—an expansion of who appeared as policymakers followed by consideration of the structural workings of race in policy formation, enactment, and implementation.[16] In addition, a challenge to state-centered studies came from a focus on the grassroots, nonelectoral, or alternative institutional spaces in which struggles for racial and racialized gendered justice have occurred. Call this policy history from below, in which the voices and aspirations of the subaltern or the disenfranchised constrain, if not make, policy.[17] But race seemed more obviously central to explications of U.S. exceptionalism; slavery and segregation were more at the heart of the national experience, even though one might argue that the sexual division of labor and the role of the heterosexual family fundamentally has structured the polity and economy no less than intimate life. Nonetheless, gender often remained silenced or neglected in studies on race and public policy until historians researching racial/ethnic women and critical race feminists highlighted the workings of racialized gender.[18]

New racial theorists, such as sociologists Michael Omni and Howard Winant, have challenged static concepts of race, emphasizing the social, economic, legal, cultural, and political circumstances by which groups gain racial or ethnic identities.[19] As Winant has explained, race is a central aspect of "the individual psyche," "relationships," "collective identities," and "social structures."[20] Research on the making of blackness under slavery and Jim Crow initially supplied the basis for reinterpretating racial formation, just as the black-white binary that historians have relied upon to explain the shaping of U.S. public policy appeared to have set the terms under which other groups have come under federal law.[21] Studies of whiteness, including changing racial designations of newcomers from southern and Eastern Europe, have provided race its own history.[22]

Work on immigrants from Asia and the Americas, though, has complicated the black-white binary. These studies have both reinforced its iron grip (with whiteness as an aspiration or distinction from blackness as a goal) and shattered its hold. They reorient us geographically away from a North-South axis to the Southwest and West, highlight numerous streams of immigration, and consider the impact on migration of U.S. foreign policy, such as the occupation of the Philippines and the colonization of Puerto Rico. Multiple racial narratives have developed, with language, education, economic resources, family structure, and condition of entry (whether temporary or permanent, documented or undocumented) generating internal differentiations among Asians and Latinas/Latinos as well as migrants from specific places, like Africa and the Caribbean.[23]

Such developments in theory, along with political struggles over work and welfare in the 1980s and 1990s, shaped the study of gender, race, and policy history. So did conceptualizations that policy history itself as an interdisciplinary practice brought to the study of the state. For policy history offered frameworks derived from political science, political sociology, and policy analysis that historians of women and gender would adapt.

These frameworks, from policy feedback to welfare regimes to a renewed attention to federalism, troubled any lingering radical feminist or nationalist formulation that equated state action with oppression models of victimization. But while "the state" as a concept gained in complexity through an expansion of its components, agents, languages, and interactions,[24] the meaning of terms like "women," "gender," "race," and "racialized gender" were taken for granted.

"Sex" or "race" have appeared self-evident because only at significant moments of contestation or crisis have the makers and implementers of policy considered their meaning, explicitly defined them, and in the process helped to construct such identities. For all sorts of policies—including apportionment, enfranchisement, military recruitment, and taxation as well as immigration, labor, marriage, education, housing, and social assistance—have depended on classification, such as knowing who is a man or a woman, who is kin or a parent or a child, who is black or nonwhite or white, who is a resident or not, and who is a citizen or a documented or undocumented immigrant. By complicating the categories of "race," "gender," and "racialized gender," I argue in this essay, gender, queer, and new racial studies can enrich a policy history that has moved from considering gender and race apart to thinking of each of these categories as integral to the other. First, I will reconsider the equality-difference debate, so central to feminist scholarship over the last quarter century, which manifested itself through the maternalist paradigm. This conceptual binary still pervaded the feminist turn to citizenship as a framework for analysis. Then I will briefly discuss recent scholarship on immigration and its racialized and heteronormative assumptions. Such work already is challenging policy history as we know it.

From Maternalism to Citizenship: What's in a Paradigm?

The rise and decline of maternalism as a framework for understanding social welfare policy illustrates the impact of feminist thought and the influence of state-centered modes of analysis on the writing of policy history.[25] The stakes in the maternalism wars revolved around women's agency in the creation of the welfare state and the place of the home and motherhood in law and social policy, as well as the very meaning of citizenship and rights in a liberal polity.[26] Questions of whether equality for women would come from being treated the same as men or whether equality could be met from taking account of female reproductive labor polarized feminists. From the late 1960s into the 1990s, the resulting equality-difference debate manifested itself through a series of clashes over "protective labor" legislation, reproductive rights at the workplace, and maternity leave, policy legacies of earlier attempts to reconcile women's wage work with family responsibilities.[27]

In the early 1980s, against the ascendancy of difference theories in feminist thought,[28] Alice Kessler-Harris powerfully argued for gender equity. She charted how the domestic claim impeded, even as it shaped, women's employment. Her interpretation on how wage and hour laws for women only enhanced occupational segregation by sex, thus restricting employment, resonated with a new labor feminism that sought higher wages and flexible hours in "female" jobs and also entrance into occupations dominated by men.[29] Kessler-Harris would continue to judge harshly the workings of what she more recently has named "the gender imagination" on public policy. With increasing theoretical sophistication and reference to Scandinavian social democratic alternatives, she critiqued early twentieth-century social feminists, the Women's Bureau, and later trade-union women for their support of hegemonic gender norms of male breadwinning and female domesticity and their situating women's labor-force participation in the context of family obligations rather than individual aspirations.[30]

Other scholars historicized difference in charting "maternalist discourses," the name that Seth Koven and Sonya Michel gave to "ideologies that exalted women's capacity to mother and extended to society as a whole the values of care, nurturance, and morality."[31] Political sociologist Theda Skocpol enshrined maternalism in the 1992 *Protecting Soldiers and Mothers*. Skocpol sought "why maternalist forces promoting social policies for mothers and women workers were considerably more effective in U.S. politics during the early 1990s than were paternalist forces that simultaneously worked for the enactment of policies targeted on male wage-earners."[32] The administrative capture by "corrupt" political parties associated with Civil War pensions, combined with limited bureaucratic capacity, she proposed, hampered the growth of a universal pension and welfare system. But the enactment of mothers' pensions suggested that the United States was an innovator, rather than a laggard, in welfare state development—albeit in a maternalist vein.[33]

Along with Linda Gordon, Kessler-Harris judged Skocpol's gender analysis as lacking. Skocpol failed to recognize that maternalists actually were paternalists, who would restrict female wage earning, whether or not women were mothers or mothers were breadwinners. Early twentieth-century women reformers supported the family wage as an alternative to the exploitative conditions faced by the mother who had to earn; they would harness the power of the law to compel men to support their families.[34] The resulting maternalist legislation targeted working-class families, conflating what was good for mothers and children with an enhanced capacity of the state to promote the dominance of elites.[35] In contrast, Kathryn Kish Sklar positively assessed early twentieth-century activists, such as Florence Kelley and Jane Addams, as "social justice feminists" for their commitment to structural change in the economy as well as the family.[36]

Gordon and Kessler-Harris were more attuned to the ideological, discursive, and "fundamental social divisions of class, race, and sex" [37] and Skocpol to the governmental and interest-group aspects of policy contestation. Still, it was not that Gordon and other women historians clung to ideological or social explanations, while Skocpol offered political ones. Each generated competing sets of binary divisions: what Skocpol saw as maternalism and paternalism, Gordon historicized as public assistance and social insurance models of welfare policy. Barbara Nelson divided social politics into two tracks, female and male, undeserving and deserving, means-tested and entitled. Suzanne Mettler more precisely characterized the welfare state as separated into state, local, and federal authorities, grounding gender norms in state structures, especially federalism.[38]

The state, then, could no longer appear as merely an instrument to maintain or extend male dominance; rather, it reinforced the racialized gender order—and women reformers, as maternalists, played a significant role in that process by defining proper homes and families. As Gordon recognized in her discussion of the casework approach that pervaded the Children's Bureau and state-level departments of public assistance, social control as well as class or racial hegemony often came along with the implementation of such programs.[39] As she put it, "white women's welfarist activity played a role in maintaining, even reinforcing, class and race exclusions." Maternalist politics sustained what Gwendolyn Mink pinpointed as "socializ[ing] motherhood rather than citizenship." Mink underscored "the origins of the American welfare state" in "gender-based solutions to what was widely perceived to be a racial problem,"[40] that is, the assimilation of ethnic/racial others.

For their part, African American women promoted maternal and child health and social support for lone mothers. As I suggested in 1989, race made a difference: white women's mother talk could reinforce dominant notions of womanhood, while black women's demands on the basis of their motherhood proved more oppositional, given their representation as workers, rather than mothers, in a world that maintained such a distinction.[41] In Chicago, black clubwomen became municipal employees, enforcing decisions of the juvenile court.[42] Immigrant women too would use mechanisms established to control their behavior for their own ends, as Gordon documented in her 1988 history of domestic violence and as Mary Odem showed in her 1995 analysis of sexual regulation of teenage women.[43] But to account for race and ethnicity as anything but exclusion or discrimination often meant shifting gears, away from the formal state apparatus to the voluntary or private realm.[44]

Moving from the social-control thesis, Michel documented how pensions functioned as an alternative to out-of-home child care.[45] In this interpretation, mothers' pensions were less about family life and caretaking and more about work and earning (though the two could not be separated easily).[46] Michel's subsequent history of child care, along with case studies of Philadelphia, Cleveland, Washington, D.C., and California, underscored policy ambivalence around maternal employment. Children's needs, especially for education and cultural assimilation, better justified nonparental care than women's right to earn.[47]

The connection of mothering and soldiering as representing services to the state equally deserving of recompense, which Skocpol saw embodying two policy paths, provided historical grounding for political scientist Wendy Sarvasy. She found in mothers' pensions the possibility for universal endowment of motherhood. Christening as social democratic feminists a multiracial group of women reformers, including Addams, Kelley, Rose Schneiderman, and Mary Church Terrell, Sarvasy reconceptualized their thought to imagine a participatory state that cared for human need outside the market, in which the service work of women offered the template for a larger citizenship.[48] Difference then provided an alternative to an equality that conflated male activities with the good.

However, in a challenge to Skocpol (no less than to Grace Abbott and other historical promulgators), legal historian Susan M. Sterett convincingly has unraveled the soldier/mother service analogy. Soldiers were unique because the federal government alone could conduct war and reward their efforts. But courts also upheld pensions for firemen, police, civil servants, and some teachers as "payments for service." Mothers' pensions, in contrast, passed muster as a form of "poor relief, payments . . . granted as a matter of charity rather than entitlements, and . . . paid only to the indigent, not to all mothers." By explicating the establishment of state-level pensions, Sterett established a long trajectory for the connection of pensions to employment. "What in other countries is a social right of citizenship," she contended, "is in the United States a return for work." She thus complicated structure of governance arguments by underscoring the significance of municipalities and state courts for defining the basis upon which the state could give pensions.[49]

Citizenship for All!

By the late 1990s, the maternalist paradigm had played itself out. In response, gender scholars followed the trajectory of other historians of the welfare state by turning to citizenship. They made two intellectual moves. First, interdisciplinary work on gender and the state reworked the Swedish political theorist Gøsta Esping-Andersen.[50] These studies looked at comparative models of welfare states, considered the political and economic resources that organized groups brought to bear upon struggles over social welfare, and evaluated the kinds of social programs, such as unemployment and pensions, which made workers less dependent on the market and better able to bargain with employers.[51] Feminist analysis questioned Esping-Andersen's emphasis on paid labor and the male unionist as ideal citizen. It shifted the terms of debate, asking about the resources women would need to achieve independence from male breadwinners and thus the ability to exit marriages. It introduced the term "defamilization," or those supports that would uncouple women from family labor by providing incentives to reorganize reproduction and caregiving. This literature, however, rarely incorporated race into its framework. For racial ethnic women, I have contended, we might reconceptualize the problem as barriers impeding the right to care, or the ability to remain outside the labor market, rather than the right to earn.[52]

Second, the influence of T. H. Marshall led women historians to disaggregate the components of citizenship, distinguishing civil from political and social rights. The right to a job (a civil right) and to living wages (a social right) has appeared central to citizenship, but feminists noted that these rights presume waged and exclude the unpaid labor of women. White women's attainment of state services before suffrage questioned Marshall's progressive narrative in which civil and then political citizenship paved the way for social citizenship. So did the simultaneous struggle of African Americans for civil, political, and social citizenship during World War II.[53] Moreover, Marshall limited the beneficiaries of "individual economic freedom," as Alice Kessler-Harris has pointed out, to men by noting how married women stood apart from the community norm. Rights thus took on different forms for women whose responsibility for childbearing and rearing often undermined accessibility to social rights constructed through wage work.[54]

Through the concept of "economic citizenship," defined as "the independent status that provides the possibility of full participation in the polity," Kessler-Harris lifted the right to work out of the general category of civil rights. She has shown how a range of public policies (including protective labor legislation, Social Security, and tax law) promoted the family wage and opposed labor-force attachment of married women. The struggle for women's rights over the course of the twentieth century, then, pivoted around "the right to earn." In this vein, Emilie Stoltzfus has presented the concept "productive citizenship," used during the early years of the Cold War to justify "subsidized child care" as "a social right." Only with legislative and legal victories in the 1960s and early 1970s did public policy attempt to correct the disadvantages that stemmed from "conceiving of women as primarily family members" that, for Kessler-Harris, led to economic discrimination and, thus, denial of citizenship rights.[55] However, African American women never appeared in the dominant culture as family members in quite the same way as did European American women. As numerous scholars have documented, including Dorothy Roberts, Johanna Schoen, and Rickie Solinger, social policies have interfered with their bodily autonomy, reproductive rights, and access to Marshall's decent standards of social citizenship.[56]

Other women of color also experienced exclusion from these rights because of labor market segregation by racialized gender that placed them and their men in uncovered occupations, with their family work further curtailing access to social citizenship.[57] Moreover, immigrants from Asia and the Americas labored in family businesses, "illegal" sweatshops, or fields, often under threat of deportation, and thus outside the law.[58] Among communities of color, the quest for economic citizenship developed a dual meaning. For African Americans and other racial/ethnic groups—for men as well as women—economic citizenship embraced not only the right to a job or fair employment, the right to fair compensation or equal pay, but also, as Evelyn Nakano Glenn has observed, escape from coercion to labor.[59]

Beginning in the 1930s, the growth of a mixed private-public welfare state that privileged employment over unpaid carework maintained the two tracks identified by scholars of the Progressive Era, with racialized gendered consequences. The first, which was federally funded and administrated, embraced the economy's core-sector workers—who were more often white men—and their dependents. The National Labor Relations or Wagner Act facilitated the collective bargaining crucial for industrial workers to wrestle better wages, working conditions, and, with World War II, fringe benefits such as pensions and health care from their employers, inscribing a private welfare state within this federal one. The second, which was left to the states and their greater arbitrariness, covered the most socially and economically disadvantaged people, who were more often men of color and women.[60] Especially in the area of health care, Jennifer Klein has documented how the private welfare state grew with the expansion of state benefits, crowding out community- and union-based alternatives such as group health and disadvantaging the vast majority of nonwhites, the nonunionized working class, and many white women whose places in the labor market made them ineligible for benefits.[61]

Sonya Michel and I attempted to bridge the employment/care divide by claiming that the civil right to work was an empty right without additional substantive rights to social services.[62] This understanding that employment required attention to dependent care historicizes insights of labor feminists before and after passage of Title VII of the Civil Rights Act of 1964, who lobbied for child care, maternity leave, and a host of other programs necessary for women to exercise their "civil" right to earn. Dorothy Sue Cobble recently emphasized how labor feminists demanded both "'equal rights' and 'special benefits,'" proposing a mixture of state regulation, social services, and collective-bargaining agreements.[63]

The equality-difference conundrum became racialized in scholarship on aid to poor women and their children. "Welfare" reflected dominant understandings of women's citizenship even as it helped generate a lesser citizenship for the needy. ADC (AFDC after the 1962 amendments) has garnered the most attention, undoubtedly because of political challenges during the last decades of the twentieth century that culminated with Bill Clinton's "ending of welfare as we know it" in 1996.[64] Kessler-Harris first highlighted the significance of the 1939 amendments that gave "dependent wives and aged widows" old-age insurance (OAI) if husbands were eligible, segregating poor lone mothers into a separate, despised category. That Congress chose to enhance the benefits of those already covered and their families rather than extend coverage to domestics and agricultural workers suggested that gendered notions of fairness trumped over racial equity.[65] Mink stressed the ways that these amendments distinguished between types of dependency, providing fuller support to widows than those deserted, divorced, or unmarried since ADC originally lacked a caretaker grant.[66] The state's formulation reflected the illiberal assumption that male household heads represented their dependents in the body politic and women without such heads were to become "wards" of the state.

By disciplining the poor and shoring up the low-waged labor supply, the racialization of welfare served political ends. Administrators denied benefits to women of color for being "undeserving," instituted behavioral and other requirements for eligibility to limit their numbers, and finally lessened the value of welfare itself through declining monetary worth and workfare.[67] Joanne Goodwin emphasized that southern states from the 1940s passed "employable mother" rules to push would-be recipients into the labor market if any form of employment was available. State agencies demanded that poor single mothers earn income as well as care for their children, especially when such mothers were black and not married.[68] Re-periodizing the movement toward workfare, Jennifer Mittelstadt has located this shift to the late 1940s, when a new group of social welfare experts sought to end dependency through employment. They offered a therapeutic approach to rehabilitate dysfunctional families and cure individual psychosis through a mother's waged labor.[69]

Naming became central to welfare politics. Comparing Louisiana's 1960 slashing of its rolls with Newburgh, New York's 1961 campaign against chiselers, Lisa Levenstein documented the power of rhetorical framing; "child aid" garnered positive public response in contrast to portrayals of "unwed mother aid."[70] In the late 1960s, liberal antipoverty forces also generated a discourse of deficient family structures. With Ruth Feldstein and Felicia Kornbluh, Marisa Chappell has rethought liberalism by delineating its adherence to traditional, if not conservative, gender ideology. Liberals distinguished between "moms and matriarchs," as Feldstein has put it.[71] While liberals hoped to provide African Americans a family wage and feminists sought a new family wage for single mothers, Reagan tax policies promoted a family wage for the wealthy. Conservatives deployed the discourse of failed families in an effort to cut government spending and dismantle the welfare state. Some blamed government largess for economic conditions that forced worthy working-class families to send wives and mothers into the labor force. Welfare, in this scenario, appeared "unfair" because the "undeserving" could stay home, but working-class women had little choice but to leave their children in day care and go out to work.[72]

Recent questions of equal rights and different obligations, at the center of the literature on the politics of care, link welfare and immigration to global trade and transnational labor regulation. This new research has complicated further the workings of equality and difference under a transformed gender system in which the wage-earning mother has become the norm. It has joined with feminist critiques of the global care deficit to interrogate how class, race, and citizenship status, abetted by public policies, has allowed some women to gain economic citizenship because other women clean their houses and care for their children, disabled, ill, and elderly.[73]

Defining Citizenship Through Sexuality and Race

Now attentive to gender, citizenship as a category of analysis is undergoing additional permeations. More scholars speak of "sexual, intimate, or reproductive citizenship." Eileen H. Richardson and Brian S. Turner divide this terrain into "theories of sexual entitlement (such as the right to reproduce under conditions of one's own choosing) and general theories of sexual citizenship in terms of lifestyle and consumerism (such as the right to sexual choice, pleasure and fulfillment)." They emphasize "the demand of gay and lesbian communities to enjoy the same rights as heterosexuals (sexual citizenship proper), and the expectation of the diversification of sexual pleasure in a more open and liberal society (intimate citizenship)."[74]

The literature on abortion, birth control, and state regulation of reproduction comes under this rubric with its racialized, class, and imperial dimensions. Work by Leslie Reagan and Rickie Solinger, for example, has highlighted the legal and legislative categorization of abortion as "a crime," while Donald Critchlow has charted the public-private making of population policy.[75] In linking the study of sex and reproduction to colonialism, Laura Briggs critiques not only state policies in Puerto Rico but also "rescue" narratives provided by mainland women reformers and later feminist critics of sterilization and population control.[76] These works are beginning to connect reproductive politics to state development.

In taking account of sexual citizenship, the structural role of marriage and heterosexuality become central to analyzing the welfare state. As Nancy Cott has noted, by 1996 there existed "more than *one thousand* places in the corpus of federal law where legal marriage conferred a distinctive status, right, or benefit."[77] Michel has been analyzing the benefits of whiteness, maleness, and heteronormativity in systems of private as well as public welfare, and Mink has stressed the ways that welfare policy relies on normative assumptions about marriage to discipline poor women.[78] In showing the Veteran's Administration interpreting the G.I. Bill—with its education, housing, and other benefits—to exclude those with "less than honorable" discharges, despite the letter of the law, Margot Canaday offers a particularly compelling analysis of structural heterosexuality. By focusing on the first direct federal exclusion of gays and lesbians from welfare state largess, she presents the social consequences of the G.I. "closet": its institutionalization of "heterosexuality by channeling resources to men so that—at a moment when women had made significant gains in the workplace—the economic incentives for women to marry remained firmly in place."[79] While John D'Emilio, William B. Turner, and Marc Stein, among others, have investigated the nexus of public policies and gay rights,[80] Canaday connects this history both to queer studies, with its emphasis on state construction of gay identities, and the larger literature on social citizenship and the welfare state.

The imperative to classify people by sexual and reproductive practices, which gender and queer theory especially have highlighted, also
has controlled immigration and naturalization policy. In considering immigration policy, we particularly witness the challenge of multiple racial
and ethnic identities to the black-white binary. Shifting classification of
South Asians and Spanish speakers reflected contradictory desires for racial "purity" and cheap labor. From the first act in 1790, which restricted
potential citizenship to whites only, through the 1875 Page Law, which
excluded Asian women "imported" for prostitution, and the 1884 Chinese Exclusion Act, which allowed only the wives of elites to join husbands, and the national quota acts of the 1920s, which disproportionately
admitted Northern Europeans, immigration policy has embedded racialized
gendered assumptions.[81] Well into the twentieth century, the citizenship
status of husbands determined wives (even for citizen women married to
noncitizens). Children of father citizens not married to their mothers born
outside the United States faced a more difficult process than those born
to citizen mothers, regardless of their location. These rules not only af-
firmed dominant gender systems, but they reinscribed the racial order by
punishing citizen women who married men ineligible for citizenship, as
many Asians were before 1950.[82]

Regulations also have upheld a racialized familialism. Pregnant women
were deemed likely to become public charges, their entry often denied.
Family reunification became the official policy, allowing the admittance
of wives, parents, children under eighteen, and other relatives of citizens
and those eligible for citizenship—a preference ensconced in 1965 reforms. Before then, it took additional acts of Congress, including the lift-
ing of Asian restrictions, for Japanese women married to GIs to come to
the United States, despite the 1945 War Brides Act. Wives, whose previous practice of prostitution disqualified entry, required special waivers.
Despite legalization provisions in 1986 immigration reform, tighter border enforcement has disrupted family formation among Mexican immigrants and made it difficult for the mothers of citizen children to become
documented. In going after those who would use the affective to cheat
quotas, the Immigration Marriage Fraud Amendment (also 1986) functioned like earlier administrative attempts to ferret out paper sons among
Chinese who had relied upon false family histories and identities to gain
admittance. As with the double sexualization of Filipino men who mi-
grated alone to the United States, charged with lusting after white women
despite being labeled as "ambiguous, inscrutable, and hermaphroditic,"
immigration and naturalization policy continued to classify by racialized
gender. It reinforced the significance of marriage for a racialized and
gendered construction of citizenship.[83]

Canaday's insight into the ways that immigration policy determined the homosexual illuminates both the creation of identities and their indeterminacy. The 1952 McCarran Walter Act defined the homosexual as a "psychopathic personality," though INS agents ascertained status through conduct that came to their attention through criminal charges, often for disorderly conduct or moral turpitude [code words for public sex], that usually led to deportation of already present migrants. This focus on conduct "destabiliz[ed] homosexuality as identity by asserting either that homosexual conduct did not make one homosexual or that homosexuals were not psychopathic, and thus not covered by the law."[84] Race, however, mattered; the two cases where work history and family ties led courts to determine individuals were not homosexuals involved Northern European men. But in 1967, the Supreme Court labeled the homosexual an identity stemming from behavior, which immigration reform in 1965 specifically included under "psychopathic" exclusions.

Appearance, rather than crime, more likely brought lesbians to the attention of the border patrol.[85] While appearance may have expressed identities, law has not recognized discriminations based on these markers of racialized gender. Rather, courts have interpreted antidiscrimination law as addressing fundamental rights, such as the right to marry and bear children, finding no right to express cultural identity on the job through hair or dress. With "race" and "gender" losing their predetermined meaning, however, law that relies on fixed categories seems less able to address grievances manifested in daily life.[86]

What are the consequences for the practice of policy history from these directions in scholarship and theory? How will our writing about bureaucracy, federalism, policy feedbacks, or a host of other standard areas be affected? More careful empirical research that explores the impact of the black-white binary on women as well as men from other racial/ethnic groups will help reassess the saliency of that model over time and across the nation. Attention to reproduction and sexualities can expand the topics of policy history and illuminate the building blocks and power relations within the welfare state itself. Bringing marriage and the family, domestic labor and bodies, into the center of policy history complicates understandings of citizenship, while a focus on immigration reminds that not all denizens are citizens. Citizenship is about exclusion as well as inclusion. At the least, the destabilization of social categories suggests self-consciousness of assumptions in ways that demand genealogies of not only the very terms and categories we deploy as historians but also new histories of the categories through which various state actors and agencies have operated that are fully attentive to racialized gender as well as age, nationality, religion, class, and other factors whose meanings have rarely remained static.

That "gay marriage" and guest-worker programs have become hotly contested issues underscore the field's origins in providing usable pasts for public deliberations. Over the last twenty years, scholars have investigated the historical roots of the work and family dilemma, argued about the consequences of equal treatment and special treatment for gender and racial equity, and complicated struggles over the right to care and be cared for no less than the right to earn. Those who write policy history will continue to take their clues from those who are making current policy and the dilemmas faced by peoples with conflicting aspirations and uneven access to power and resources.

University of California at Santa Barbara

Notes

1. The best account of the development of policy history is Julian E. Zelizer, "Clio's Lost Tribe: Public Policy History Since 1978," *Journal of Policy History* 12 (2000), 369–94; for a personalistic one hostile to gender analysis, see Guy Alchon, "Policy History and the Sublime Immodesty of the Middle Age Professor," *Journal of Policy History* 9 (1997): 358–74.

2. Carroll Smith Rosenberg, "The Female World of Love and Ritual: Relations Between Women in Nineteenth-Century America," *Signs: A Journal of Women in Culture and Society* 1 (1975): 1–29; Daniel Scott Smith, "Family Limitation, Sexual Control, and Domestic Feminism in Victorian America," *Feminist Studies* 1 (1973): 40–57; Nancy Cott, "Passionlessness: An Interpretation of Victorian Sexual Ideology, 1790–1850," *Signs: A Journal of Women in Culture and Society* 4 (1978): 219–36.

3. Judith R. Walkowitz, "Introduction: Politics and Culture in Women's History: A Symposium," *Feminist Studies* 6 (1980): 26ff.

4. Steven P. Erie, Martin Rein, and Barbara Wiget, "Women and the Reagan Revolution: Thermidor for the Social Welfare Economy," in Irene Diamond, ed., *Families, Politics, and Public Policy: A Feminist Dialogue on Women and the State* (New York, 1983), 94–119; Michel K. Brown, ed., *Remaking the Welfare State: Retrenchment and Social Policy in America and Europe* (Philadelphia, 1988).

5. This was the context in which Peter Bardaglio and I wrote "The Transformation of Patriarchy: The Historic Role of the State," in Diamond, *Families, Politics, and Public Policy*, 70–93.

6. Susan Ware, *Beyond Suffrage: Women in the New Deal* (Cambridge, 1981); Judith Sealander, *As Minority Becomes Majority: Federal Reaction to the Phenomenon of Women in the Work Force, 1920–1963* (Westport, Conn., 1983); Cynthia Harrison, *On Account of Sex: The Politics of Women's Issues, 1945–1968* (Berkeley and Los Angeles, 1988).

7. One way to trace this trajectory is Linda Nicholson, ed., *The Second Wave: A Reader in Feminist Theory* (New York, 1997), in comparison with Carole McCann and Seung-Kyung Kim, *Feminist Theory Reader: Local and Global Perspectives* (New York, 2003).

8. Joan Wallach Scott, "Gender: A Useful Category of Historical Analysis," in Scott, *Gender and the Politics of History* (New York, 1988), 49–50.

9. Even Carroll Smith-Rosenberg engaged in this change; see "Dis-Covering the Subject of the 'Great Constitutional Discussion,' 1786–1789," *Journal of American History*

79 (1992): 841–73. War and taxes of course come to mind: for example, Carol Cohn, "Sex and Death in the Rational World of Defense Intellectuals," *Signs* 12 (1987): 687–718; Lee Ann Whites, "The Civil War as a Crisis in Gender," in *Divided Houses: Gender and the Civil War*, ed. Catherine Clinton and Nina Silber (New York, 1992); Alice Kessler-Harris, "'A Principle of Law But Not of Justice': Men, Women, and Income Taxes in the United States, 1913–1948," *Southern California Review of Law and Women's Studies* 6 (1997): 331–60.

10. For an excellent explication, see Nan Enstad, *Ladies of Labor, Girls of Adventure: Working Women, Popular Culture, and Labor Politics at the Turn of the Twentieth Century* (New York, 1999), 109–10.

11. Judith Butler, "Critically Queer," in *Bodies That Matter* (New York, 1993), 224–25. See also idem, *Gender Trouble: Feminism and the Subversion of Identity* (New York, 1989).

12. Of course, these scholars draw upon Michael Foucault, *The History of Sexuality* (New York, 1980), vol. 1. See the impact of the law in the now-classic work of George Chauncey, *Gay New York: Gender, Urban Culture, and the Making of the Gay Male World, 1890–1940* (New York, 1994), and, more recently, Nan Alamilla Boyd, *Wide Open Town: A History of Queer San Francisco to 1965* (Berkeley and Los Angeles, 2003).

13. Eileen Boris, "Labor's Welfare State: Defining Workers, Constructing Citizens," in Michael Grossberg and Christopher Tomlins, eds., *Cambridge Encyclopedia of American Law*, vol. 3 (New York, forthcoming).

14. Eileen Boris, "The Racialized Gendered State: Constructions of Citizenship in the United States," *Social Politics* 2 (1995): 160–80.

15. For the concept of racialized gender, I have extrapolated from such scholars as Evelyn Nakano Glenn, "From Servitude to Service Work: Historical Continuities in the Racial Division of Women's Work," *Signs* 18 (1992): 1–43, Fiona Williams, *Social Policy: A Critical Introduction to Issues of Race, Gender, and Class* (Cambridge, 1989), and Gwendolyn Mink, *The Wages of Motherhood: Inequality in the Welfare State, 1917–1942* (Ithaca, 1995). See also Tessie Liu, "Teaching Differences among Women from a Historical Perspective: Rethinking Race and Gender as Social Categories," *Women's Studies International Forum* 14 (1991): 265–76, and my "'You Wouldn't Want One of 'Em Dancing With Your Wife': Racialized Bodies on the Job in WWII," *American Quarterly* 50 (1998): 77–108. For marriage, see Rachel F. Moran, *Interracial Intimacy: The Regulation of Race and Romance* (Chicago, 2001), and Peggy Pascoe, "Miscegenation Law, Court Cases, and Ideologies of 'Race' in 20th-Century America," *Journal of American History* 83 (1996): 44–69.

16. For example, Jill Quadagno, *The Color of Welfare: How Racism Undermined the War on Poverty* (New York, 1994); Dona C. Hamilton and Charles V. Hamilton, *The Dual Agenda: Race and Social Welfare Policies of Civil Rights Organizations* (New York, 1997); Robert C. Lieberman, *Shifting the Color Line: Race and the American Welfare State* (Cambridge, 1998); and Michael K. Brown, *Race, Money, and The American Welfare State* (Ithaca: 1999).

17. See my "'The Right to Work Is the Right to Live!' Fair Employment and the Quest for Social Citizenship," in Manfred Berg and Martin H. Geyer, eds., *Two Cultures of Rights: The Quest for Inclusion and Participation in Modern America and Germany* (New York, 2002), 121–41, in which I consider "working-class voices" in the conception of fair employment; and Felicia Kornbluh, "'To Fulfill Their Rightly Needs': Consumerism and the National Welfare Rights Movement," *Radical History Review*, no. 69 (1997): 76–113, for poor women's reconceptualization of their rights. These also take the form of local history or case studies: for one model, see Rhonda Williams on mid-century Baltimore, *The Politics of Public Housing: Black Women's Struggles Against Urban Inequality* (New York, 2005); for another, George Lipsitz, *A Life in the Struggle: Ivory Perry and the Culture of Opposition* (Philadelphia, 1988). Much of the literature on civil rights organizing can be reread through a policy history perspective.

18. For example, Kimberle Crenshaw, "Demarginalizing the Intersection of Race and Sex: A Black Feminist Critique of Anti-discrimination Doctrine, Feminist Theory, and Anti-racist Politics," *University of Chicago Legal Forum* 139 (1989): 139–67.

19. This process they name "racialization." Michael Omni and Howard Winant, *Racial Formation in the United States*, 2d ed. (New York, 1994). See also Howard Winant, *The World Is a Ghetto: Race and Democracy Since World War II* (New York, 2001).

20. Howard Winant, *Racial Conditions: Politics, Theory, Comparisons* (Minneapolis, 1994), 23, as quoted by Linda Gordon, *The Great Arizona Orphan Abduction* (Cambridge, 1999), 99. Gordon provides an excellent summary of the social constructionist theory of race and of competing and changing racial systems in the Southwest a century ago.

21. For example, Vicki L. Ruiz, "Tapestries of Resistance: Episodes of School Segregation and Desegregation in the U.S. West," in Peter Lau, ed., *From Grassroots to the Supreme Court: Exploration of Brown V. Board of Education and American Democracy* (Durham, forthcoming), provides a new context for civil rights based on Latina/Latino struggles, showing that these did not necessarily follow the black freedom movement but existed in tandem and perhaps helped to shape its legal strategy.

22. This literature is huge, not usually thought of as part of policy history, but often addresses the impact of policy or state action. See, for example, Barbara Jeanne Fields, "Slavery, Race, and Ideology in the United States of America," *New Left Review* 181 (1990): 95–118; David Roediger, *The Wages of Whiteness: Race and the Making of the American Working Class* (New York, 1991); James R. Barrett and David Roediger, "Inbetween Peoples: Race, Nationality, and the "New Immigrant" Working Class," *Journal of American Ethnic History* 16 (1997): 3–45; Matthew Frye Jacobson, *Whiteness of a Different Color: European Immigrants and the Alchemy of Race* (Cambridge, 1998); Ian F. Haney López, *White by Law: The Legal Construction of Race* (New York, 1996); George Lipsitz, *The Possessive Investment in Whiteness: How White People Profit from Identity Politics* (Philadelphia, 1998); Karin Bodkin, *How Jews Became White Folks and What That Says About Race in America* (New Brunswick, 1998); and Grace Elizabeth Hale, *Making Whiteness: The Culture of Segregation in the South, 1890–1940* (New York, 1999). For a critical assessment, see Eric Arnesen, "Whiteness and the Historian's Imagination," *International Labor and Working-Class History* 60 (2001): 3–32,and the rejoinders in the rest of that issue, 33–92.

23. Evelyn Nakano Glenn, *Unequal Freedom: How Race and Gender Shaped American Citizenship and Labor* (Cambridge, 2002), and, most powerfully, Mae M. Ngai, *Impossible Subjects: Illegal Aliens and the Making of Modern America* (Princeton, 2004), nicely exemplify these trends. See also Henry Yu, *Thinking Orientals: Migration, Contact, and Exoticism in Modern America* (New York, 2001); Lisa Lowe, *Immigrant Acts* (Durham, 1996); Neil Foley, *The White Scourge: Mexicans, Blacks, and Poor Whites in Texas Cotton Culture* (Berkeley and Los Angeles, 1997); Susan Koshy, "Morphing Race into Ethnicity: Asian Americans and Critical Transformations of Whiteness," *boundary 2*, no. 28 (2001): 151–91; David Palumbo-Liu, *Asian/American: Historical Crossings of a Racial Frontier* (Stanford, 1999); David Gutiérrez, *Walls and Mirrors: Mexican Americans, Mexican Immigrants, and the Politics of Ethnicity* (Berkeley and Los Angeles, 1995); and Tómas Almaguer, *Racial Fault Lines: The Historical Origins of White Supremacy in California* (Berkeley and Los Angeles, 1994).

24. The other essays in this special issue testify to that generative scholarship.

25. Margaret Weir, Ann Shola Orloff, and Theda Skocpol, *The Politics of Social Policy in the United States* (Princeton, 1988).

26. This discussion of maternalism elaborates upon Eileen Boris and S. J. Kleinberg, "Mothers and Other Workers: (Re)Conceiving Labor, Maternalism, and the State," *Journal of Women's History* 15 (2003): 100–103.

27. For one excellent account, see Dorothy Sue Cobble, *The Other Women's Movement: Workplace Justice and Social Rights in Modern America* (Princeton, 2003), esp. 215–19.

28. Carol Gilligan, *In a Different Voice* (Cambridge, 1982).

29. Alice Kessler-Harris, *Out to Work: A History of Wage-Earning Women in the United States* (New York, 1982); for how this argument became twisted against her in the 1986

drama of *EEOC v. Sears, Roebuck and Co.* and the impact of this case on feminist theory, see Joan W. Scott, "Deconstructing Equality-Versus-Difference: or, the Uses of Poststructuralist Theory for Feminism," *Feminist Studies* 14 (Spring 1988): 32–50.

30. Alice Kessler-Harris, *A Women's Wage: Historical Meanings and Social Consequences* (Lexington, 1990); idem, *In Pursuit of Equity: Men, Women, and the Quest for Economic Citizenship in 20th-Century America* (New York, 2001).

31. Seth Koven and Sonya Michel, "Womanly Duties: Maternalist Politics and the Origins of Welfare States in France, Germany, Great Britain, and the United States, 1880–1920," *American Historical Review* 95 (October 1990): 1076–109.

32. Theda Skocpol, *Protecting Soldiers and Mothers: The Political Origins of Social Policy in the United States* (Cambridge, 1992), 56.

33. Ann Shola Orloff made a similar argument for old-age pensions; see *The Politics of Pensions: A Comparative Analysis of Britain, Canada, and the United States, 1880–1940* (Madison, 1993).

34. More recently Michael Willrich has explored the use of the courts to control the working-class, predominantly urban European immigrant, in "Home Slackers: Men, the State, and Welfare in Modern America," *Journal of American History* 87 (2000): 460–89. See also my *Home to Work: Motherhood and the Politics of Industrial Homework in the United States* (New York, 1994).

35. Alice Kessler-Harris, review of Theda Skocpol, *Protecting Soldiers and Mothers: The Political Origins of Social Policy in the United States, The Journal of American History* 80 (December 1993): 1035–37.

36. Kathryn Kish Sklar, Anja Schuler, and Susan Strasser, *Social Justice Feminists in the United States and Germany: A Dialogue in Documents, 1885–1933* (Ithaca, 1998), 5–7. See also Joanne Goodwin, *Gender and the Politics of Welfare Reform: Mothers' Pensions in Chicago, 1911–1929* (Chicago, 1997). For other rejections of maternalism, see Landon R. Y. Storrs, *Civilizing Capitalism: The National Consumers' League, Women's Activism, and Labor Standards in the New Deal Era* (Chapel Hill, 2000), who uses feminist, and Sybil Lipschultz, "Social Feminism and Legal Discourse: 1908–1923," *Yale Journal of Law and Feminism* 2 (1989): 131–60, who refers to industrial feminism.

37. For a fuller critique, see Linda Gordon, "Gender, State, and Society: A Debate with Theda Skocpol," *Contention* 2 (1993), reprinted in Nikki R. Keddie, ed., *Debating Gender, Debating Sexuality* (New York, 1996), 129–46, quote at 141.

38. Barbara J. Nelson, "The Origins of the Two-Channel Welfare State: Workmen's Compensation and Mothers' Aid," in Linda Gordon, ed., *Women, the State, and Welfare* (Madison, 1990), 123–51; Suzanne Mettler, *Dividing Citizens: Gender and Federalism in New Deal Public Policy* (Ithaca, 1998).

39. Linda Gordon, *Pitied But Not Entitled: Single Mothers and the History of Welfare* (New York, 1994); see also Andrew J. Polsky, *The Rise of the Therapeutic State* (Princeton, 1991).

40. Linda Gordon, "The New Feminist Scholarship on the Welfare State," in Gordon, ed., *Women, the State, and Welfare*, 25; Gwendolyn Mink, "The Lady and the Tramp: Gender, Race, and the Origins of the American Welfare State," in ibid., 93, 111. She elaborates her thesis in *The Wages of Motherhood*.

41. See Eileen Boris, "The Power of Motherhood: Black and White Activist Women Redefine the 'Political,'" *Yale Journal of Law and Feminism* 2 (Fall 1989): 25–49, reprinted in Seth Koven and Sonya Michel, eds., *Mothers of a New World*, 213–45.

42. Patricia A. Schechter, *Ida B. Wells-Barnett and American Reform, 1880–1930* (Chapel Hill, 2001).

43. Linda Gordon, *Heroes of Their Own Lives: The Politics and History of Family Violence, Boston, 1880–1960* (New York, 1988); Mary Odem, *Delinquent Daughters: Protecting and Policing Adolescent Female Sexuality in the United States, 1885–1920* (Chapel Hill, 1995).

44. For one excellent example of self-help and grassroots efforts, Nancy Hewitt, *Southern Discomfort: Women's Activism in Tampa, Florida, 1880s–1920s* (Urbana, 2001).

45. Sonya Michel, "The Limits of Maternalism: Policies toward American Wage-Earning Mothers during the Progressive Era," in Koven and Michel, eds., Mothers of a New World, 298–300.

46. S. J. Kleinberg, "The Economic Origins of the Welfare State, 1870–1939," in Hans Bak, Frits van Holthoon, and Hans Krabbendam, eds., Social and Secure? Politics and Culture of the Welfare State: A Comparative Inquiry (Amsterdam, 1996), 94–116.

47. Sonya Michel, Children's Interests, Mothers' Rights: The Shaping of America's Child-Care Policy (New Haven, 1999); Elizabeth Rose, A Mother's Job: The History of Day Care, 1890–1960 (New York, 1999); Emilie Stoltzfus, Citizen, Mother, Worker: Debating Public Responsibility for Child Care After the Second World War (Chapel Hill, 2003).

48. Wendy Sarvasy, "Social Citizenship from a Feminist Perspective," Hypatia: A Journal of Feminist Philosophy 12 (1997): 54–74. See also her "Beyond the Difference versus Equality Policy Debate: Postsuffrage Feminism, Citizenship, and the Quest for a Feminist Welfare State," Signs 17 (1992): 329–63.

49. Susan M. Sterett, Public Pensions: Gender and Civic Service in the States, 1850–1937 (Ithaca, 2003), esp. 105–6, 102.

50. Gøsta Esping-Andersen, The Three Worlds of Welfare Capitalism (Princeton, 1990).

51. Ann Shola Orloff, "Gender and the Social Rights of Citizenship," American Sociological Review 58 (1993): 303–28; Julia O'Connor, Ann Shola Orloff, and Shelia Shaver, States, Markets, Families: Gender, Liberalism, and Social Policy in Australia, Canada, Great Britain, and the United States (Cambridge, 1999).

52. For a friendly critique, see my "The Racialized Gendered State Revisited," in Mark Shackleton and Maarika Toivonen, eds., Roots and Renewal: Writings by Bicentennial Fulbright Professors (Helsinki, 2001), 45–57.

53. Kathryn Kish Sklar, "The Historical Foundations of Women's Power in the Creation of the American Welfare State, 1830–1930," in Koven and Michel, eds., Mothers of a New World, 43–93; Boris, "'The Right to Work Is the Right to Live!'"

54. T. H. Marshall, Citizenship and Social Class (Cambridge, 1952); Alice Kessler-Harris, "Gender Identity: Rights to Work and the Idea of Economic Citizenship," Schweizerische Zeitschrift fur Geschichte 46 (1996): 414–17. For modifications, see also Nancy Fraser and Linda Gordon, "Contract Versus Charity: Why Is There No Social Citizenship in the United States?" Socialist Review 22 (1992): 45–68; Ruth Lister, "Tracing the Contours of Women's Citizenship," Policy and Politics 21 (1993): 3–16; Linda K. Kerber, "The Meanings of Citizenship," Journal of American History 84 (1997): 833–54, most completely accounts for race, class, gender, and nation, offering a model synthesis.

55. Stoltzfus, Citizen, Mother, Worker, 14; Kessler-Harris, In Pursuit of Equity, 5, 288.

56. Dorothy Roberts, Killing the Black Body: Race, Reproduction, and the Meaning of Liberty (New York, 1999): Johanna Schoen, Choice and Coercion, Birth Control, Sterilization, and Abortion in Public Health and Welfare (Chapel Hill, 2005); Rickie Solinger, Beggars and Choosers: How the Politics of Choice Shapes Adoption, Abortion, and Welfare in the United States (New York, 2001). See also my "Citizenship Embodied: Racialized Gender and the Construction of Nationhood in the United States," in Norbert Finzsch and Dietmar Schirmer, eds., Identity and Intolerance: Nationalism, Racism, and Xenophobia in Germany and the United States (New York, 1998), 325–29.

57. Boris, "'The Right to Work Is the Right to Live!'"

58. For example, Grace Chang, Disposable Domestics: Immigrant Women Workers in the Global Economy (Boston, 2000).

59. Nakano Glenn, Unequal Freedom.

60. Here I draw upon my "Changing Debate on Work and Family Lives: A Historical Perspective," in Christopher Beem and Jody Heymann, eds., Unfinished Work: Building Equality and Democracy in an Era of Working Families (New York, forthcoming 2005); see also Mettler, Dividing Citizens, and Lieberman, Shifting the Color Line.

61. Jennifer Klein, For All These Rights: Business, Labor, and the Shaping of America's Public Private Welfare State (Princeton, 2003.)

62. Eileen Boris and Sonya Michel, "Social Citizenship and Women's Right to Work in Postwar America," in *Women's Rights and Human Rights: International Historical Perspectives*, ed. Pat Grimshaw, Marilyn Lake, and Katie Holmes (New York, 2001), 199–219.

63. Cobble, *The Other Women's Movement*, 223–25.

64. For one declension narrative, see William Graebner, "The End of Liberalism: Narrating Welfare's Decline, from the Moynihan Report (1965) to the Personal Responsibility and Work Opportunity Act (1960)," *Journal of Policy History* 14 (2002): 170–90; for its invention, see Michael B. Katz and Lorrin R. Thomas, "The Invention of Welfare in America," *Journal of Policy History*, 10 (1998): 399–418.

65. Kessler-Harris, *In Pursuit of Equity*, 130–56, quote from 132; see also her earlier essay, "Designing Women and Old Fools: The Construction of the Social Security Amendments of 1939," in *U.S. History as Women's History: New Feminist Essays*, ed. Linda K. Kerber, Alice Kessler-Harris, and Kathryn Kish Sklar (Chapel Hill, 1995), 87–106.

66. Mink, *Wages of Motherhood*, 137.

67. On this point, see also Frances Fox Piven, "Welfare and Work," *Whose Welfare?* 83–99; Kenneth J. Neubeck and Noel A. Cazenave, *Welfare Racism: Playing the Race Card Against America's Poor* (New York, 2001), 35–36.

68. Joanne Goodwin, "'Employable Mothers' and 'Suitable Work': A Re-evaluation of Welfare and Wage-earning for Women in the Twentieth-Century United States," *Journal of Social History* 29 (1995): 253–74, quote at 545; Nancy Rose, *Workfare or Fair Work: Women, Welfare, and Government Work Programs* (New Brunswick, 1995), 73–75; Ellen Reese, "The Politics of Motherhood: The Restriction of Poor Mothers' Welfare Rights in the United States, 1949–1960," *Social Politics: International Studies in Gender, State, and Society* 8 (2001): 65–11.

69. Jennifer Mittelstadt, "'Dependency as a Problem to Be Solved': Rehabilitation and the American Liberal Consensus on Welfare in the 1950s," *Social Politics: International Studies in Gender, State, and Society* 8 (2001): 228–57.

70. Lisa Levenstein, "From Innocent Children to Unwanted Migrants and Unwed Moms: Two Chapters in the Public Discourse on Welfare in the United States, 1960–1961," *Journal of Women's History* 11 (2000): 10–33.

71. Ruth Feldstein, *Motherhood in Black and White: Race and Sex in American Liberalism, 1930–1965* (Ithaca, 2000), 9; Felicia Kornbluh, "The Rise and Fall of Welfare Rights: Gender, Law, and Poverty in Postwar America," manuscript draft in author's possession.

72. Marisa Chappell, *From Welfare Rights to Welfare Reform* (Philadelphia, forthcoming).

73. Rhacel Salazar Parreñas, "Transgressing the Nation-State: The Partial Citizenship and 'Imagined (Global) Community' of Migrant Filipina Domestic Workers," *Signs* 26 (2001): 1129–54; Barbara Ehrenreich and Arlie Russell Hochschild, *Global Woman: Nannies, Maids, and Sex Workers in the New Economy* (New York, 2002); Pierrette Hondagneu-Sotelo, *Doméstica: Immigrant Workers Cleaning and Caring in the Shadow of Affluence* (Berkeley and Los Angeles, 2001). See also Parreñas, *Servants of Globalization: Women, Migration, and Domestic Work* (Stanford, 2001).

74. Eileen H. Richardson and Bryan S. Turner, "Sexual, Intimate, or Reproductive Citizenship?" *Citizenship Studies* 5 (2001): 329–30, 333.

75. Leslie Reagan, *When Abortion Was a Crime: Women, Medicine, and Law in the United States, 1867–1973* (Berkeley and Los Angeles, 1997); the more popular, Rickie Solinger, *The Abortionist: A Woman Against the Law* (New York, 1994); Donald Critchlow, *Intended Consequences: Birth Control, Abortion, and the Federal Government in Modern America* (New York, 1999).

76. Laura Briggs, *Reproducing Empire: Race, Sex, Science, and U.S. Imperialism in Puerto Rico* (Berkeley and Los Angeles, 2002).

77. Nancy F. Cott, *Public Vows: A History of Marriage and the Nation* (Cambridge, 2000), 2.

78. Sonya Michel, "The Benefits of Race and Gender: Retirement in Postwar America," unpublished work in progress, 2002, in possession of the author; Gwendolyn

Mink, "Violating Women: Rights Abuse in the Welfare Police State," in Randy Albelda and Ann Withorn, *Lost Ground: Welfare Reform, Poverty, and Beyond* (Boston, 2002), 95–112. See also Jill Quadagno, "Women's Access to Pensions and the Structure of Eligibility Rules: Systems of Production and Reproduction," *Sociological Quarterly* 29 (1988): 541–58.

79. Margot Canady, "Building a Straight State: Sexuality and Social Citizenship under the 1944 G.I. Bill," *Journal of American History* 90 (2003): 235–57. A number of historians already stressed how gendered restrictions on military service and the inequalities of a Jim Crow army disadvantaged women and African American men. See Linda Kerber, *No Constitutional Right to Be Ladies: Women and the Obligations of Citizenship* (New York, 1998), 221–302; Lizabeth Cohen, *A Consumer's Republic: The Politics of Mass Consumption in Postwar America* (New York, 2003), 137–46, 166–73; and David H. Onkst, "'First a Negro . . . Incidentally a Veteran': Black World War II Veterans and the G.I. Bill of Rights in the Deep South, 1944–1948," *Journal of Social History* 31 (1998): 517–44. For the "lesbian menace" during World War II, see Leisa D. Meyer, *Creating GI Jane: Sexuality and Power in the Women's Army Corps During World War II* (New York, 1996).

80. For example, John D'Emilio, William B. Turner, and Urvashi Vaid, *Creating Change: Sexuality, Public Policy, and Civil Rights* (New York, 2000); Marc Stein, *City of Sisterly and Brotherly Loves: Lesbian and Gay Philadelphia, 1945–1972* (Chicago, 2000).

81. For a good summary, see Eithne Luibhéid, *Entry Denied: Controlling Sexuality at the Border* (Minneapolis, 2002).

82. Virginia Sapiro, "Women, Citizenship, and Nationality: Immigration and Naturalization Policies in the United States," *Politics & Society* 13 (1984): 1–26; Candice Lewis Bredbenner, *A Nationality of Her Own: Women, Marriage, and the Law of Citizenship* (Berkeley and Los Angeles, 1998), Kerber, *No Constitutional Right*, 33–46.

83. Luibhéid, *Entry Denied;* Nancy F. Cott, "Marriage and Women's Citizenship in the United States, 1830–1934," *American Historical Review* 103 (1998): 1440–74; Erika Lee, *At America's Gates: Chinese Immigration During the Exclusion Era, 1882–1943* (Chapel Hill, 2003); Ngai, *Impossible Subjects*, esp. 109–16 on Filipinos, 202–24 on Chinese, quote at 113.

84. Margot Canaday, "'Who Is a Homosexual?' The Consolidation of Sexual Identities in Mid-Twentieth-Century Immigration Law," *Law and Social Inquiry* 28 (2003): 351–86, quote at 354–55.

85. Luibhéid, *Entry Denied*, 77–101.

86. I am currently exploring this issue as part of a larger project on bodies on the job. But see Taunya Lovell Banks, "The Black Side of the Mirror: The Black Body in the Workplace," in *Sister Circle: Black Women and Work*, ed. Sharon Harley and The Black Women and Work Collective (New Brunswick, 2002), 13–28; Alan Hyde, *Bodies of Law* (Princeton, 1997), 125–30; Karl E. Klare, "Power/Dressing: Regulation of Employee Appearance," 26 *New England Law Review* 1395 (1992).

ROBERT J. McMAHON

Diplomatic History and Policy History: Finding Common Ground

It is difficult to imagine two fields of scholarly inquiry with so much in common and yet so little interaction as diplomatic and policy history. Policy, policy process, policymakers, policy origins, policy intentions, policy consequences—those terms and ones of a similar stripe roll just as easily off the tongues and word processors of diplomatic historians as of self-described policy historians. Moreover, the questions asked and the methods employed by the two groups of scholars bear a striking resemblance. Both fields focus perforce on the state and state-centered actors, concern themselves with elite-level decision making, interrogate fundamental issues of power within societies, and concentrate overwhelmingly on the twentieth century to the relative neglect of earlier periods. Each field occupies as well an embattled position within the larger historical profession, where social and cultural history have predominated since the 1960s.

One might expect, under the circumstances, strong bonds to be forged and fruitful cross-fertilization to develop between these two fields. Instead, a rather puzzling, if artificial, division has kept them separated. Diplomatic historians, so eager of late to expand the boundaries of their field to encompass some of the preoccupations of social and cultural history, have shown little inclination to explore the more obvious common turf on which they and their colleagues in policy history stand. Plainly, the older, more established field of historical scholarship has not rushed to embrace the newer field. Yet neither have policy historians shown much inclination to enter into a sustained dialogue, or explore shared interests, with specialists in foreign policy.

The landmark Harvard University conference of November 1978, which, as Julian Zelizer has recorded, "marked the first 'self-conscious discussion' of policy history as a distinct subfield of either history or the policy sciences," held out the promise of fruitful interchange among and

THE JOURNAL OF POLICY HISTORY, Vol. 17, No. 1, 2005.

collaboration between scholars of foreign and domestic policy. Indeed, the consensus reached by participants at that founding meeting certainly appeared to fold both dimensions of policy within the new field's boundaries. It held that "policy historians should define themselves around a common set of issues, including the distinction between the public and private realms, the role of professionals in policymaking, the role of crisis in policy development, how changes in process influence policy, the impact of institutional structure on policies, the relations between government and nongovernmental actors, the changing definition of policy over time, and the relations of policies to 'contemporaneous' intellectual assumptions."[1] Each of those issues had, of course, long been—and indeed remain—major areas of analysis within diplomatic history, as the participants surely recognized. The active involvement at that gathering of Ernest May, the distinguished historian of U.S. foreign relations, combined with the signal importance for the policy history field of his co-authored book, *Thinking in Time: The Uses of History for Decision Makers* (1986), offered the promise of a genuine intellectual convergence between diplomatic and policy history.[2]

As readers of the *Journal of Policy History* are doubtless well aware, however, there has been no such convergence. Instead, policy history has evolved over the past quarter-century in such a manner that it has become essentially synonymous with the study of domestic policy. Specialists in the field write about welfare, Social Security, and education; about civil rights, health care, and housing; about environmental issues, tax and fiscal policies, and about a host of other subjects that mostly fall within the purview of federal- and state-level policy-making organs. Curiously, foreign policy and national security/defense matters have for all practical purposes remained outside the field's scope. Yet those have absorbed the lion's share of the U.S. federal budget for more than sixty years now, with U.S. defense spending currently amounting to 40 percent of the world's total and projected to reach a staggering $451 billion in 2007.[3] Diplomatic historians investigate the latter realms, policy historians the former—with disappointingly little overlap. In practice, a de facto division of labor has characterized policy-oriented scholarship that echoes the British Government's separation of responsibilities between its aptly named Home and Foreign Offices.

This essay is concerned principally with explaining how this state of affairs has developed and highlighting some of the advantages that could redound to the benefit of each branch of the policy history community from a greater awareness of the insights, approaches, methods, and interpretive debates of the other. I begin with a brief discussion of what appear to be the chief factors that have led to the compartmentalization of the two fields. Next, I present an overview of U.S. diplomatic history's evolution. I then try to account for the striking reinvigoration and transformation of the U.S. foreign relations field in recent years, with particular attention to the implications of those changes for the policy history community. I end with some general thoughts about how more connection to and interaction with scholars of domestic policy might help further strengthen and invigorate the work of foreign relations historians.

Why have two fields with so many obvious shared interests become so compartmentalized? The artificial divide between policy history and diplomatic history stems, in significant measure, from the former's emergence out of political history—and from the major professional and intellectual currents prevailing at the time of its emergence. It bears remembering that policy historians' first, self-conscious organizing efforts in the late 1970s coincided with, and indeed were spurred by, the larger historical profession's palpable indifference to—even outright disdain for—studies of the state, high-level politics, and elite behavior. As first social and then cultural history eclipsed more traditional modes of historical inquiry, those laboring in the policy history trenches were forced on the defensive. "The status of the political historian within the profession," wryly commented William Leuchtenberg in his 1986 presidential address to the Organization of American Historians, had "sunk somewhere between that of a faith healer and a chiropractor."[4]

In the time-honored manner of academic subdisciplines under siege, policy historians circled the wagons. They began to develop a common scholarly outlook and identity, pinpointed shared interests, sought to identify particular audiences for their work (especially government decisionmakers themselves), and found some solace in interdisciplinarity. Policy historians tried to secure an important scholarly niche for their specialization by straddling the disciplines of history and the burgeoning policy sciences. "Policy history became," Zelizer writes, "an interdisciplinary arena for scholars from many different fields to interact."[5] The particular time and context in which the policy history field emerged thus militated against any inclination to forge a unified scholarly front with a group of scholars whose interest in the diplomatic and defense dimensions of policy not only seemed quite distinct, but who belonged to a field that was itself under siege. Why, to put it crudely, hitch one's sails to what looked like another sinking ship?

The very same intellectual and professional trends that made political history's preoccupation with the state and with elites seem retrograde had a comparably galvanizing effect on foreign relations history. Diplomatic historians, too, began to circle the wagons. Their struggles to regain lost status pushed in a number of different directions. Some moved into a more diffuse international realm, aiming to contextualize U.S. foreign policy by scrutinizing more fully the actions of other states. Others explored intercultural aspects of international affairs or examined some of the deep cultural, societal, and ideological roots of American foreign policy. At the same time, diplomatic historians formed institutions outside the mainstream profession, constructing a strong professional association—the Society for Historians of American Foreign Relations (SHAFR)—which built solidarity within an embattled guild, organized well-attended annual meetings, and oversaw the flourishing of *Diplomatic History*. None of those developments, however, prompted diplomatic historians to reach out to other similarly marginalized groups, least of all a policy history contingent that visualized government policymakers and academic policy experts housed in public policy centers as key target audiences for their scholarship.

Regrettably, both branches of the policy history community therewith missed an opportunity to develop mutually beneficial connections and establish a sustained scholarly dialogue. The separate ground occupied by each of the two groups of scholars has been shifting constantly ever since, along with the vicissitudes of broader intellectual and academic currents, making such a convergence more difficult. That diplomatic and policy historians remain predominantly concerned with policy, however, gives cause for at least guarded optimism to those who see merit in stronger connections, closer dialogue, and more direct collaboration—for both sets of scholars.

The centrality of policy for U.S. diplomatic historians has, until very recently, been a defining feature of the field. Since an engagement with great power relations, questions of war and peace, diplomacy, and high politics characterized the earliest historical studies, going back to Thuycidides and the ancients, historiographers routinely depict diplomatic history as one of the discipline's most venerable, if not fossilized, branches. Yet, within the United States, the professionalization of the diplomatic history field actually developed quite late. From the 1930s to the early 1950s, a mere four scholars dominated the field: Samuel Flagg Bemis, Dexter Perkins, Thomas A. Bailey, and Julius Pratt. Not until the 1950s and 1960s, coincident of course with America's burgeoning global power, did the training of graduate students as specialists in foreign relations history and the production of historical monographs and articles begin to approach critical mass.[6]

Bemis, Perkins, Bailey, and Pratt, the scholars so instrumental to the field's early development, each focused in their writings on the formation and implementation of the foreign policy of the U.S. government. Their work established a set of core questions: Why were particular foreign policies pursued, and how were they made and implemented? Beyond the broad consensus that obtained regarding the nature of the subject under study and the cardinal questions to be addressed, however, this small band of first-generation luminaries actually divided quite sharply in their conceptual approaches. Bemis and Perkins, on the one hand, concentrated primarily on the state itself in their scholarship, and especially on those top-level government officials involved in the formal policy-making process. Bailey and Pratt, on the other hand, explored the role that the larger society played in U.S. foreign policy. They examined public opinion, Congress, and various interest groups, laboring to pinpoint the influence exerted on state actors from outside the executive branch of government.

That early bifurcation has persisted to this day, a telling reflection of the field's dualistic nature. Diplomatic history is, intrinsically, a Janus-faced field, one that looks both outward and inward for the wellsprings of America's behavior in the global arena. Put another way, the history of American foreign relations has always encompassed studies focused on the state and state-to-state relations as well as studies examining the internal constellation of forces and influences that shape state policy. In the widest sense, all students of foreign relations need to choose between, or blend, externalist and internalist approaches. In accounting for the formation and implementation of policy, they must analyze the external forces that influence and constrain relations with the larger world while explicating the internal pressures and values that shape the policies executed by governmental decision makers.[7]

Although not mutually exclusive, to be sure, the first approach tends more toward an international history framework, the second more toward a national history framework. The very nature of the subject matter of foreign relations history thus creates an ambiguous identity for U.S. diplomatic historians, especially since most find themselves housed in history departments demarcated along geographic lines of expertise. Are they primarily specialists in U.S. national history? Or do they belong within the more expansive, if amorphous, subject area of international history? Or should they, to the extent possible, try to straddle successfully each and assiduously avoid pigeonholing? In short, where exactly do historians of American foreign relations "fit"? The field's Janus-faced nature has fostered healthy intellectual tension within the diplomatic history guild about method and approach. It has also helped fuel the interpretive divisions for which the field has become notorious.

The dominant interpretive paradigm among scholars of U.S. foreign relations, from the early postwar era right up to the present, has been

realism. Within its ranks can be found such notable authors as diplomat-
scholars George F. Kennan and Henry A. Kissinger, political scientists
Hans Morgenthau and Kenneth Waltz, and historians Norman Graebner,
Robert Ferrell, John Lewis Gaddis, Marc Trachtenberg, and many more.
Realists believe that foreign policy is determined by a relatively small
policy-making elite that responds objectively to the mix of dangers and
opportunities it apprehends in the international environment.
Policymakers seek to advance broad national interests in an inherently
complex and conflict-ridden international system. The state, for most realists, often functions as a near-autonomous entity within U.S. society.
The intensive examination of governmental policy records thus forms an
essential research strategy for realists; the policy-making process and gov-
ernment-to-government relations constitute the primary objects of study.

Progressive, or revisionist, historians take a radically different tack,
concentrating instead on the critical role played by nongovernmental elites
and the deeper material and intellectual context for the nation's external
actions. Charles Beard, one of the most influential American historians
of the interwar years (though not per se a specialist in diplomatic history), helped establish in the 1930s a robust progressive critique of U.S.
foreign policy as the product of business interests and their governmental
allies. In books such as *The Idea of National Interest* and *The Open Door at
Home*, he argued that corporate-state elites together forged a strategy of
overseas economic expansion to meet what they identified as the nation's
fundamental needs.[8] That critique fell into disfavor during the patriotic
resurgence ushered in by World War II and the early Cold War years, only
to reemerge with a vengeance during the 1960s and 1970s. The advent of
a neo-Beardian revisionism, associated especially with the towering figure of William Appleman Williams, was abetted by growing popular dis-
satisfaction with the Vietnam War and the nation's global interventionism.
Some of the most vituperative interpretive debates within the diplomatic
history field over the past several decades have continued to pit revision-
ists against their critics: the former emphasizing the material and ideological bases of American foreign policy, the latter typically insisting upon
the importance of security and other noneconomic variables. The gaping
chasm separating the interpretive paradigms offered for American Cold
War foreign policy by Thomas J. McCormick, on the one hand, and
staunchly antirevisionist John Lewis Gaddis, on the other, serves as a prime
case in point.[9]

For all the raucous interpretive disputes these competing approaches
inspired in the 1960s, 1970s, and after, the seemingly polar-opposite realist and revisionist paradigms have actually operated from some of the same
basic epistemological premises. For all their differences, notes Frank

Ninkovich, "they shared the assumption that objective forces, on the basis of which interests could be rationally calculated, mattered most." Realist and revisionist scholars were, additionally, "committed to objectivist conceptions of truth in which historical knowledge was defined in terms of a close fit between fact and the historian's account."[10] Further, they each shared the conviction that elite interests, values, and behavior were what counted in the realm of foreign policymaking—even if they disagreed, and they often did so quite strenuously, about the relative importance of governmental and nongovernmental actors and the relative weight that should be attached to material and nonmaterial variables. Such broad common ground, abetted by an abiding commitment to empiricism, lent a conceptual stability to the field that has only recently been challenged. But it came at a high price since diplomatic history, as practiced in the United States, appeared increasingly insular, stale, and old-fashioned to many scholars outside the field.

By the late 1970s, the field's insularity and its preoccupation with elites and the state made diplomatic history seem out of step with a historical profession that was by then preoccupied with "new" histories of the less powerful: blacks, native Americans, women, workers, immigrants, and other, formerly voiceless nonelites. Critics began castigating foreign relations history as a stagnant, insular, undertheorized field. At a meeting of the American Historical Association in the late 1970s, prominent social historian Peter Stearns remarked that diplomatic history was languishing in an advanced state of decay.[11] The overwhelmingly white, male elites who dominated most foreign relations histories also posed an acute political problem for the field. Those elites, along with the power they wielded, became suspect in the eyes of many of the "new" historians who emerged with the intellectual ferment of the 1960s, determined as they were to write history from the bottom up. "History from the bottom up takes its toll in a field of human activity that is still largely executed, if not ultimately shaped, from the top down," Charles S. Maier observed perceptively in a seminal 1980 essay. "Throughout the culture one might expose power or resist it, but hardly seek it, or even comfortably describe it without implicit condemnation."[12]

It bears emphasizing that the very same intellectual and professional trends also placed American political history, and its policy history offspring, on the defensive. "A new generation of historians, coming of age in the baby-boom era and socialized in the insurgency of social movements," notes Hugh Davis Graham, "lost interest in the state and turned away from political history."[13] Some political historians tried to keep pace by turning to the investigation of the electoral behavior of rank-and-file voters, especially as a window into deep-seated social, ethnic, and religious tensions and identities.[14] Others explored the concept of political culture as a bridge between the political and the cultural.[15] Studying either high-level politics or public policy, on the other hand, rapidly lost both professional esteem and active practitioners. Those tradition-bound subjects seemed somehow tainted in the eyes of social and cultural historians committed to recapturing the lived experiences of ordinary folk— little more than a "celebratory and exclusionary" exercise, in Joel Silbey's apt description.[16]

The parallels with diplomatic history's precipitous fall from professional grace and fashion could hardly be closer. In each case, a field that traditionally pivoted on the exploration of elites and the state had come under attack, in large measure because of the core subjects that had long formed its *raison d'être*. "There clearly has emerged a distinct and inflexible antagonism to the study of politics," observed Silbey in 1999, "of great intensity and breadth." The "indifference, hostility, and neglect" that continue to exist toward political history, at least among the still-dominant social and cultural historians, plainly extended to diplomatic history as well.[17]

Diplomatic and political-policy historians have of course each responded vigorously and imaginatively to the criticism, neglect, and indifference that their respective fields have suffered over the past generation. For historians of U.S. foreign relations, withering critiques from within the field itself made the problem particularly acute and the need for some refashioning imperative. Charles S. Maier surveyed the historiography of foreign relations history in 1980 and found it languishing. He depicted the field as a "stepchild" at some remove from "the cutting edge of scholarship." Maier, Sally Marks, Christopher Thorne, Michael H. Hunt, and several other prominent diplomatic history specialists, all of whom penned stinging critiques of the field in the 1980s, disparaged what they characterized as the parochialism, narrowness, and one-sidedness of so many U.S. diplomatic histories. A key problem, they agreed, was epitomized by the limited use of foreign-language sources and archives, which fostered both an insularity and a tendency to accept uncritically the views of Washington decision makers about the world beyond America's shores. Revisionist and nonrevisionist U.S. diplomatic historians alike, the critics complained, took for granted the international environment that U.S. policymakers confronted and dealt with but failed to probe carefully its actual nature or the extent to which it might have imposed constraints on U.S. ambitions.[18]

The charges hit the mark. Certainly, compared to their diplomatic history counterparts in Britain, Canada, and throughout much of Western Europe, scholars of U.S. foreign relations *were* markedly less internationalist in orientation. Broadly cast works by Ernest R. May, Akira Iriye, and other preeminent scholars served as notable exceptions, to be sure.[19] Yet, as a group, specialists in U.S. diplomatic history proved much less inclined to paint on a multinational canvas or to consult archives outside the United States. For those situated within what I have described as the externalist realm—namely, those dealing principally with state-to-state relations—the criticisms proved especially telling. By relating U.S. policymaking "more rigorously and systematically to the international environment," as Hunt rightly noted, such historians could more effectively address two essential questions: "How have international developments influenced U.S. policy? And what consequences, unintended no less than intended, has that policy had for the broader world?"[20] Surely one cannot discuss with any degree of authority the *impact* of American policies on other nation-states and regions unless one possesses some degree of expertise in the histories and cultures of those areas.

Over the past decade and a half, the internationalist dimension of U.S. diplomatic history has undergone a quiet renaissance. Partly in response to the hotly debated broadsides launched against the field and the prescriptive agendas behind them, and partly in response to an ancillary intellectual movement aimed at decentering the United States and jettisoning exceptionalist assumptions, a growing number of U.S. diplomatic historians have expanded the internationalist scope of their work. The 1990s and the opening years of the new century have witnessed a sharp spike in broadly cast, internationalist-oriented monographs and articles. Much of this new work has been based upon sufficient binational or multinational archival research to meet the most exacting standards of the international history advocates.[21] Concomitant with this development, the number of U.S. diplomatic historians with a dual specialization in the history of another country or region has increased substantially as well. A glance at recent programs of the annual meetings of the Society for Historians of American Foreign Relations (SHAFR), which have regularly featured the work-in-progress of dozens of Ph.D. candidates, offers unmistakable evidence that much more work in this vein will soon be forthcoming, as do the ambitious research projects undertaken by recent recipients of the highly competitive SHAFR dissertation fellowships. Relatedly, the U.S. foreign relations field has shown itself quite open to those whose principal scholarly homes lie elsewhere, but whose work speaks directly to at least some of the issues and concerns of the diplomatic history community—whether they be Asian, European, or Middle Eastern historians, political scientists, or anthropologists. A growing number of European-, Asian-, or Latin American–born scholars now belong to the

U.S. diplomatic history community, moreover, offering further testimony to the internationalization of the field. Taken together, these developments suggest a more open, fluid, and cosmopolitan field, a field marked by greater diversity, more scholarly collaboration, and abundant interdisciplinary cross-fertilization.

One especially important development that encapsulates many of the above trends is the flowering of the Cold War International History Project (CWIHP). Established in 1991 at the Woodrow Wilson International Center for Scholars in Washington, D.C., the project's central aim has been the dissemination of "new information and perspectives on the history of the Cold War emerging from previously inaccessible sources on 'the other side' of the superpower rivalry that dominated international relations after World War II."[22] The CWIHP has labored assiduously to achieve that goal, publishing in its *Newsletter* English-language translations of key documents from Eastern Europe, the former Soviet Union, China, and elsewhere, along with interpretive essays about those documents. It has also published a series of stimulating working papers, made additional documents available on its Web site, and organized a host of international conferences to debate the significance of the new evidence for our comprehension of the global dimensions of the Cold War. Since many of the scholars closely involved in these efforts have been specialists in Russian, Eastern European, or Asian history, rather than U.S. diplomatic history, the CWIHP's various initiatives have led to a fruitful blending of the different perspectives and scholarly preoccupations of area experts and foreign relations historians. Our understanding of the Korean War, the Cuban missile crisis, Soviet-American clashes in Africa, and much more has been fundamentally altered by this new scholarship.[23]

A burgeoning literature has also begun to appear on the impact of the United States on the wider world. Much of this work has focused on the cultural realm, including important, prize-winning books by Reinhold Wagnleitner and Jessica C. E. Geinow-Hecht on postwar Austria and Germany.[24] The enormous influence of American popular culture, in its various guises, has featured prominently in much of this work, a focus doubtless spurred by the unmistakable significance of this force during our age of ubiquitous globalization/Americanization. The work of Dutch scholar Rob Kroes on America's cultural impact on Europe has been especially noteworthy in that regard.[25]

The strengthened internationalist orientation within U.S. foreign relations history carries important implications for any prospective scholarly dialogue between diplomatic and policy historians. On one level, U.S. diplomatic history's shift into the wider, international realm makes such a dialogue more problematic. Situating American foreign policy in a broad, global frame of inquiry means a corresponding pulling away, at least relatively speaking, from the domestic realm; and since the domestic policy-making arena constitutes the prime putative common ground of the two fields, this intellectual trend renders that ground less certain and less stable. Those foreign relations scholars exploring subjects of a transnational nature—the Cold War, international politics in the Middle East, globalization, evolving trade regimes, to take but a few prominent examples—will perforce be much less exclusively focused on the American state and its policy-making organs. The points of potential scholarly convergence with those studying the domestic elements of state policy will, consequently, be reduced. The growing interest in America's impact on other peoples, nations, and regions, although not yet a predominant trend within U.S. diplomatic history, further muddies the picture since the complex subject of policy consequences demands altogether different approaches, sources, and methods.

On another level, however, this internationalist trend opens possibilities for fresh kinds of scholarly interchange between diplomatic and policy historians. American policy historians have themselves recently begun to move away from an exclusive focus on the United States. They have shown themselves open to comparativist perspectives and welcoming to the work of scholars investigating domestic policy development and state formation in other national contexts. Indicative of that trend is the inclusion in this issue of Peter Baldwin's essay on comparative European policy history. A broader intellectual move toward the international, the transnational, and the comparative among students of American history in fact appears to be influencing policy and diplomatic historians alike. Leading historians of the United States have, in recent years, sought to overturn the venerable traditions, habits, assumptions, and narrative strategies of American exceptionalism. Rather than viewing the American historical experience as unique, they propose, in the words of Thomas Bender, that "we imagine an American historical narrative that situates the United States more fully in its larger transnational and intercultural global context."[26] Bender led a series of meetings, sponsored by the Organization of American Historians, that resulted in the issuance of the influential La Pietra Report of 2000. It concluded that contemporary globalization made clear the need for a basic reconceptualization of American history and called for the deployment of broad transnational and comparative frames of reference in order to historicize the national experience of the United States.

The core conviction impelling this intellectual thrust outward has direct relevance to diplomatic and policy historians, and to the prospects for greater collaboration between them. It can be boiled down to the basic notion that a wider angle of vision can yield new interpretive perspectives and insights since certain subjects cannot be fully understood if viewed through too exclusionary a national lens. Plainly, the state, the subject at the heart of both fields, forms one of those. There is nothing unique about the range of problems faced by the modern American state: not in terms of the challenges posed by immigration, urbanization, and industrialization; and certainly not in terms of the need to deal with such complicated but unavoidable matters as poverty, education, health care, social welfare, criminal justice, environmental regulation, taxation, trade, national security, military affairs, and bilateral and multilateral diplomacy. By discarding the notion of American exceptionalism and instead entertaining comparative perspectives, as some diplomatic and policy historians have already begun to do, scholars of state policy can more accurately grasp the truly distinctive as well as the not-so-distinctive ways in which the American state has ordered its priorities and has pursued particular policies to meet a wide range of problems, challenges, and opportunities.[27]

International, transnational, and comparative perspectives can also help identify more effectively some of the *interconnections* between domestic and foreign policy. Jeremi Suri's recent study of the organic link between common fears about domestic disorder among American, Soviet, Chinese, and European leaders and the rise of detente richly illuminates the value of such explorations.[28] Since the state's highest-level actors rarely isolate or compartmentalize the domestic and foreign policy issues that they confront, students of the state—whether they style themselves as diplomatic or as policy historians—should consider exploring more fully the interrelationships between the two and the manifold ways in which politics, bureaucratic as well as electoral, impinge on both. In his prize-winning book, *Choosing War*, Fredrik Logevall expertly elucidates how these interrelationships influenced the Lyndon B. Johnson administration's lurch toward intervention in Vietnam.[29]

The subject of the political context for policy can of course be fitted just as easily into diplomatic history's internalist branch as it can within the new internationalism. That branch of foreign relations scholarship, with its primary focus on society-wide determinants of the nation's external behavior, has undergone a resurgence and transformation of its own in recent years. Influenced by the theories, methods, and analytical categories of cultural studies, critical theory, and postmodernism, a growing number of U.S. foreign relations scholars have explored such previously understudied matters as the role of culture, ideology, race, gender, language, and emotion. Some have posited a powerful link between the race-, gender-, and class-based contours of American society and the deeply rooted ideological presuppositions and cultural values and biases that have conditioned America's encounters with foreign states and societies.[30] Although much too diverse and complex to allow for simple categorization, the scholarship associated with this cultural turn within U.S. diplomatic history has mounted a powerful challenge to some of the most basic epistemological assumptions of the field. To what extent, this work forces us to ask, are such widely used reference points as interests, security, and threats as much constructed concepts as terms that connote something fixed, tangible, and "real"? To what extent do diplomatic history's well-established empiricist and positivist inclinations need to be adjusted in light of poststructuralist challenges?

This trend, too, creates obstacles for those who advocate more explicit connections between diplomatic and policy historians. On the one hand, some of the new "culturalists" have discarded policy altogether as a focus for their work; they are quite consciously striving to move beyond the preoccupation with state actors that has long defined the field of diplomatic history. U.S. foreign relations scholars are currently exploring so expansive a range of topics that they include, as one keen observer has catalogued, "the international implications of Broadway musicals; modernization; sports; world's fairs; tourism; art; food; the environment; movies; cultural relations and intellectual encounters; trans-national interest groups and organizations, and more."[31] Much of this newer work, insofar as it pushes toward a kind of internationalization of cultural and social history and jettisons the state as the prime subject of analysis, seems unlikely to resonate with policy historians. Michael J. Hogan, the former, longtime editor of *Diplomatic History* and recent SHAFR president, recently applauded this move away from the state in his June 2003 presidential address to the association. "If we are truly historians of foreign relations, not just diplomacy," Hogan declared, "then the global crusade for human rights, the international woman's movement, religious movements, and ethnic conflicts, to name just a few, must become the subjects of our inquiry, quite apart from any connection to government policy." Paraphrasing the influential Akira Iriye, who has pioneered the investigation of nongovernmental organizations and intercultural relations, Hogan proclaimed that "the history of international relations need not be the history of government relations, or even the history of individuals and organizations acting on behalf of their governments or in the context of government policy." In short, he celebrated those diplomatic historians who are eagerly anticipating "a de-centered history that is less preoccupied with the state or with the national project and more preoccupied with non-state actors and international relations."[32]

Yet this trend, too, is multidirectional. All those who might be lumped within the culturalist camp are not abandoning the state as a legitimate object of study. Rather, some are striving to more fully contextualize state behavior; and, in that important sense, they are treading on territory that a handful of policy historians have already blazed. Diplomatic history's multifaceted inward turn, consequently, may not be quite so alien to the interests and concerns of those working on domestic aspects of policy as it might appear at first glance. To the extent that some of this newer foreign relations scholarship aims to deepen our appreciation for the deep-seated connections between state actors and the wider society that they represent and that produces and sustains them, significant points of convergence between the two fields emerge.

One can find important commonalities, for example, between those who see a direct relationship between discourses about race, gender, class, religion, and culture within American society and the development of particular policies. Such prominent scholars of domestic policy as Linda Gordon and Jill Quadagno have insisted that American social welfare programs were shaped to a significant degree by deep-seated assumptions, values, and biases regarding race, gender, and class.[33] Likewise, and quite independently, such notable scholars of American foreign policy as Michael H. Hunt, Thomas Borstelmann, Mary Dudziak, Robert Dean, and Andrew Rotter have explored ways in which the same factors conditioned American policy toward development, revolution, decolonization, nation-building, nonalignment and other critical foreign policy issues.[34] The conjoined issues of civil rights at home and rising race consciousness abroad offer a superb example of why domestic and foreign policy cannot so easily be separated. The influence of policy communities and the importance of the broader political culture, subjects that policy historians have devoted increasing attention to of late, are no less germane to the work of diplomatic historians—even if the latter have been slow to recognize that fact. So, too, one can discern arresting parallels in the efforts aimed at gradualist state-building, in a strongly antistatist political culture, that Julian E. Zelizer has highlighted in his study of governmental fiscal policy and Michael J. Hogan has illuminated in his work on the construction of a national security state.[35]

Scholars of the domestic and foreign dimensions of policy, in sum, have far more in common than most of them recognize. They have been traveling along somewhat separate and distinct paths for some time now, to be sure. Each of the two fields has responded differently to the comparable professional and intellectual pressures and challenges they have faced over the past quarter-century. Each of the fields, as a consequence, has become increasingly diverse and pluralistic—and, arguably, more sophisticated. Still, for all the serious impediments that stand in the way of greater collaboration and interchange, one need not be an inveterate dreamer to imagine a future in which more diplomatic historians present papers at the Policy History Conference and publish in the *Journal of Policy History*, and in which more policy historians whose work touches upon or overlaps with the foreign relations field present papers at annual SHAFR conventions and publish in *Diplomatic History*. If one considers diplomatic history and policy history as fields that each are comprised of a series of concentric circles, such circles representing the various interests, concerns, and approaches of practitioners, then one can easily pinpoint areas in which the circles overlap. It is those areas in which common ground can be found and most usefully cross-fertilized.

University of Florida

Notes

1. Julian E. Zelizer, "Clio's Lost Tribe: Public Policy History Since 1978," *Journal of Policy History* 12 (2000): 373–74.
2. Richard E. Neustadt and Ernest R. May, *Thinking in Time: The Uses of History for Decision Makers* (New York, 1986).
3. James Chace, "In Search of Absolute Security," in *The Imperial Tense: Problems and Prospects of American Empire*, ed. Andrew Bacevich (Chicago, 2003), 120.
4. William E. Leuchtenberg, "The Pertinence of Political History: Reflections on the Significance of the State in America," *Journal of American History* 73 (December 1986): 585–600. See also Steven M. Gillon, "The Future of Political History, *Journal of Policy History* 9 (1997): 239–55.
5. Zelizer, "Clio's Lost Tribe," 369.
6. See especially Walter LaFeber, "The World and the United States," *American Historical Review* 100 (October 1995): 1015–24.
7. These points and some of what follows are adapted from Robert J. McMahon, "Toward a Pluralist Vision: The Study of American Foreign Relations as International History and National History," in *Explaining the History of American Foreign Relations*, ed. Michael J. Hogan and Thomas G. Paterson (2d rev. ed., New York, 2004), 35–50.
8. Charles Beard and George H. E. Smith, *The Idea of National Interest: An Analytical Study of American Foreign Policy* (New York, 1934); Charles Beard, *The Open Door at Home* (New York, 1935).
9. Thomas J. McCormick, *America's Half-Century: United States Foreign Policy in the Cold War* (Baltimore, 1989); John Lewis Gaddis, *We Now Know: Rethinking Cold War History* (Oxford, 1997). For useful overviews, see Michael H. Hunt, "The Long Crisis in U.S. Diplomatic History: Coming to Closure," in *America in the World: The Historiography of American Foreign Relations Since 1941*, ed. Michael J. Hogan (New York, 1995); LaFeber, "The World and the United States"; Campbell Craig, "The Not-So-Strange Career of Charles Beard," *Diplomatic History* 25 (Spring 2001): 251–74. For an up-to-date survey of the historiography, see Robert D. Schulzinger, ed., *A Companion to American Foreign Relations* (Malden, Mass., 2003).
10. Frank Ninkovich, "Paradigms Lost: The Cultural Turn and the Globalization of U.S. Diplomatic History" (forthcoming).
11. Ibid.

108   ROBERT J. McMAHON

12. Charles S. Maier, "Marking Time: The Historiography of Internaitonal Relations," in *The Past Before Us: Contemporary Historical Writing in the United States*, ed. Michael Kammen (Ithaca, 1980), 356.
13. Hugh Davis Graham, "The Stunted Career of Policy History: A Critique and an Agenda," *Public Historian* 15 (Spring 1993): 26.
14. See, for example, Samuel P. Hays, *American Political History as Social Analysis: Essays* (Knoxville, Tenn., 1980).
15. Glen Gendzel, "Political Culture: Genealogy of a Concept," *Journal of Interdisciplinary History* 28 (Autumn 1997): 225–50.
16. Joel H. Silbey, "The State and Practice of American Political History at the Millennium: The Nineteenth Century as a Test Case," *Journal of Policy History* 11 (1999): 26.
17. Ibid., 3, 9.
18. Sally Marks, "The World According to Washington," *Diplomatic History* 11 (Summer 1987): 265–67, 281–82; Christopher Thorne, "After the Europeans: American Designs for the Remaking of Southeast Asia," *Diplomatic History* 12 (Spring 1988): 206–8; Michael H. Hunt, "Internationalizing U.S. Diplomatic History: A Practical Agenda," *Diplomatic History* 15 (Winter 1991): 1–11.
19. Ernest R. May, *The World War and American Isolation, 1914–1917* (Cambridge, Mass., 1959); Akira Iriye, *After Imperialism: The Search for a New Order in the Far East, 1921–1931* (Cambridge, Mass., 1965).
20. Hunt, "The Long Crisis in U.S. Diplomatic History," 110.
21. Some representative recent work includes William Stueck, *The Korean War: An International History* (Princeton, 1995); Chen Jian, *Mao's China and the Cold War* (Chapel Hill, 2001); Fredrik Logevall, *Choosing War: The Lost Chance for Peace and the Escalation of the War in Vietnam* (Berkeley and Los Angeles, 1999); Mark Philip Bradley, *Imagining Vietnam and America: The Making of Postcolonial Vietnam, 1919–1950* (Chapel Hill, 2000); Timothy Naftali and Alexandr Furchenko, *"One Hell of a Gamble": Kennedy, Castro, and Khrushchev, 1958–1964* (New York, 1997); Lester Langley, *The Americas in the Age of Revolution, 1750–1850* (Athens, Ga., 1996); Norman E. Saul, *War and Revolution: The United States and Russia, 1914–1921* (Lawrence, Kan., 2001); Jeremi Suri, *Power and Protest: Global Revolution and the Rise of Detente* (Cambridge, Mass., 2003).
22. Jim Hershberg letter, *Cold War International History Project Bulletin* (Spring 1992): 1, 6.
23. See, for example, Stueck, *The Korean War*; Naftali and Furchenko, *"One Hell of a Gamble"*; Piero Gleijeses, *Conflicting Missions: Havana, Washington, and Africa, 1959–1976* (Chapel Hill, 2002).
24. Reinhold Wagnleitner, *Coca-Colonization and the Cold War: The Cultural Mission of the United States in Austria after the Second World War*, trans. Diana M. Wolf (Chapel Hill, 1994); Jessica C. E. Gienow-Hecht, *Transmission Impossible: American Journalism as Cultural Diplomacy in Postwar Germany, 1945–1955* (Baton Rouge, 1999).
25. Rob Kroes, *If You've Seen One, You've Seen the Mall: Europeans and American Mass Culture* (Urbana, Ill., 1996). See also "The American Occupation of Germany in Cultural Perspective: A Roundtable," *Diplomatic History* 23 (Winter 1999): 1–77; "Roundtable: Cultural Transfer or Cultural Imperialism?" *Diplomatic History* 24 (Summer 2000): 465–528; Michael J. Hogan, ed., *The Ambiguous Legacy: U.S. Foreign Relations in the "American Century"* (New York, 1999); Reinhold Wagnleitner and Elaine Tyler May, eds., *"Here, There and Everywhere": The Foreign Politics of American Popular Culture* (Hanover, N.H., 2000).
26. Thomas Bender, "Introduction: Historians, the Nation, and the Plenitude of Narratives," in *Rethinking American History in a Global Age*, ed. Thomas Bender (Berkeley and Los Angeles, 2002), 10.
27. An excellent example of such a work is Daniel Rogers, *Atlantic Crossings: Social Politics in a Progressive Age* (Cambridge, Mass., 1998). See also Don H. Doyle, *Nations Divided: America, Italy, and the Southern Question* (Athens, Ga., 2002); and the essays in Bender, ed., *Rethinking American History*.

28. Suri, *Power and Protest.*

29. Logevall, *Choosing War.*

30. Representative works include Frank Ninkovich, *Modernity and Power: A History of the Domino Theory in the Twentieth Century* (Chicago, 1994); Emily Rosenberg, *Financial Missionaries to the World: The Politics and Culture of Dollar Diplomacy, 1900–1930* (Cambridge, Mass., 1999); Andrew J. Rotter, *Comrades at Odds: The United States and India, 1947–1964* (Ithaca, 2000); Michael E. Latham, *Modernization as Ideology: American Social Science and "Nation Building" in the Kennedy Era* (Chapel Hill, 2000); Frank Costigliola, "'Unceasing Urge for Penetration': Gender, Pathology, and Emotion in George Kennan's Formation of the Cold War," *Journal of American History* 83 (March 1997): 1309–39; idem, "The Nuclear Family: Tropes of Gender and Pathology in the Western Alliance," *Diplomatic History* 21 (Spring 1997): 163–83.

31. Ninkovich, "Paradigms Lost."

32. Michael J. Hogan, "The 'Next Big Thing': The Future of Diplomatic History in a Global Age," *Diplomatic History* 28 (January 2004): 1–21.

33. Linda Gordon, *Pitied But Not Entitled: Single Mothers and the History of Welfare* (New York, 1994); Jill Quadagno, *The Color of Welfare: How Racism Undermined the War on Poverty* (New York, 1994).

34. Michael H. Hunt, *Ideology and U.S. Foreign Policy* (New Haven, 1987); Thomas Borstelmann, *The Cold War and the Color Line: Race Relations and American Foreign Policy Since 1945* (Cambridge, Mass., 2001); Mary Dudziak, *Cold War Civil Rights: Race and the Image of American Democracy* (Princeton, 2000); Robert Dean, *Imperial Brotherhood* (Amherst, Mass., 2001); Rotter, *Comrades at Odds.*

35. Julian E. Zelizer, *Taxing America: Wilbur D. Mills, Congress, and the State, 1945–1975* (Cambridge, Mass., 1998); Michael J. Hogan, *A Cross of Iron: Harry S. Truman and the Origins of the National Security State, 1945–1954* (New York, 1998).

REUEL SCHILLER

"Saint George and the Dragon": Courts and the Development of the Administrative State in Twentieth-Century America

In January 1938, James Landis, Dean of Harvard Law School, author of much of the New Deal's securities legislation, and a former member of the Securities and Exchange Commission, traveled to New Haven, Connecticut, to deliver the prestigious Storrs Lectures at Yale Law School. His subject was "The Administrative Process." Of particular interest to Landis was defining the correct relationship between courts and the administrative state. According to Landis, the interaction between agencies and courts "gives a sense of battle."[1] He continued: "Here one is presented with decisions that speak of contest between two agencies of government—one, like St. George, eternally refreshing its vigor from the stream of democratic desires, the other majestically girding itself with the wisdom of the ages."[2]

Landis's simile tipped his hand as to his opinion about who should win this contest. Like many New Dealers, he saw the judiciary as a reactionary institution, intent on thwarting both the democratic desire of Americans to establish a vigorous administrative state and the expert opinions of scientific administrators who were trying to pull the nation out of the Great Depression. Later generations of reformers might have been inclined to switch the parties in Landis's allegory, portraying administrative bureaucracy as the rapacious dragon and courts as the chivalric guardians of freedom and democracy. No one, however, would deny that elemental to the study of the administrative process was understanding the relationship between courts and the administrative state. Indeed, thirty years later, another New Deal alum, Louis Jaffe, would note that judicial review was "the necessary condition . . . of a system of administrative power that purports to be legally valid."[3] By the mid-1970s, the notion that courts

THE JOURNAL OF POLICY HISTORY, Vol. 17, No. 1, 2005.
Copyright © 2005 The Pennsylvania State University, University Park, PA.

and agencies were "partners" in the administrative process was common-place among both judges and legal academics.[4]

Yet despite the fact that at least three generations of administrative lawyers have viewed the nature of the interaction between courts and agencies as an integral part of the study of the administrative state, social scientists who have focused their attention on the development of the American governmental bureaucracy have essentially ignored the judiciary. In particular, historical institutionalists, who have sought to "bring the state back in" to the study of American political history seem to have pushed the judiciary out of the narrative of American political history altogether. In much of this scholarship, courts as a variable in the policy-making process are relegated to the periphery. When they are mentioned at all, it is in one of two marginal contexts. First, courts are portrayed as significant actors only in the premodern, nineteenth-century state.[5] During the twentieth century their policy-making functions are taken over by bureaucratic, administrative actors. Second, when courts do appear in the twentieth century, they are pushed into limited policy pigeonholes (civil rights and civil liberties, for example) that are viewed as unrelated to the main narrative of state-building in twentieth-century America.[6]

This vision of the judiciary's role in the modern, administrative state profoundly underestimates the significance of courts in the administrative process. Scholars within the legal academy have written historical accounts of the relationship between the judiciary and the administrative state.[7] Yet these seem to go unread by institutionalist historians and social scientists. Throughout the twentieth century, courts imposed their own, semi-autonomous interests on the policy-making process, bending and warping policy inputs like any other state institution. Accordingly, if we are truly to bring the state back into American political history, we need to include courts.

To bring the state back in, we must identify the institutional interests that courts sought to impose on the administrative process. This will then allow us to see how these interests shaped bureaucratic capacity and the development of the administrative state. At the broadest level, courts had an interest in retaining control over the administrative process. In the early twentieth century, this interest manifested itself as a refusal to allow certain agencies—such as railroad or workman's compensation commissions—to act as anything more than a fact finder for the courts.[8] In the postwar period, this impulse cropped up more modestly as an insistence on relatively rigorous judicial review of administrative action.

There are several reasons why the judiciary insisted on retaining control in this manner. First, judges and lawyers seemed to have feared a loss of status and power if large portions of the judicial business disappeared into the maw of the administrative state. Certainly, Landis suggested that this was a concern of judges who reviewed administrative action too strictly.[9] Similarly, Ronen Shamir has demonstrated that many New Deal–era lawyers worried that the status of their profession (and, presumably, the size of their wallets) would be diminished if the rise of the administrative state resulted in a decrease in the need for lawyerly expertise.[10]

Second, courts attempted to control the administrative process throughout the twentieth century because judges believed that peculiarly "legal" forms of reasoning were better than the methods of decision-making that agencies used. For example, New Deal–era judges resisted the inclination of administrative agencies to replace common law–style methods of thinking—reasoning by analogy or syllogism—with more empirical, pragmatic, or, alternatively, political reasoning.[11] After all, legal education and professional culture suggested to judges that legal reasoning was the best, fairest way to achieve just policy outcomes.

This judicial reluctance to endorse administrative methods of reasoning explains the desire of the judiciary to assert its control over the administrative process. It also defines the nature of the requirements that courts have repeatedly placed on agencies. Shamir, among others, has demonstrated how the legislative proposals to create uniform judicial controls over the administrative state that began in the 1930s each attempted to make agencies behave more like courts.[12] Indeed, the culmination of these proposals, the Administrative Procedure Act (APA), passed in 1946, placed many courtlike procedural requirements (cross-examination, rules of evidence, formal records) on federal agency adjudications. During the 1960s and 1970s, judges sought to impose similar procedures on the rulemaking process.[13]

A third, related phenomenon stimulated the judicial desire to control the administrative process and helped to define the nature of that control: a judicial commitment to the principle of the rule of law. The rule of law is, of course, a pretty abstract idea. However, what is clear from studying the interaction of courts and the administrative state during the twentieth century is that judges did not think that agencies followed it. The very aspects of the administrative process that made it so appealing to its advocates—its informality, its disdain for general principles, and the way it marshaled expertise in an attempt to tailor state action to a particular set of facts—consistently troubled lawyers and judges. In the 1930s, for example, the American Bar Association repeatedly attacked agency actions that seemed to it to be "non-legal": ignoring rules of evidence and the principle of *stare decisis*, making decisions without a record, blending legislative, judicial, and executive functions in a single administrative actor.[14] After World War II, similar critiques emerged from more liberal quarters. New Dealers like William O. Douglas and Robert Jackson, both writing from the bench of the Supreme Court, decried the tendency of agencies to engage in case-by-case, ad hoc decision-making, and to reject rules that would bind them in the future. Such behavior, Justice Jackson wrote, was an "assertion of power to govern the matter *without law*" and, as such, was nothing more than "administrative authoritarianism."[15]

Thus, the tradition of due process, the ideal that judges should apply the law neutrally, and the principles of *stare decisis* and the rule of law did not jibe well with the functionalist administrative aphorism that "the ultimate test of the administrative is the policy that it formulates; not the fairness as between the parties."[16] Judges were thus inclined to see judicial, lawyerly ways of doing things as not only generating better public policy but also as doing it in a manner that was consistent with just, democratic values.[17] Thus, judges sought to control agencies by imposing judicial procedures that were traditionally seen as generating fair outcomes or protecting the rights of the parties.

Of course the vigor with which courts sought to limit administrative autonomy waxed and waned over the course of the twentieth century just as the specific requirements that courts imposed on agencies changed.[18] Additionally, the subject matter of administrative action seems to have affected the potency of judicial supervision. In areas of regulation that fit comfortably within a traditional reading of the police powers (protecting public health, safety, and morals), courts were quite deferential to agencies. The intensity of judicial review was elevated primarily in more novel areas of regulation, particularly economic regulation or regulation that had a redistributive effect.[19] Regardless of these variables, however, courts remained part of the administrative process throughout the twentieth century.

Thus, to gain an accurate understanding of state-building and policy creation in twentieth-century America, we must examine how judicial interests are imposed on the administrative process. To demonstrate how this process should work, I will take two examples of institutionalist scholarship and show how the story each tells can be improved by paying more attention to the judicial role in the administrative process.

My first example comes from Daniel P. Carpenter's wonderful book in the state-building genre of historical institutionalism, *The Forging of Bureaucratic Autonomy*. Carpenter shows that, under certain circumstances, mid-level agency officials have been successful at shaping public policy according to their own preferences, regardless of wishes of Congress or the President. He demonstrates this point by reference to specific policy innovations that occurred during the Progressive Era at the Post Office, the United States Department of Agriculture (USDA), and the Department of the Interior. For example, he shows how Harvey Wiley, the chief chemist of the Department of Agriculture, was able to overcome presidential and congressional resistance to pure food and drug laws. According to Carpenter, Wiley was able to do this because his ties to political, economic, scientific, and charitable organizations gave him "reputational autonomy" that allowed him to outflank intransigent politicians.[20]

Carpenter tells this story, and many others, with admirable detail. There is no doubt that he is correct. "Mezzo-level" bureaucrats were able to carve out autonomous spaces for themselves in federal executive agencies and essentially legislate. However, Carpenter ignores the fact that the federal judiciary put limits on that autonomy. Indeed, these limits could be particularly potent because unelected federal judges could not be politically outmaneuvered by mid-level administrators deploying their reputation-based authority. Consider, for example, the problems that Wiley had enforcing the pure food sections of the Pure Food and Drug Act during the first decade of its existence.

In order to limit the Secretary of Agriculture's power, Congress divided the authority to enforce the Pure Food and Drug Act among the Department of Agriculture, the Justice Department, and the federal courts.[21] The USDA did not actually have the power to punish a person who violated the act. Nor was it able to seize and destroy adulterated or misbranded goods. Only the Justice Department had the power to institute proceedings in federal court that would result in punishment or seizure. The Secretary of Agriculture had a more limited role. He was to examine the goods at issue and then hold a hearing (known as a section 4 hearing) at which the party who produced the goods had a right to appear. If the secretary determined that the goods were adulterated or misbranded, he was to forward his finding, along with the record he compiled, to the Justice Department. Then the Justice Department could bring a case against the manufacturer in federal district court.

Congress's decision to force the Department of Agriculture to work through the judiciary gave courts the opportunity to impose procedural requirements on the agency. Indeed, because Congress did not define the relationship between the section 4 hearing and the Justice Department's decision to bring a case in federal court, the courts themselves got to define that relationship. Thus, in the first years after the act was passed, courts were divided over whether or not a section 4 hearing was a prerequisite for bringing a prosecution under the act. Some courts held that it was[22]; others held that it was not.[23] Still others held that a section 4 hearing was required before a criminal prosecution occurred but not before a seizure.[24] Ultimately, in 1911, the Supreme Court held that section 4 hearings were not required under any circumstances. The only significance of the hearing was that if the USDA did it, the Justice Department was obligated to bring the case. Under other circumstances, individual U.S. Attorneys were free to use their discretion.[25]

This interaction between courts and the USDA nicely illustrates how courts could limit agency autonomy. Obviously, when courts forced the agency to use section 4 hearings, they undermined agency autonomy by foisting procedural requirements on it that it did not want. Yet even when the Supreme Court lifted this requirement, it replaced the procedural requirement with a requirement of substantive review: if the administrative procedure that led to the seizure of adulterated goods was to pass constitutional muster, courts had to have the power to review the agency's findings from scratch.[26] Thus, even as the USDA gained procedural autonomy, it lost substantive autonomy. The judiciary, as it turned out, had no trouble simply rejecting the agency's positions in Pure Food and Drug cases on their substance even if the procedural hurdles were satisfied.[27]

What does this expedition into an antique, obscure area of administrative procedure tell us about Carpenter's story? It demonstrates that the web of connections and affiliations that mezzo-level bureaucrats at the USDA used to carve out areas of autonomy for themselves were ineffective when it came to disarming the judiciary. Despite the split among the courts in these cases, each court was interested in imposing some form of due process on the agency: either administrative due process (i.e., the section 4 hearing was mandatory) or constitutional due process (i.e., courts must review the substance of administrative decisions from scratch). The imposition of due process values was a limitation on agency autonomy that the agency could not avoid by invoking political clout or scientific expertise, the currencies that Carpenter so ably demonstrates were used against resistant political actors.

For my second example of the benefits of studying the relationship between courts and agencies, I draw on the institutionalist studies of bureaucratic capacity that focus on how the underdeveloped nature of American bureaucratic structures has limited policy impulses. Some of the most interesting literature in this area relates to the development of the American welfare state. In particular, scholars such as Theda Skocpol, Anna Shola Orloff, and Jill Quadagno have attempted to demonstrate that the underdevelopment of America's welfare state, as compared to those in Europe, cannot be explained simply with reference to American ideology.[28] Instead, these scholars focus on how American institutions were structured in a manner that prevented egalitarian political impulses from turning into egalitarian policies. They examine the way in which the localism and fragmentation of power resulting from our decentralized system of government inhibited the growth of the welfare state. They also demonstrate that America's lack of preexisting bureaucratic capacity made establishing a welfare state difficult even during a time—the Great Depression—when most political and ideological impulses pointed in that direction. Additionally, these factors dictated the form of those welfare programs that were established (local control and self-funding insurance programs, for example).[29]

Despite the strengths of this scholarship, it ignores courts and the role the judiciary has played in the development of the American welfare state. The actions of courts are hardly irrelevant to the administration of social services. Indeed, in some cities the entire systems of social welfare provision operate under judicial supervision.[30] More significant, the institutional mechanisms for providing welfare have been profoundly shaped by judicial oversight.

Bureaucratic capacity is deeply affected by the values that courts impose on administrative agencies. The administrative reaction to the Supreme Court's famous 1970 opinion *Goldberg v. Kelly* provides an excellent example of this phenomenon. In *Goldberg* the Court held that welfare recipients were entitled to trial-like adversarial hearings before the state could remove them from the welfare rolls. This decision should be of interest to those who study the development of social welfare bureaucracies, particularly if they are concerned with the issue of administrative capacity. By imposing the requirements of due process on the administrative process, *Goldberg* had the unintended consequence of straining administrative capacities. Agencies had to change not only their procedures but also their allocation of resources and, in some instances, how agency employees interacted with their clients.[31] Thus just as a structural constitutional impediment (federalism, for example) affected the development of social welfare programs in the United States, so to did judicial attitudes about the applicability of due process.

Goldberg is a famous constitutional law case with far-reaching implications for entitlement programs. Consequently, it should not be surprising that it had profound effects on the development of social policy. It may be, however, that the plethora of mundane interactions between courts and social service providers has an even greater effect. The mechanisms of the social welfare bureaucracy in the twentieth century developed as a dialogue between courts and agencies. Courts prevented or allowed particular administrative innovations in a manner that directly affected both administrative autonomy and capacity. When faced with rapidly increasing caseloads in the 1970s, could the Department of Health and Human Services speed up the processing of disability claims by limiting an applicant's testimony? What evidentiary rules was the Department of Labor supposed to use in adjudicating worker's compensation claims? Courts and agencies answered these questions together.[32] The agency suggested innovations that it believed would promote efficiency and accuracy. Courts then tempered these innovations through the process of constitutional and statutory interpretation. In doing so, they imported peculiarly judicial values into the administrative process, thereby shaping bureaucratic capacity and limiting bureaucratic autonomy.

Nor was the effect of the judicial imposition of procedures on agency autonomy and capacity limited to social service bureaucracies. For example, in the 1970s, courts made agency rulemaking considerably more difficult by adding a slew of procedural dictates to the modest requirements of the APA and by increasing the intensity of their substantive review of agency rules. As a result, the National Highway Traffic Safety Administration stopped issuing safety regulations and instead began recalling unsafe vehicles in an ad hoc fashion—a remarkably inefficient method of regulation that profoundly limited the effectiveness of motor vehicle safety regulation.[33] Similarly, these requirements threatened to derail the Environmental Protection Agency's attempts to implement the Clean Air Act by limiting the effective participation of important constituencies in the administrative process and by creating procedural disincentives for responding to such constituencies.[34] In each case, judicial action limited administrative capacity in the same way that underdeveloped bureaucratic structures might have.

Each of these examples demonstrates how an awareness of institutional autonomy must include both bureaucratic and judicial institutions. Both institutions act as prisms through which policy inputs are refracted. Each institution brings its own autonomous interests to the process of policy creation and implementation. Thus, only by identifying the autonomous judicial values that courts impose on the administrative process can we truly "bring the state back in" to the study of American political history.

The judicial imposition of legalistic values on the administrative state is not the only role that courts play in state-building. The power that courts have over agencies allows them to impose not only their own internal values. They also can act as a conduit by which political, social, and cultural ideas make their way into the administrative process. Of course, this is not the only way that agencies are buffeted by the ideological currents in which they sit. Courts, however, can force agencies to comply with a particular idea in a manner that other institutions cannot. Additionally, judges are forced to articulate their rationale for a given instance of oversight of the administrative process in a written opinion. Accordingly, these opinions can provide scholars with wonderful evidence of the ideological context of state-building and bureaucratic action. Indeed, by examining the way that courts and agencies interact, scholars can begin to address a criticism often leveled at historical institutionalism: that it is insufficiently sensitive to the social and ideological context in which agencies sit.[35]

It is not difficult to find revealing examples of the utility of studying the interaction between courts and agencies to provide a broader context for understanding the development of the administrative state. Judicial opinions are rich sources to mine for ideals of political culture—liberalism versus statism, or assumptions about how policy should be created, for example—since judges often try, both with and without success, to mold agencies in the form of these ideals. Consider two examples: how courts imposed anti-totalitarian ideology on the administrative state in the 1940s and how these same courts attempted to force agencies to adhere to ideals of participatory democracy during the 1960s.

A number of legal historians have demonstrated the dramatic effect that the rise of European totalitarianism had on American judges. In particular, scholars of constitutional law have shown how courts' increasing receptiveness to civil liberties claims stemmed in part from a desire to distance the American legal system from that of Nazi Germany, a system that had become part and parcel of the totalitarian state.[36] Courts reacted in a similar fashion with respect to administrative law. Just as totalitarian legal systems rejected civil libertarian notions of freedom of speech or racial and ethnic equality, so too did they reject legal controls on the administrative actions of the dictator. Consequently, American courts began to embrace these roles.

Even before the passage of the Administrative Procedure Act in 1946, itself influenced by anti-totalitarian ideology,[37] federal courts began curtailing administrative discretion by broadening standing to challenge agency actions and by increasing the intensity with which courts reviewed these actions.[38] Several decisions explicitly linked calls for a more vigorous judicial role to the fight against fascism. As early as 1940, a Ninth Circuit panel made up entirely of Roosevelt appointees accused the National Labor Relations Board of "the kind of administrative absolutism denounced in democratic assemblies . . . as characteristic of the totalitarianism of the Central European powers." The panel continued: "We do not belive [sic] that . . . the National Labor Relations Act intended to make a long start on the road to where our civil liberties are regarded as the 'pale phantoms of objective law' which no longer control our deliberations, as the German Chief Justice . . . of the newly constituted court in conquered Poland is reported to have told his colleagues."[39] Indeed, throughout the 1940s and 1950s, Justices of the Supreme Court used antitotalitarian rhetoric to justify decreasing judicial deference to the administrative state.[40]

A similar interaction among ideology, judicial decision-making and the administrative process can be identified in the 1960s. During the immediate postwar period, public intellectuals spilled a great deal of ink extolling the virtues of the pressure group. Interest groups were, in the words of the particularly effusive John Chamberlain, "the corporate age's analogue to the individual freeholder of Jeffersonian times."[41] These groups transformed otherwise atomized voters into forces that politicians would respond to. At the same time, they promoted liberty and stability through a system of "countervailing power," to use John Kenneth Galbraith's term.[42] They were thus the building blocks of representative, responsive, stable democracy—America's self-image in the years following World War II.

By the 1960s, of course, most Americans had a very different view of interest-group pluralism. Critics on both the right and the left acknowledged that government responded to interest groups but denied that these groups were genuinely representative. Instead, thinkers from Gabriel Kolko to Mancur Olson argued that the pressure group was simply the mechanism by which entrenched elites manipulated the state to serve their interests.[43] Many intellectuals demanded that American democracy become genuinely participatory.[44] Indeed, these thinkers seemed to reflect a tendency in the political culture at large—as manifest, for example, in the civil rights movement and the free speech movement—to demand that a broader swath of Americans be allowed to participate in the political process.

During the 1960s, the federal judiciary attempted to impose this value on the administrative state. In a series of opinions, federal appellate courts limited agency discretion to exclude parties from administrative adjudications simply because their direct economic interests were not at stake. The Federal Communications Commission had to respond to viewers as well as station owners.[45] The Federal Power Commission had to listen to environmentalists as well as power companies.[46] The Civil Aeronautics Board had to consider the comments of people living near airports as well as those of the airlines.[47] For the administrative process to work, it had to become more participatory: "[Community groups]," wrote the Court of Appeals for the D.C. Circuit, "usually concern themselves with a wide range of community problems and tend to be representative of broad as distinguished from narrow interests, public as distinguished from private or commercial interests."[48]

In each of these instances courts took a rather nebulous ideological trend (anti-totalitarianism or participatory democracy) and converted it into a legal doctrine (more intense judicial review or increased administrative standing) that limited administrative autonomy. Courts acted as a conduit for elements of American political culture, converting these abstractions into concrete rules for deciding cases. Thus, just as courts imposed their own, internal autonomous interests on the administrative state, so too they imposed general societal interests. Surely there are a host of social, political, cultural, or ideological factors that courts imposed on agencies as they created and implemented public policy. By examining the interaction between courts and the administrative state, we can complete the narrative of state-building not only by acknowledging bureaucracy's autonomous elements but also by situating it in a social and ideological context.

The possibilities suggested by the integration of the judiciary into the study of state-building help to outline a research agenda for scholars who are interested in this project. First, I have suggested that an examination of the interaction between courts and the administrative state will allow us to see how courts imposed their own autonomous legal values on the administrative process. Accordingly, scholars need to identify the nature of these values as they changed over time. Additionally, we need to know how successful courts were at forcing agency adherence. How did agencies resist? Second, I have argued that courts acted as conduits for broader ideological and social forces, imposing the nonlegal policy preferences, social norms, and political theories on the administrative bureaucracy. Once again, we must identify what these forces were, how they changed over time, and how agencies responded to them.

There are two general approaches to answering these questions. First, we need a broad narrative of the development of administrative law from the late nineteenth century to the present. Chunks of this narrative exist,[49] but they are only beginning to approach the subject with the sort of methodological and historiographical sophistication that has been brought to bear on other areas of legal history, such as the development of constitutional law during this same period. Ideally, scholars who explore this narrative will discover both the distinctly legal values and the broader social values that courts sought to impose on agencies, see how these values changed over time, and show how agencies reacted to judicial oversight.

Second, scholars should undertake monographic studies of particular agencies and the way they have interacted with the judiciary. Certainly there are plenty of examples of close examinations of particular agencies or the regulation of particular subject matters. However, as I have indicated, few of these studies explore the relationship between courts and the agency. There are a few exceptions,[50] but for the most part the people who study courts are segregated from those who study agencies.

It is possible to speculate about why historical institutionalism has ignored the role of courts in the development of the administrative state. To the extent that many legal historians have focused on the intellectual history of the law, they have committed themselves to a very different methodology than have the institutionalists. Furthermore, until quite recently, the legal history of twentieth-century America has been underexamined. This is particularly true of the postwar period. The scholarship that has been done has focused on constitutional issues such as changes in the judicial protection of civil rights and civil liberties. Perhaps this explains why institutionalist scholars eject courts from the administrative arena and consign them to these areas. It is not because courts are not an integral part of the administrative state. Instead it is because legal historians have not generated secondary materials about administrative law. Finally, I am sure that many scholars shy away from administrative law because of its reputation for being both complicated and dull—hardly an inviting subject for extended historical research. This reputation is undeserved. Indeed, to the contrary, the development of administrative law in the twentieth century is a rich and interesting area of research. By examining it in detail, scholars will be able to tell the story not only of the development of legal doctrines and institutions but also of the development of the administrative state in twentieth-century America. After all, the story of Saint George or the story of the Dragon is not half as interesting as the tale of what happened when the two met.

University of California, Hastings College of Law

Notes

1. James M. Landis, *The Administrative Process* (New Haven, 1938), 123.
2. Ibid.
3. Louis L. Jaffe, *Judicial Control of Administrative Action* (Boston, 1965), 320.
4. See, for example, *Portland Cement Ass'n v. Ruckelshaus*, 486 F.2d 375, 394 (D.C. Cir. 1973); Henry J. Friendly, "Some Kind of Hearing," *University of Pennsylvania Law Review* 123 (1975): 1311 n. 221.

5. See, for example, Stephen Skowronek, *Building a New American State: The Expansion of National Administrative Capacities, 1877–1920* (Cambridge, 1982), 24–31.

6. Ibid., 287, 289.

7. Richard B. Stewart, "The Reformation of American Administrative Law," *Harvard Law Review* 88 (1975): 669; Robert L. Rabin, "Federal Regulation in Historical Perspective," *Stanford Law Review* 38 (1986): 1189; Thomas W. Merrill, "Capture Theory and the Courts: 1967–1983," *Chicago-Kent Law Review* 72 (1997): 1039; Martin Shapiro, *Who Guards the Guardians? Judicial Control of Administration* (Athens, Ga., 1988); Reuel E. Schiller, "Reining in the Administrative State," in Daniel R. Ernst and Victor Jew, eds., *Total War and the Law: The American Home Front in World War II* (Westport, 2002), 185; idem, "Rulemaking's Promise: Administrative Law and Legal Culture in the 1960s and 1970s," *Administrative Law Review* 53 (2001): 1139; idem, "Enlarging the Administrative Polity: Administrative Law and the Changing Definition of Pluralism, 1945–1970," *Vanderbilt Law Review* 53 (2000): 1389.

8. For some prominent examples form the U.S. Supreme Court's docket, see *Smyth v. Ames*, 169 U.S. 466 (1898); *Ohio Water Valley v. Ben Avon Borough*, 253 U.S. 287 (1920); *Crowell v. Benson*, 285 U.S. 22 (1930).

9. Landis, *The Administrative Process*, 154–55.

10. Ronen Shamir, *Managing Legal Uncertainty: Elite Lawyers in the New Deal* (Durham, 1995), 131–32. See also George B. Shepherd, "Fierce Compromise: The Administrative Procedure Act Emerges from New Deal Politics," *Northwestern Law Review* 90 (1996): 1571–72.

11. Nicholas S. Zeppos, "The Legal Profession and the Development of Administrative Law," *Chicago-Kent Law Review* 72 (1997): 1139–51.

12. Shamir, *Managing Legal Uncertainty*, 109–13; Shepherd, "Fierce Compromise," 1649–52; Schiller, "Reining in the Administrative State," 198–99.

13. Schiller, "Rulemaking's Promise," 1139.

14. The ABA's critique was expressed most forcefully in the 1938 Annual Report of the Special Committee on Administrative Law, chaired by Roscoe Pound. "Report of the Special Committee on Administrative Law," *American Bar Association Annual Report* (1938): 342. For an account of the ABA's general hostility to administrative action, see Shepherd, "Fierce Compromise," 1569–78.

15. *Securities and Exchange Commission v. Chenery*, 332 U.S. 194, 216 (1947), (Jackson, J., dissenting). See also Justice Douglas's opinion for the Court in *Estep v. United States*, 327 U.S. 114 (1946).

16. Landis, *The Administrative Process*, 39.

17. Schiller, "Rulemaking's Promise," 1166–68.

18. In addition to the materials cited in note 7, see G. Edward White, "Allocating Power Between Agencies and Courts: The Legacy of Justice Brandeis," in G. Edward White, *Patterns of American Legal Thought* (Indianapolis, 1978), 227–87.

19. See, for example, Reuel E. Schiller, "Free Speech and Expertise: Administrative Censorship and the Birth of the Modern First Amendment," *Virginia Law Review* 86 (2000): 1; and Charles W. McCurdy, "The Roots of Liberty of Contract Reconsidered: Major Premises in the Law of Employment, 1867–1937," *Yearbook of the Supreme Court Historical Society* (1984): 20.

20. Daniel P. Carpenter, *The Forging of Bureaucratic Autonomy: Reputations, Networks, and Policy Innovation in Executive Agencies, 1862–1928* (Princeton, 2001), 257–75.

21. Pure Food Act of 1906, 34 Stat. 768, 769, section 4; Gustavus A. Weber, *The Food, Drug, and Insecticide Administration: Its History, Activities, and Organization* (Baltimore, 1928), 41–43.

22. *United States v. Twenty Cans of Grape Juice*, 189 F. 331 (2d Cir. 1911); *United States v. Certain Cans of Syrup*, 192 F. 79 (E.D. Penn 1911).

23. *United States v. Morgan*, 181 F. 587 (S.D.N.Y. 1910); *Schraubstadter v. United States*, 199 F. 568 (9th Cir. 1912).

24. *United States v. Nine Barrels of Olives*, 179 F. 983 (E.D.Penn. 1910); *United States v. Seventy-Four Cases of Grape Juice*, 181 F. 629 (W.D.N.Y. 1910); *United States v. Fifty Barrels of Whiskey*, 165 F. 966 (D.Md. 1908); *United States v. Sixty-Five Casks Liquid Extracts*, 170 F. 449 (N.D. W.Va. 1909).

25. *United States v. Morgan*, 222 U.S. 274 (1911).

26. *National Remedy Co. v. Hyde*, 50 F.2d 1066 (D.C. Cir. 1931).

27. See, for example, *United States v. St. Louis Coffee and Spice Mills*, 189 F. 191 (E.D.Mo. 1909); *In re Wilson*, 168 F. 566 (D.R.I. 1909); *United States v. Northwestern Fisheries*, 224 F. 274 (W.D.Wash. 1915); *French Silver Dragee Co. v. United States*, 179 F. 824 (2d Cir. 1910).

28. For a selection of essays on this subject by these and other authors, see Margaret Weir, Ann Shola Orloff, and Theda Skocpol, eds., *The Politics of Social Policy in the United States* (Princeton, 1988).

29. Ann Shola Orloff, "The Political Origins of America's Belated Welfare State," in Weir, Orloff, and Skocpol, *The Politics of Social Policy in the United States*, 73–80.

30. Ross Sandler and David Schoenbrod, *Democracy by Decree: What Happens When Courts Run Government* (New Haven, 2003).

31. Jerry L. Mashaw, *Due Process and the Administrative State* (New Haven, 1985), 32–41; William H. Simon, "The Rule of Law and the Two Realms of Welfare Administration," *Brooklyn Law Review* 56 (1990): 784–88.

32. These two examples come from *Heckler v. Campbell*, 461 U.S. 458 (1983), and *Director, Officer of Workers' Compensation Programs v. Greenwich Collieries*, 512 U.S. 267 (1994).

33. Jerry L. Mashaw and David L. Harfst, *The Struggle for Auto Safety* (Cambridge, Mass., 1990).

34. Bruce A. Ackerman and William T. Hassler, *Clean Coal, Dirty Air* (New Haven, 1981), 111–14.

35. Ira Katznelson, "The State to the Rescue? Political Science and History Reconnect," *Social Research* 59 (1992): 719; Daniel R. Ernst, "Law and American Political Development, 1877–1938," *Reviews in American History* 26 (1998): 205.

36. Herman Belz, "Changing Conceptions of Constitutionalism in the Era of World War II and the Cold War," *Journal of American History* 59 (1972): 640, 641, 646–47; William E. Nelson, "The Changing Meaning of Equality in Twentieth-Century Constitutional Law," *Washington and Lee Law Review* 52 (1995): 3, 21–28; David M. Bixby, "The Roosevelt Court, Democratic Ideology, and Minority Rights: Another Look at United States v. Classic," *Yale Law Journal* 90 (1981): 762–67; Michael J. Klarman, "Brown, Racial Change, and the Civil Rights Movement," *Virginia Law Review* 80(1994): 25–26 and nn.73–75.

37. Schiller, "Reining in the Administrative State," 196–99.

38. Schiller, "Enlarging the Administrative Polity," 1417–42.

39. *NLRB v. Sterling Electric Motors*, 112 F.2d 63, 68 (9th Cir. 1940). All three members of the panel, judges Denman, Mathews, and Healy, were Roosevelt appointees. *Who's Who in America* 21 (1940–41): 755, 1209, 1713. Judge Healy dissented.

40. See, for example, *Estep v. United States*, 327 U.S. 114, 121–22 (majority opinion) and 131–32 (Murphy, concurring); *SEC v. Chenery*, 332 U.S. 194, 216–17 (1947) (Jackson, J., dissenting); *New York v. United States*, 342 U.S. 882, 884 (1951) (Douglas, J., dissenting).

41. John Chamberlain, *The American Stakes* (New York, 1940), 27.

42. John Kenneth Galbraith, *American Capitalism: The Concept of Countervailing Power* (Boston, 1956).

43. Gabriel Kolko, *The Triumph of Conservatism* (Chicago, 1967) (originally published in 1963), 287–305; Mancur Olson, *The Logic of Collective Action* (Cambridge, Mass., 1965), 132–67. See also Schiller, "Enlarging the Administrative Polity," 1411–12.

44. See, for example, Grant McConnell, *Private Power and American Democracy* (New York, 1966), 366–69; Henry S. Kariel, *The Decline of American Pluralism* (Palo Alto, 1961),

273–91; Edmond Cahn, *The Predicament of Democratic Man* (New York, 1961), 116; E. E. Schattschneider, *The Semisovereign People: A Realist's View of Democracy in America* (New York, 1960), 105, 141; James McGregor Burns, *The Deadlock of Democracy* (Englewood Cliffs, 1963), 235–40, 323–40.

45. *Office of Communications of the United Church of Christ v. FCC*, 359 F.2d 994 (D.C.Cir. 1965).

46. *Scenic Hudson Preservation Conference v. FPC*, 345 F.2d 608 (2d. Cir. 1965).

47. *Palisades Citizens Ass'n v. CAB*, 420 F.2d 188 (D.C.Cir. 1969).

48. *Church of Christ*, 1004–5.

49. See note 7 above.

50. See, for example, Lucy Salyer, *Laws Harsh as Tigers: Chinese Immigrants and the Shaping of Modern Immigration Law* (Chapel Hill, 1995). Although Stephen Skowronek's germinal study of state-building generally pushes courts to the periphery, his examination of the relationship between the federal judiciary and the Interstate Commerce Commission does an excellent job of demonstrating how courts can have a profound effect on the development of governmental institutions. Skowronek, *Building a New American State*, 259–67.

JACOB S. HACKER

Bringing the Welfare State Back In: The Promise (and Perils) of the New Social Welfare History

The welfare state—the complex of policies that, in one form or another, all rich democracies have adopted to ameliorate destitution and provide valued social goods and services—is an increasingly central subject in the study of American history and politics. The past decade has unleashed a veritable tidal wave of books on the topic, including, from historians, Alice Kessler-Harris's *In Pursuit of Equity* and Michael Katz's *The Price of Citizenship*, and, from political scientists, Robert Lieberman's *Shifting the Color Line* and Peter Swenson's *Capitalists Against Markets*.[1] Journals ranging from the *American Historical Review* to *Political Science Quarterly* (and, with less regularity, even the *American Political Science Review*) now routinely feature analyses of U.S. social policy. And going back just a few years more, the early 1990s saw the publication of several influential works on the subject, notably Paul Pierson's *Dismantling the Welfare State?* and Theda Skocpol's *Protecting Soldiers and Mothers*, each of which won major book prizes in political science.[2] If any moment deserves to be seen as a heady time for writing on the American welfare state, this is it.

As natural as this state of affairs has come to be seen, it was not always so. Writing in 1991, the historian Edward Berkowitz lamented that the American welfare state "commands little attention from today's students, who view it as a confusing, highly technical, and dry subject that cannot compete with the exploits, often heroic, of the blacks and women who have emerged as major figures in the history classroom over the course of the last twenty years."[3] Although Berkowitz was writing of historians, his complaint applied more broadly. Indeed, what is striking in retrospect—

My thanks to Paul Pierson and Julian Zelizer for extremely valuable comments on a previous draft of this essay, though their assistance should not, of course, be construed as endorsement. Pearline Kyi provided very helpful research assistance.

THE JOURNAL OF POLICY HISTORY, Vol. 17, No. 1, 2005.
Copyright © 2005 The Pennsylvania State University, University Park, PA.

not to mention, in light of the huge share of the economy the welfare
state represents, even in its famously stingy U.S. incarnation—is precisely
how *few* major works concerned themselves with the American welfare
state in the years before Berkowitz's words were penned. Today, however,
Berkowitz's complaint rings anachronistic: no current observer would say
that students of American public affairs bypass social welfare policy.

The explanation for this reversal is at once simple and complex. The
simple reason concerns the world outside the academy. Once protected
by a real, if uneasy, postwar consensus, the welfare state came under increasing political and economic strain in the 1980s and 1990s. In the
process, it has also become the kind of hot, front-page news topic that
academics, for all their avowed eschewal of flashy subjects, love to wade
into. At the same time, the tenor of policy debates grew sharply more
conservative, making it ever harder to accept the once-common conceit
that the United States was simply a "laggard" on a universal path toward
expanded state responsibility. What master narrative replaced this well-
worn story line was, of course, anything but obvious. But at the very least,
the welfare state suddenly seemed open to fresh approaches.

The less obvious reason for increased interest in the welfare state
concerns a set of shifts within the academic world itself. The birth of
policy history as a self-conscious field, the increasing prominence of the
political science subfield of "American political development," the rise of
"institutional political history," and the increasing sophistication of scholarship on gender and race—all were critical spurs to the explosion of interest in welfare state development. But perhaps most important, scholars
simply woke up to a fact so obvious that it was frequently overlooked: the
welfare state is a central element of modern society and politics. The seminal trigger for this new wave of analysis was Gøsta Esping-Andersen's landmark sociological study, *The Three Worlds of Welfare Capitalism*.[4]
Esping-Andersen replaced the common unilinear conception of welfare
state development with a hugely influential threefold typology that con-
trasted the "social-democratic" welfare states of Scandinavia with the "conservative" model of welfare provision in Continental Europe and the
"liberal" model found in Britain and the United States. Much as John
Rawls's *A Theory of Justice* revitalized American political theory, *The Three
Worlds of Welfare Capitalism* provided a major impetus for criticism, praise,
and refinement of arguments about the welfare state both old and new.

And yet a curious thing has happened to the welfare state on its way
from the periphery to the center of scholarly concern. Historians and political scientists are now writing about the American welfare state, but
they are not really all that concerned with the welfare state as such. For
most, instead, the welfare state has become a convenient window into

some larger relation of power—between blacks and whites, between women and men, between capital and labor. Nor, indeed, are most scholars really writing about *the* welfare state. Some concern themselves with public assistance for the poor, others with social insurance programs like Social Security, still others with labor policies, such as rules governing unions. An increasing number, in fact, are interested in policies well *beyond* the typical conception of the welfare state, such as tax policies and workplace benefits. In short, the near-perfect silence on the welfare state that once reigned has given way not to a single or harmonious tune, but to a cacophony of sometimes discordant notes that occasionally threatens to drown out the very subject of the melody.

This is perhaps not so surprising. The very diversity of the welfare state as a subject and the sheer sweep of U.S. social welfare history guarantee that scholars will pursue myriad research avenues. The question is whether these diverse inquiries are also leading to a more general picture of American welfare state development, or simply making more complex and foreboding the topography that has to be traversed. The argument of this essay is that while work on the American welfare state has dramatically improved our understanding of U.S. social policy development, there is a real risk that the stories that emerge will read like "one damn thing after another"—study piled upon study, fact upon fact, without adequate integration, explanation, or advancement.

The positive message, however, is the one to emphasize up front: studies of the American welfare state have revolutionized our understanding of American history and politics—and, indeed, have a good claim to represent the strongest area of scholarship in history and political science more generally. I begin the article, therefore, with a review of the amazingly rich and fertile avenues of inquiry that students of the American welfare state have pursued in the last decade or so. Collectively as well as individually, these recent works testify to the tremendous progress in understanding U.S. social policy that has marked the past decade—a conclusion that I want to stress far more than any specific qualms I have about recent work. Given how much of value has been written, in fact, my review will of necessity be highly selective. Yet there can be little dispute that each of the areas I take up—race and the welfare state, gender and social policy, the role of business, and the interplay of public and private benefits—has witnessed signal advances that, together, offer a far broader and deeper view of the American welfare state.

Nonetheless, all is not perfect in the world of welfare state research, and two concerns in particular emerge from my survey. The first is that a number of major lines of research are developing in almost complete isolation from one another. We have arguments about race and gender, about the role of business, about the interplay of private and public social benefits. These claims are not always mutually exclusive, to be sure. But they are not all wholly compatible either; nor are they all equally applicable to all areas of U.S. social policy. More important, because they are rarely set against each other or mapped onto policy areas different from those they were developed to explain, it is nearly impossible to adjudicate among or synthesize the competing claims they make.

This situation leads to the second general weakness of recent scholarship: a notable absence of explanatory integration. Not only are whole veins of research proceeding in largely unreflective independence from each other, but, in addition, even mid-level propositions that could connect these disparate research enterprises remain largely undeveloped. This is all the more striking because recent scholarship tends to exhibit characteristic explanatory faults that are remarkably similar across different areas of inquiry. In what follows, I argue that four such weaknesses—confusion of intentions and effects; hazy and slippery conceptions of power; failure to pursue relevant cross-national, cross-policy, or historical comparisons; and ahistorical styles of argumentation (even in deeply historical research)—are particularly common and debilitating. And I argue that each of these deficiencies could be at least partially rectified by refashioning arguments and approaches around the issue of *social policy development*—how policies, as both outcomes and causes of crucial social processes, evolve over long periods of time.

It goes without saying that these deficiencies are by no means unique to social welfare history. And lest I be misinterpreted, my message is not that historians should share the same interests or methods as political scientists, or that political scientists should discard their theories and dive into the archives (though I encourage diving in once in a while). My premise—as uncontroversial to historians, I hope, as it is to political scientists—is that the goal of research on the American welfare state is to better understand its character, causes, and consequences, and that attention to what other scholars are arguing and to basic rules of evidence and inference are necessary to achieve that goal. For reasons I shall outline, I believe this aim can best be achieved by constructing general claims about processes of long-term social policy development. But my core argument is simply that students of the American welfare state ignore what others are writing and how they can convince others of their views at their peril— and, more important, at the peril of a deeper and broader understanding of U.S. history and politics.

Revisiting Race

Students of American history have long recognized race as a distinctive "American dilemma," in the famous words of Gunnar Myrdal.[5] For good reason: while the U.S. historical experience is certainly not unique, slavery and segregation have left enduring scars on the American body politic and produced stubbornly persistent patterns of black exclusion and disadvantage within American society. Today, few would deny that race has been a leading subtext of welfare state debates since at least the New Deal, or that it plays an important, if often covert, role in current discussions of social policy.

Recent scholarship on race and the welfare state, however, moves beyond these uncontroversial observations to map out exactly *how* race matters in social policy. Race and racism, we learn, informed the original design of many programs and continues to shape public perceptions of them. Moreover, because racial disadvantage is embedded in the larger political economy that these programs seek to shape, race enters into social policy even when it is not on the minds of citizens or elites. Not only, then, do perceptions of racial difference undermine the "social solidarity" that is the cement of the welfare state; equally important, many features of the world that social policies seek to change are "race-laden," in the words of political scientist Robert Lieberman, and hence ostensibly race-neutral policies may have deeply racialized effects.[6]

The new scholarship on race has made major contributions to our understanding of American social welfare history. Yet when it comes to placing race in the context of other forces shaping U.S. social policy, it tends to falter. Few scholars, of course, are so bold as to claim that race is the motor force of American welfare state development. But in their emphases and their arguments, they generally echo the argument of Michael K. Brown that "the problems of race, on the one hand, and the failure to create broadly inclusive social policies for all Americans, on the other, have become entwined."[7] Martin Gilens, in *Why Americans Hate Welfare*, argues, for example, that distrust of welfare reflects the twin beliefs of white Americans that "most people who receive welfare are black" and that "blacks are less committed to the work ethic than are other Americans."[8] While Gilens's point is restricted to welfare (that is, public assistance for the poor), the general tenor of the new work on race and social policy is that welfare is the leading case for a basic relationship: the welfare state and debates about it are explicable first and foremost through the lens of racial analysis.

In pointing toward this more ambitious claim, the new scholarship on race risks running aground on two opposed shoals. On the one hand, relatively straightforward arguments about how racist beliefs inform the formation and evolution of social programs are clear in their mechanisms and in their implications about what supportive evidence should look like. Yet they are also limited in their reach, for many areas of the American welfare state do not appear racialized in the sense of being motivated by explicitly racist intentions. On the other hand, the claim that social policies are "race-laden" because they intersect with larger features of American society marked by racial hierarchy has considerable—indeed near-total—reach, but the political mechanisms it highlights are diffuse and quite problematic as subjects of empirical inquiry. Ironically, in fact, the broadest of such claims are quite similar in their observational implications to the discussions of dissenting scholars who have argued that what is notable about American social policy development is the general *absence* of explicit attention to race.[9] If race is everything—hidden, all-encompassing, unchanging—then it risks being nothing, too.

Robert Lieberman's generally exemplary work on the role of race in the development of the American welfare state is a case in point.[10] At times, Lieberman emphasizes the racist motives that led to key policy decisions in the 1930s and after (for example, the initial exclusion of agricultural and domestic workers from the old-age insurance program created in the Social Security Act). Yet at other points, Lieberman seems content merely to show the huge racial implications of seemingly race-neutral policies—an important point but one with a very different meaning for our understanding of U.S. social welfare history. It is not that both arguments cannot be true. Yet one suspects that the back-and-forth dance between the two is as much an attempt to "prove" that race matters as it is an effort to explain when and why race matters (and sometimes does not matter) in social policy debates.

Grasping Gender

While race has long been a central theme in the study of the American welfare state, gender, surprisingly, has not. This is so despite the fact that women have played a large and obvious role in the development of U.S. social policy, as well as representing the chief beneficiaries of its major antipoverty programs. This absence of attention can no doubt be chalked up in part to the blinders of traditionally male-dominated and -oriented historical research. Yet this explanation is incomplete. Long after gender was a major focus of work in American history, the welfare state was mostly viewed through the lens of male wage-earners and their struggle for expanded social protection.

To understand this, it helps to recognize that the major theoretical current in welfare state scholarship until recently drew from Marx in emphasizing class struggle as the root cause of welfare-state building. Social policies, on this view, were primarily means of "decommodification," a way of freeing workers from wage dependence by providing them with income when they are unable to engage in well-paid work.[11] Like much labor-oriented theorizing, women, if they entered into the analysis at all, were subsumed within the larger category of "worker"—a move that ignored the extent to which women's relationship to the labor market differed from men's and the degree to which ostensibly self-supporting male workers were supported by female domestic work.

This blinkered perspective is no longer tenable. In welfare state research, "feminist" scholarship has had a major impact over the last decade or so, and a good deal of it has concerned the American experience.[12] Symptomatic of the shift is Skocpol's *Protecting Soldiers and Mothers*—which, while controversial within feminist scholarly circles, details the role played by women's groups and reformers at the turn of the last century in promoting what she calls a "maternalist" vision of the welfare state oriented around state protection for women and children.[13] Against Skocpol's interpretation, other scholars have emphasized the repressive elements of the maternalist vision, while a growing body of writing has reinterpreted the post-1930s development of the welfare state in light of the taken-for-granted subordinate position of women.[14] Recent work has emphasized, for example, that many social insurance and employment programs initially excluded female workers, focused on risks and needs distinctive to men, and were built on the assumption that women would remain home to support male breadwinners.[15]

In comparative research, too, gender has become a central frame of reference.[16] Welfare states do not merely "decommodify," this new comparative work argues. They can also "defamilialize," lessening the extent to which women are required to remain home and care for children by providing public day care and structuring policies in gender-neutral ways. Put simply, welfare states not only affect citizens' place and power in the economy; they also affect their place and power in the household—and, indeed, it is at the nexus of these two realms that women's distinctive role, and dilemma, lies.

The success of feminist scholarship in reorienting existing theories and suggesting new historical interpretations cannot be gainsaid. Nonetheless, this work has also suffered from a number of common weakness, many of which it shares with recent scholarship on race. The first is that the singular emphasis on gender, like the singular emphasis on race, tends to occlude other forces that shape policy and politics, and to limit analysis to certain corners of the social welfare field—in this case, again, overwhelmingly poverty relief. As with work on race, feminist scholars are also often less than clear whether they are talking about sexist beliefs held by citizens and elites or about the impact of ostensibly gender-neutral policies in a world marked by vast gender inequalities, or both.[17] Indeed, far more than recent research on race, feminist scholars face the challenge of interpreting *absence*, for what is striking in many early social policy debates is precisely how little was said distinguishing women and men. This contrasts with the clear, repeated, and often breathtakingly crude and biased references to race in many of the same political debates.

Capturing Capitalists

Work on gender challenges the laborist perspective for its alleged sins of omission. New writings on the role of business, by contrast, tackle it for its alleged sins of commission. The essence of these works' critique is that previous scholarship has overstated the antimony of interests between capitalists and labor and, in doing so, missed the strong capitalist bases of support for domestic social reform.[18]

This argument has two main variants, which are not mutually exclusive. One says that businesses sometimes demand social programs to impose costs on competitors—for example, by requiring that all firms pay for benefits that they already provide.[19] The other says that businesses sometimes demand social programs to off-load their costs onto the public fisc—for example, by socializing the cost of risks to which they are particularly susceptible.[20] Both variants argue, however, that some (but, crucially, not all) businesses want generous social programs.[21] To be sure, organized labor demands social programs, too. But its success hinges on the emergence of "cross-class alliances" with capitalists.[22] Only when the bourgeoisie are on board does the proletariat get what it wants.

The recent sweeping work of Peter Swenson, *Capitalists Against Markets*—which compares the fate of social reforms in the United States during the 1930s and in Sweden immediately after World War II—exemplifies, while deepening, the new business-power thesis. Swenson argues that during the Great Depression, a significant segment of the business community was at least latently supportive of new social insurance programs that would cripple their low-wage, low-price domestic competitors. The original turn in Swenson's argument is not so much his identification of a capitalist interest in reform, but his attempt to tease out the bases of capitalist influence. Swenson argues that neither the so-called instrumental power of business (its lobbying prowess and resources) nor its "structural" power (its control over investment and jobs, about which politicians care regardless of whether business organizes to press for policy change) were crucial.[23] Rather, it was New Dealers' anticipation of long-term capitalist support for—and fear of long-term capitalist opposition to—domestic social reforms that, Swenson argues, represents the primary means by which the largely unexpressed pro-reform sentiments of the business community shaped the making of 1930s social policy.[24]

As this brief summary indicates, there is more than a whiff of the New Left to Swenson's provocative thesis. Yet unlike earlier New Left scholars who argued that Progressive Era and New Deal social reforms were essentially conservative creatures of business interests, Swenson and those who make related claims do not believe that the progressive ambitions of social reformers were hijacked by corporate America.[25] They want to argue instead that underlying business interests were largely consistent with what reformers wanted. This, of course, raises the issue of how one demonstrates *influence*. If reformers want what business wants, that could evidence influence or simply preference congruence. And indeed, in much of the recent literature, Swenson's contribution included, surprisingly scant and circumstantial evidence is offered that reformers actually responded to actual or anticipated business power in crafting their proposals.

No less serious, for all the close attention to historical detail that characterizes recent business-power accounts, these works are often at their core notably ahistorical. Swenson, for example, uses large employers' eventual acceptance of the Social Security Act as an important piece of evidence in favor of his thesis that the act was initially consistent with their interests. But, of course, the eventual business response to the New Deal is hardly an accurate gauge of initial interests. Once legislation is in place, after all, employers may simply believe they cannot realistically overturn it, or the policy may in fact change what employers want by altering market conditions, reshaping the population of employers, or encouraging new conceptions of business interests.

Similarly, many works that stress employers' influence tend to begin the story when reform gets on the agenda, then trace the direct interventions of business on specific policy choices. But this "snapshot" approach to the role of business makes it nearly impossible to judge the true power of employers, because it leaves unanswered the profound question of whether the policy terrain on which business operates at any particular moment is tilted in its favor or against it.[26] In broader historical relief, for example, what is arguably most striking about social policymaking during the New Deal is the marked *weakness* of employers relative to the position that they enjoyed in the decentralized political economy of the prior decades.[27] Nonetheless, the renewed emphasis on the role of business does powerfully call into question the traditional assumption that capitalists are merely recalcitrant stumbling blocks on the road to social reform.

Heralding the Hidden

In at least one respect, new work on business emulates older theories of the welfare state—and that is in its emphasis on public spending programs like Social Security. In this, the business-power literature is of a piece with nearly everything that has been written on the welfare state. While scholars often note the importance of taxation and of policy tools besides direct social spending, studies of the welfare state are, almost without exception, studies of social spending, with little attention paid either to tax policy (including the actual provision of benefits through the tax code) or to the wide range of "publicly subsidized and regulated private social benefits," such as employment-based health insurance, that tax policy usually helps underwrite.[28]

On one level, this conflation of social policy and public spending is understandable. Much of what welfare states do, after all, is spend—as much as two-fifths of GDP in some Nordic countries. But on another level, it is unexpected, for taxation and the role of the private sector have probably been the most consistently explosive issues in welfare state development. It is also surprising because one of the most influential theoretical writings on the welfare state—Richard Titmuss's famous *Essays on the "Welfare State"*—placed tax policy (which he termed "fiscal welfare") and private social benefits (which he called "occupational welfare") on par with spending as a means of achieving social welfare ends.[29] Yet Titmuss's insights on this point, unlike many of his other contributions, have produced relatively little follow-up analysis.

That situation has started to change, but not nearly as quickly or as fully as in the other areas we have reviewed. Much of the credit for the shift must go to Christopher Howard's 1997 *The Hidden Welfare State*, which examines the use of tax breaks with social welfare aims, such as the Earned Income Tax Credit (EITC) for the working poor.[30] Howard begins his analysis with a startling finding: federal social spending is perhaps 150 percent as large as official spending figures indicate when tax breaks with social welfare aims are included in the tally. Through an analysis of the origins and development of four such tax breaks—the EITC, the targeted jobs tax credit, the special tax treatment of employer-sponsored pensions, and the home mortgage interest deduction—Howard concludes that these measures emerge and evolve quite differently than public social programs. Most notably, in contrast with public programs, they generally emerge with little debate or conflict as part of congressional revenue bills.

Howard's signal contribution was to stress a point that students of public policy know well, but which welfare state scholars had generally overlooked: governments have alternative instruments for achieving their ends. The welfare state literature had, not implausibly, identified spending as the key instrument of social policy. But in the process, it had missed other means by which policymakers could achieve their goals—from regulation to tax breaks, to judicial empowerment, to the use of government credit and insurance. Moreover, these less-studied instruments appeared to be *particularly* characteristic of the American social welfare framework, with its embedded aversion to the robust exercise of visible government power. Thus, for example, law professor Robert Kagan emphasized that the American welfare state was, in fact, unusually *interventionist*—but not in its spending role.[31] It was, rather, America's strong tradition of "adversarial legalism"—the use of courts and legal procedures to adjudicate societal disputes and alter behavior—that defined the distinctive U.S. social policy landscape.[32]

But while Howard and others examined the tools at policymakers' disposal, they had relatively little to say about the vast private-sector field of social welfare, including employer-sponsored benefits and charitable activities, that these tools were often designed to shape. Ironically, then, a line of research designed to showcase the limits of focusing on big government interventions has tended to direct attention back at public leaders and their choice of instruments, rather than to highlight the degree to which many social welfare outcomes are the product of an *interplay* between the goals of political leaders, on the one hand, and the aims of the organizations and actors—from corporations to nonprofits to private individuals—that these leaders hope to influence, on the other.

Recent scholarship, however, has started to highlight this even more "hidden" realm of U.S. social policy. Michael Katz's sweeping new history, *The Price of Citizenship*, for instance, mostly consists of a learned exploration of the standard social welfare concerns.[33] Yet it also devotes a long chapter to the growth and retrenchment of private social benefits in the nonprofit "third sector" and the workplace. Other recent historical works, including Colin Gordon's *Dead on Arrival*, Sanford Jacoby's *Modern Manors*, and Jennifer Klein's *For All These Rights*, place the evolution of private benefits at the center of their story of American welfare-state building, directly challenging the older historical view that these benefits became irrelevant when older forms of "welfare capitalism," increasingly enfeebled, were swept aside by government social programs during the

New Deal.[34] Political scientists, for their part, have been slower to move into the field, perhaps because there is so little secondary historical work to build on. But work by Michael K. Brown, Marie Gottschalk, Beth Stevens, and myself indicates a growing interest in incorporating the role of private social benefits into theories of the welfare state.[35]

In the process, this new scholarship has fundamentally challenged the prevailing verdict on the American welfare state—that it is much smaller that its European counterparts. In my book, *The Divided Welfare State*, I show, to the contrary, that American social welfare spending is at or above the average for comparable advanced industrial democracies when properly measured. "Properly measured," in this case, means adjusting for relative tax burdens and including private employer-provided benefits that are substantially regulated or subsidized by government. Because U.S. tax levels are comparatively low and its private social welfare sector is far and away the largest in the world, these two simple adjustments, as Figures 1 and 2 show, raise U.S. social spending from approximately 17 percent of GDP to nearly 25 percent. The conclusion I reach is that "what is distinctive about U.S. social spending is not the *level* of spending, but the *source*."[36] Building on this finding, Christopher Howard has recently gone even farther, arguing that the "question for future researchers . . . may not be why the U.S. government does relatively little compared to European governments. Rather, the question is why governments of similar size devote comparable resources to pursue similar policy objectives through such a diverse mix of policy tools."[37]

I would not go so far. Whether the policy approaches characteristic of the American social welfare framework really do "pursue similar policy objectives" as those pursued by direct-spending programs abroad is a highly open question, and on the available evidence the answer is no. The United States may spend as much as many European governments when private social benefits and tax policy are taken into account, but the distribution of these benefits is fundamentally different. For one, the *vertical* distribution of benefits—up and down the income ladder—is almost certainly much less favorable toward lower-income citizens. Employment-based benefits are much more prevalent and generous at higher ends of the wage scale, and tax subsidies, because they forgive tax that would otherwise be owed, are generally worth the most to taxpayers in the highest tax brackets. For another, the *horizontal* distribution of benefits across similarly situated workers is also almost certain to be much less equal. Employers decide whether to provide benefits, and there are whole industries and categories of employment where they are quite rare. Overall, only about two-thirds of workers receive health insurance through employment, and fewer than that have a pension plan at work, much less contribute to it.[38] Per-

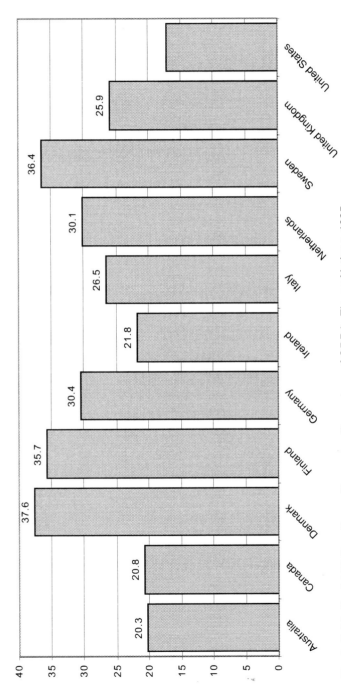

Fig. 1. Public Social Welfare Expenditures as a Percentage of GDP in Eleven Nations, 1995

Source: Calculated from Willem Adema, "Net Social Expenditure," *Labour Market and Social Policy-Occasional Papers No. 39* (Paris: OECD, August 1999), 30.

Notes: Public social welfare expenditures exclude education. They include cash benefits for a wide range of social contingencies—disability, old age, death of a spouse, occupational injuries, disease, sickness, childbirth, unemployment, poverty—as well as spending on housing, health care, services for the elderly and disabled, active labor-market policies, and other similar social benefits.

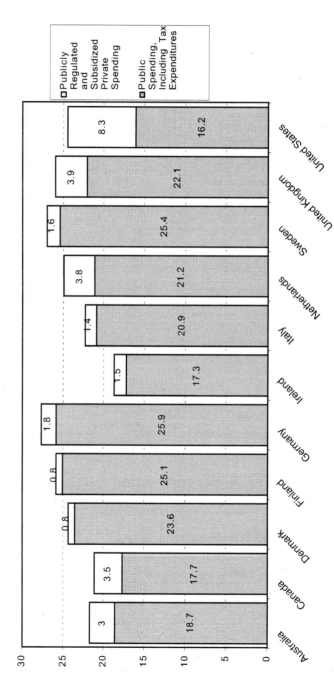

Fig. 2. After-Tax Public and Private Social Welfare Expenditures as a Percentage of GDP in Eleven Nations, 1995

Source: Calculated from Willem Adema, "Net Social Expenditure," *Labour Market and Social Policy-Occasional Papers No. 39* (Paris: OECD, August 1999), 30.

Notes: Private social welfare expenditures are payments for purposes similar to those of public social programs that are made by employers and other nongovernmental organizations, provided that such payments are mandated, subsidized, or regulated by government. To prevent double-counting, tax breaks for private benefits are not included in the public spending estimate.

haps not surprisingly, then, comparative figures on redistribution suggest that taxes and government transfers in the United States reduce inequality significantly less than in any other rich democracy.[39]

Howard's assertion also raises a deeper question: By what standard are we to call the indirect policy tools and government-supported private benefits that are characteristic of American social provision part of that body of state activity conveniently, if often imprecisely, termed the "welfare state"? The scholarship just reviewed makes a strong case for thinking that these distinctive aspects of U.S. social policy should, indeed must, be analyzed in studies of U.S. social policy. But despite frequent use of the evocative (and highly contestable) term "private welfare state" to describe workplace benefits, much of this recent work has surprisingly little to say about why these benefits and tax breaks are on par with the public programs that students of the welfare state usually study. To the extent, moreover, that it simply assumed that the concept of the welfare state can be "stretched" to include all these diverse instruments and policies, then it is not immediately clear why it could not or should not stretch even further—to include almost anything that government does to affect social welfare.[40] Certainly, once the rubric of the welfare states opens up, it cannot be assumed that the generalizations about welfare state development advanced to explain public programs hold equally well in explaining other realms of social provision. Yet why and how indirect policies and private benefits differ from traditional programs—enough that they require new theories and histories, but not so much that they fall outside the bounds of social welfare policy—are questions scholars have only started to explore.

In this respect, the literature on hidden forms of social policy runs into a problem that all of the literature we have reviewed faces: how at once to do justice to the complexities of U.S. social welfare history and provide relatively simplified historical and conceptual accounts that add to our common knowledge. It is fair to say that this is a problem that scholarship on indirect policy tools and private social benefits faces acutely. But failure to advance general claims that can unify disparate research agendas is a notable characteristic of nearly all the scholarship taken up thus far. Ironically, the clearest indication of this difficulty is not the *diversity* of recent scholarship, but the *common* problems into which it runs— confusion of intentions and effects, incomplete investigations of power, lack of comparative leverage, and ahistorical argumentation—problems that I shall argue could be at least partly addressed by thinking more seriously about the dynamics and determinants of over-time processes of policy development.

Intentions and Effects

To write about social welfare policy is to write about why people support and design policies that have specific real-world effects. There are, to be sure, purely symbolic policies that do not change the material world at all, but they are not without effect either. Responding symbolically is responding, and symbolic policies can have very real effects on how people think and act. In every discussion of public policy, therefore, two subjects are at least implicitly under consideration: why a particular course of action (or inaction) was pursued and what effects it had.

Most scholarship on public policy, unfortunately, is interested in only half of this simple equation. Economists and policy analysts, for example, have developed a rich body of theory and evidence concerning the effects of policies on income, wealth, employment, family structure, and so on. But they typically have little or nothing to say about why a policy was adopted in the first place.[41] By contrast, political scientists and other students of public affairs have developed a rich body of theory and evidence concerning the political processes that lead up to the passage of policies, including elections, the formation and expression of public opinion, congressional voting, and interest-group lobbying. But they typically have little or nothing to say about what *effects* a policy has once it is in place. Indeed, while coming at the problem from the completely opposite direction than that followed by economists and policy analysts, they make much the same assumption: that policy effects will flow from political intentions.[42]

Students of policy history are not so bifurcated in their interests. They usually look at the origins and development of important areas of public policy, and in that inherently developmental focus, they have an important comparative advantage. And yet policy historians, too, routinely fall prey to the temptation to conflate intentions and effects. Consider, for instance, the issue already introduced of whether discriminatory policy effects or discriminatory policy intentions are the most relevant evidence of racial or gender bias in social policy. On the one hand, we may emphasize the racist or sexist motives of policymakers, assuming that policies grounded in racist or sexist motives will be racist or sexist in operation. One the other, we may say that public policies are so race- or gender-"laden," because they intersect with elements of society deeply structured by race or gender, that we do not really have to attend to motives. The proof of racism or sexism is in the pudding, so to speak, of outcomes. Neither alternative, however, gets at what is truly important for understanding the role of race or gender in social policymaking: the actual, ongoing relationship between biased motives and biased effects. And, as noted in fact, most work that advances one or the other stance seems to do so less for theoretical reasons than to make a persuasive case for the importance of their favored factor—an effective technique, but one more prosecutorial than scientific.

Or consider the new literature on business power. As already noted, scholars in this tradition often point to the long-term benefits of social policies for sectors of the business community as evidence in favor of the thesis that these favored employers were supportive in the first place. This, however, is a classic non sequitur. It may well be true, but it is not inherently so. Indeed, reading preferences off of results invites an additional analytic error: failure to investigate the extent to which the preferences are in fact a product, rather than a producer, of the policies to which they putatively gave rise.

In short, two barriers stand in the way of the facile equation of policy preferences and outcomes: effects may not reflect preferences, and preferences may flow from policy as well as the other way around. The great virtue of a long-term developmental approach is that, used carefully, it allows us to examine each of these potential relationships and to begin to explain when and why they hold true sometimes and not others.

Perils of Power Analysis

At root, most analyses of U.S. social policy are interested in power. Who set the agenda? Who decided which alternatives to consider? Who won out in debate over these alternatives? Who benefited or lost under the policies finally chosen, or not chosen? These are the classic questions of social welfare history. And most social welfare historians are hardly shy about answering these questions. "The limited development of the American welfare state reflects the weakness of U.S. labor." "The highly decentralized and limited quality of American antipoverty policies is a result of the institutional power of Southern Democrats." "The major social programs of the New Deal were shaped and bounded by the continuing power of business." Statements like these, and debates over their veracity, are the bread and butter of the field.

But that does not mean that we are consistently moving closer to definitive, or even tentatively agreed-upon, answers to such questions. Paradoxically, in fact, the more we know about the history of particular episodes, the less in agreement the field seems to be about who actually won out. Put simply, the problem in many cases is not that we lack sufficient knowledge, but that the frameworks within which we are interpreting this knowledge miss basic problems in the definition and measurement of power.

The most revealing example is the debate over the role of business during the New Deal, which has given rise to perhaps the best historiographic record we have on any important example of American policy formation. Understandably, much of the discussion has focused on fights over particular pieces of legislation. Yet political influence means something far broader than triumph in a "head-to-head" conflict over a particular provision. It means the ability to achieve ends consistent with one's underlying preferences, and that ability is often quite difficult to read off of individual policy fights.

The principal justification for widening our view is the concept of anticipated reactions. All political participants are in a position to calculate (with at least some degree of accuracy) the reactions of other actors. Given this capacity, a group's actions often will not reveal its preferences, but rather its strategic calculations of what is the best that can be accomplished given existing circumstances. An actor's expressed policy preferences may in fact be "induced" or "strategic"–that is, they reflect accommodations to circumstances that constrain what can be achieved. And an actor's capacity to achieve its induced preferences should not necessarily be construed as a sign of great influence.

Consider Figure 3, which depicts the policy preferences of two political actors over a range of policy options stretching from A_0 to B_0. Actor A favors, in decending order, those policies grouped toward the left end of the spectrum, while Actor B favors those at the right end. At any point, however, only a narrow subset of these alternatives is likely to be on the decision agenda. In one context, the conflict may be between options A_1 and A_2, while in another the choice is between options B_1 and B_2. Although the final choice between these two "viable" alternatives is the most visible part of the policymaking process, it is often not the crucial one. Rather, the most significant aspect of influence involves moving the decision-making agenda toward an actor's preferred end of the spectrum. A particular group may get its preferred outcome among those considered at this final stage, but only because it has recognized its weak position and made concessions that allow it to hold off a still-worse alternative. Thus, focusing only on the actual conflict between contending alternatives may give a very misleading impression of relative influence. For example, if Congress chose B_2 over B_1, we would be mistaken to conclude that Actor A has more influence than Actor B, even though Actor A obtained a

Actor A _____ Actor B
Prefers A_0 A_1 A_2 B_2 B_1 B_0 Prefers

Fig. 3. Ranked Policy Preferences of Two Political Actors

preferred outcome within this particular subset. The crucial issue is to determine why the "viable" options were those at the right end of the spectrum, rather than why one of the options broadly favorable to Actor B was finally selected.

For the most part, the debate over the role of business has failed to embrace this fundamental point. The admirable focus on the details of policy development necessarily draws attention to the particular choices made within a narrow range of options, rather than to the question of why only that particular subset was considered feasible. Not surprisingly, this focus also encourages confusion about what the historical record shows. In the fight between relatively narrow alternatives, there will be some victories for each side. Even the lines dividing the "sides" are likely to become ambiguous as different actors within groups take a variety of stances because of uncertainty or because they are situated somewhat differently. In the resulting confusion, both advocates and opponents of the business-power position will find evidence to support their claims.

Recognizing the significance of anticipated reactions makes the study of influence more difficult. The exertion of power often means convincing opponents that they cannot hope to accomplish their true goals, and must instead aim for something less ambitious. We need to determine whether a particular policy stance reflects a genuine preference or reluctant acquiescence in light of a weak political position.[43] We need to focus attention on agenda-setting and the identification of viable alternatives.[44] We need to know why the set of "feasible" initiatives comes to rest at a particular place—and we especially wish to know if this reflects indirect sources of influence. And we need to distinguish preferences from strategic courses of action that actors adopt to get as close as they can to their desired outcomes in a particular context. In all these inquiries, the long-term perspective encouraged by an emphasis on policy development can be invaluable.

Missing Obvious Comparisons

Particularly useful in making judgments about the distribution of influence, as well as about the relation between intentions and effects, are comparisons—comparisons over time, and comparisons across nations or other relevant political units. Policy historians, I have noted, too often overlook the obvious sources of analytic leverage that a long historical view permits. However, comparisons across nations (or across subnational political units, like states) are even less exploited. Much of the scholarship on social policy, to put it bluntly, is remarkably parochial.[45] While often justified by a concern with why the United States did not develop a "Western European-style welfare state," in the language of Margaret Weir,

Ann Orloff, and Theda Skocpol, analysts usually engage with little more than a highly stylized conception of other countries' policies before delving into the specific of the U.S. case.[46] In the process, they often forfeit the chance to refine claims that could be easily examined in the context of other nations' experiences.

The reasons for this are not hard to fathom. The time and energy required to look into even a small aspect of U.S. social policymaking are formidable—which is why, one suspects, so few political scientists spend much time studying policy details. And the American welfare state often looks so exceptional in comparative relief that cross-national investigation seems unproductive or even misguided. The mistake, however, is to think that comparative inquiry necessarily has to involve entire systems of social provision in other nations—or even other nations at all. Rather, the goal should be to draw out the key implications of arguments made about U.S. social policy and then see if they hold in contexts different from the ones in which they were formulated. These alternative contexts can, and often should, be other nations. But they can also be policies at the state level, other national-level policies, and policy episodes at other times. In fact, they can even be hypothetical alternative scenarios—so-called counterfactuals—in which one or more factors deemed casually crucial are altered.[47]

Edwin Amenta's *Bold Relief* displays the benefits of these more limited comparative inquiries.[48] Amenta's thesis is that public-works programs at the national level were stymied by the emergence of a concerted conservative coalition, uniting antigovernment Republicans and southern Democrats intent on protecting the racial hierarchy and low-wage economy of southern states. To test this relatively familiar claim, however, he turns to traditionally untapped comparisons—looking, first, across the Atlantic to contrasting developments in Britain and then, within the United States, across state lines, in a careful comparative investigation of the implementation of work programs in southern and nonsouthern states. Through these internal and "shadow" comparisons, Amenta provides much stronger and richer support for his argument than he could otherwise, and he shows that full-scale cross-national comparative work is not necessary to overcome the well-known limitations of studies of a single nation or policy.

In my own work, I use a similar strategy to explore the effect of private social benefits on the political development of U.S. public social programs.[49] My thesis is that when employer-provided benefits become a core source of social protection for citizens, it is very difficult for government to assume responsibility in this area, both because the demand for government action becomes more muted and divided and because the providers and sponsors of private benefits become formidable opponents of government incursions onto their territory. My principal strategy for testing this claim is to compare policy developments between pension policy, where Social Security emerged before the widespread development of private pension plans, and health policy, where private health insurance covered a majority of Americans before public programs passed. Yet I also undertake more limited comparisons between the United States and Britain and Canada, to show how the particular development of private benefits in these nations did not pose as significant a hurdle to government action as it did in the United States, especially in the context of these nation's more facilitative political institutions.

Because studies of policy development are so deeply historical, scholars of policy history are often dismissed as "mere" storytellers or journalists. Yet it is precisely *because* of their long-term historical perspective that policy historians are uniquely situated to deal with the problems of causal complexity that plague all students of social life. This is so because the long historical view that policy historians typically adopt allows them to see and test relationships that more narrowly focused work too often misses—if, that is, they exploit the full power of their approach.

Failing to Historicize History

Perhaps the most common theme of recent works on the political development of U.S social policy is that contemporary debates have their roots in the past. Yet *why* the past is so important, and its effects so enduring, is much less clear. In some cases, the argument appears to be merely that past conflicts created present policies. In others, it seems deeper: that past policies have given rise to self-reinforcing dynamics that have helped push the American welfare state down highly resilient historical tracks. This does not, of course, exhaust the possibilities. In some cases, the claim is not about endurance but fragility—for example, the relative political *weakness* of the work-oriented focus of the New Deal relief policies highlighted by Amenta. But what is at stake in all these claims is the place of history, if you will, in policy history. Why must we take the long view in analyses of the American welfare state? Why are some policies resilient, while others are not? What explains continuity and change within specific policies? And how do policies reshape political life after they are enacted?

The deepest failure of social welfare history to date is its inability or unwillingness to engage with these seminal issues. This failure is all the more glaring because, in the last decade, mainly because of the pathbreaking scholarship of Harvard political scientists Paul Pierson and Theda Skocpol, a relatively powerful set of generalizations has emerged about the effect of public policies, once implemented, on political dynamics going forward.[50] This notion of "policy feedback" has built upon and furthered a related theoretical enterprise in the social sciences: the exploration of processes of "path dependence" in which early developments structure later ones by giving rise to institutions and dynamics that are inherently difficult to reverse. For the most part, however, policy historians have not engaged with these theoretical currents, and in the rare cases when they are invoked, they are usually treated quite superficially.

As Pierson argues in a 1993 article, the idea that "policies make politics" has a distinguished lineage in political science. Yet much of the writing on the subject, including recent works that use the term, remains extremely vague about *why* and *how* policies remake politics. Pierson's main contribution in his 1993 article was to flesh out the meaning of policy feedback, identifying three main categories of feedback effects: consequences for governing elites, effects on interest groups, and impacts on the mass public. In subsequent writings, Pierson has deepened this framework by linking it to the concept of "path dependence." The long-term feedback effects of policies, he argues, are a powerful example of a so-called path-dependent social process. By pushing policymaking down enduring, self-reinforcing tracks, early policy choices—for example, the creation of a pension system reliant on future workers' contributions to meet its benefit obligations and sustain its finances—can shape what elites consider viable and possible, what interest groups demand (and whether they form at all), and how the public thinks about state activity and responds to competing policy alternatives.[51]

It is no coincidence that Pierson formulated his argument in the context of his work on welfare state retrenchment, *Dismantling the Welfare State*, for social welfare policies are probably among the most likely to produce long-term feedback effects.[52] As I argue in *The Divided Welfare State*, social policies generally entail the creation of large-scale institutions with substantial set-up costs, benefit sizable and resourceful organized groups of citizens, and create long-lived expectations on which individuals premise crucial life and organizational decisions—each factors that increase the chance that early policy choices will be consequential down the line. Importantly, however, not only government programs share these characteristics. Many private social benefits, such as employer-provided pensions and health insurance, have similar features. In fact, because these benefits are generally less visible and their development in response to subsidy and regulatory policies harder to predict, they are in some respects more prone to path dependence. Early choices taken with little foresight or in pursuit of goals quite different from those eventually achieved can create powerful organizations and vested interests that subsequently become important players on the political landscape.[53]

Not all social policies share these features, of course. Social Security pensions, for example, have promoted widespread mobilization among the aged, who are well poised to fight cuts. Their generosity, lack of stigma, visibility, and receipt by a large and easily identifiable group—all, as Andrea Campbell has argued in a recent important book, have encouraged the formation of an extremely powerful support coalition poised to protect and enlarge the program.[54] Cash assistance for the poor, in contrast, has given rise to an extremely weak, fragmented, and politically demobilized constituency, which was unable to present an effective and united front against the 1996 welfare-reform law.[55] Antipoverty benefits are ungenerous, they carry significant stigma, and they are received by a fluctuating population of citizens who, in general, have meager political capacity. Little wonder, then, that the main barrier to the alteration of welfare benefits has not been resistance from beneficiaries but lack of agreement among would-be reformers.[56]

A common criticism leveled against path-dependence claims is that they are overly static. Yet the concept presents a vision that is far from static. Rather, the crux of the claim is that path-dependent processes make some courses of action more likely and others less likely. Options that were once feasible no longer are, but other options may well *emerge* as a result of past policy choices. Indeed, the next frontier for research on policy feedback and path dependence is to specify more precisely when policies are highly resilient to change and when they are not, and in what ways previous policies will influence future policy choices when policies are in fact open to revision.

Happily, this appears to be the direction in which institutionally minded political scientists are heading. Pierson, for example, has written a new book, *Politics in Time*, that lays out his own arguments about how path dependence creates change as well as continuity.[57] Kathleen Thelen and Eric Schickler, in very different ways, have pushed forward the study of institutional development by tracing the evolution of German labor-market institutions and the U.S. Congress, respectively.[58] In my own recent writings, I have argued for a fourfold model of policy change that builds on the work of these authors.[59] Once policies with strong support coalitions are in place, I argue, "big bangs" of policy reform or replacement are rare, requiring as they do a consolidation of political power that most nation's political institutions, but particularly the United States's, make difficult. Nonetheless, even without epochal transformations, social policies may change markedly through three less studied processes, as outlined in Figure 4. The first is what Thelen calls "conversion"—the internal transformation of policies without formal policy change. In programs run by private organizations or front-line caseworkers, there are numerous opportunities to reorient programs without going through the

Barriers to Internal Policy Conversion

	High (Low levels of policy discretion, strong policy support coalitions)	Low (High levels of discretion, weak support coalitions)
High (Many veto players)	**Drift** (Transformation of stable policy due to changing circumstances) Illustrative Example: Erosion of Scope of Protection of Existing Public Social Programs and Private Benefits	**Conversion** (Internal adaptation of existing policy) Illustrative Example: Employers' Restructuring of Publicly Subsidized Voluntary Workplace Benefits
Low (Few veto players)	**Layering** (Creation of new policy without elimination of old) Illustrative Example: Creation and Expansion of Tax Subsidies for Private Retirement Accounts	**Revision** (Formal reform, replacement, or elimination of existing policy) Illustrative Example: 1996 Welfare Reform

Left axis label: Barriers to Authoritative Policy Change

Fig. 4. Four Modes of Policy Change

normal legislative process, and many of the most consequential changes in U.S. social policy over the past two decades—such cutbacks in anti-poverty benefits and the decline and restructuring of tax-subsidized work-place benefits—have occurred through such conversion processes.

The second process of change that occurs without formal transformation of the existing program is what Schickler terms "layering," the creation of new policies that can alter the operation of older policies. "Layering" requires legislative action, but it does not require dismantling older programs—a far more difficult prospect. Thus, for example, conservative critics of Social Security have been consistently rebuffed in their effort to scale back the program significantly, but they have succeeded handsomely at capitalizing on periods of conservative ascendance to enact new policies encouraging highly individualized tax-subsidized retirement accounts, like 401(k) pension plans.

The third process of change is perhaps the least recognized, and often the most important—what I call "drift" within the bounds of formally stable policies. Drift occurs when changes in the environment of policies make them less capable of achieving their initial goals, but the policies are not updated, either because the gap between goals and reality is not recognized or, more interesting still, is recognized, but there is active opposition to the updating of policies to reflect their context.[60] In the past three decades, the employment market and structure of families have changed dramatically. Yet most of the American welfare state has not. The result is a growing gulf between the new social risks that citizens face and the existing framework of social benefits on which they depend. This gulf is no accident: Opponents of the welfare state have faced great difficulties in cutting it back. But they have proved extremely capable of blocking the updating of social policies to reflect changing social realities—as they did, for example, when they decisively defeated President Clinton's ill-fated 1993 health plan.[61]

Although the issue of institutional development is moving to the center of the debate in political science, it is certainly premature to declare that robust generalizations about processes of institutional change are destined to sift into studies of policy history, much less that generating arguments of this sort will become a primary concern of social welfare historians. Yet for social policy historians to ignore these emerging issues would be to pass up a tremendous opportunity not only to learn from work in other fields but also to inform it, as well as to develop a set of explanatory tools that could create greater cohesion and clarity in a field that, for all its richness and depth, still needs both.

The Promise of a Policy-Development Approach

Once, the story of American welfare-state building was clear and agreed upon. The United States scarcely had a welfare state at all. The social policies enacted in many European nations had foundered on the shoals of America's antigovernment heritage. And what programs had emerged were the product of two great spasms of twentieth-century liberal achievement: the New Deal and the Great Society—the first of which challenged the privileged position of business in the American political economy; the second of which attacked the structures of hierarchy that had subjugated women and blacks, denying them an equal place in American civic and social life.

The last decade of research has upended this traditional master narrative. The racially biased aspects of the welfare state did not just vanish; they remain part and parcel of the language, and the dilemmas, of the welfare state today. Women were not just subjects of the welfare state; they helped construct it, and in distinctive ways. Business was not always monolithically opposed to social programs. Plenty of welfare-state building was done during the calm eddies of social welfare history—before, after, and between the big bangs. And antigovernment values were never as fixed or as determinative as once suggested. A "weak" state sometimes made "strong" policies. Above all, it made policies that were not simply a pale imitation of European experience but often were singularly distinctive in their justification, structure, and effects.

Yet while the traditional linear story of hampered yet inexorable progress is no longer tenable, we should not pretend that the loss of that larger narrative has come without cost. In this case, the cost has been a fragmentation of the field, a proliferation of nonintersecting claims, and an eschewal of the broader perspective that once cast the welfare state as a window into bigger scholarly questions and vaster historical tides.

Just as widely distributed social policies always resist undoing, there can be no going back to the less complicated social welfare history of the past. Nor should we. As the scholarship reviewed in this article shows, the gains in knowledge are breathtaking. The study of the American welfare state is now among the most vibrant, broad-ranging, sophisticated, and engaging areas of history and political science—and one in which an unusually diverse range of disciplines and perspectives inform one another. But in any field, there are times for pushing forward in multiple directions regardless of the resulting fragmentation, and there are times for bringing together the insights thus won to construct a more compelling overall picture. The contention of this article is that we have reached the second of these times, and serious effort should be made to integrate the fruits of the multipronged, creative, and amazingly productive research endeavors of the last decade.

Where should such an effort begin? At the beginning, so to speak—with the foundational issue of what the American welfare state looks like and why. In responding to this enduring puzzle, four insights of recent scholarship will need to be front and center: the pivotal role of the United States's fragmented and decentralized political institutions, the special character and place of race in American social life, the heavy U.S. reliance on hidden or indirect policy tools, and the distinctive prominence of business in the making (and perhaps unmaking) of the American welfare state. Our aim, in bringing these insights to bear, should be to move beyond black-and-white portraits of state weakness or state strength. Scholars should seek to uncover the fault lines in even the strongest exercises of state power and the hidden wellsprings of power in even the seemingly weakest policy interventions. The goal should also be to move beyond the focus on "leading" policy issues and debates—those prominent moments of contention and change about which so much is written.[62] Instead, scholars should trace the unfolding historical development of specific policies across long periods of attention and inattention, action and inaction. And finally, in doing so, the aspiration should be to construct general claims about U.S. social policymaking that are formulated and examined in the context of explicit comparisons across time and space, whether the comparative contrast be other nations, other policies, other times, or all three.

In all this, our eyes should remain fixed on the ultimate goal: to understand not merely the details of social welfare policies, but what they do—to and for citizens and to and for polities and societies. The welfare state expresses, at root, a sense of solidarity, a belief in shared fate. At this moment, when our fates seem shared more in fear than in hope, the link between policies and the collective commitments that they reflect and nurture is as vital a subject for American politics and society as it is for policy historians.

Yale University

Notes

1. Alice Kessler-Harris, *In Pursuit of Equity: Women, Men, and the Quest for Economic Citizenship in 20th-Century America* (Oxford, 2001); Michael B. Katz, *The Price of Citizenship: Redefining the American Welfare State* (New York, 2001); Robert Lieberman, *Shifting the Color Line* (Cambridge, Mass., 1998); Peter Swenson, *Capitalists Against Markets: The Making of Labor Markets and Welfare States in the United States and Sweden* (New York, 2002).

2. Paul Pierson, *Dismantling the Welfare State? Reagan, Thatcher, and the Politics of Retrenchment* (New York, 1994); Theda Skocpol, *Protecting Soldiers and Mothers: The Political Origins of Social Policy in the United States* (Cambridge, Mass., 1992).

3. Edward D. Berkowitz, *America's Welfare State: From Roosevelt to Reagan* (Baltimore, 1991), xi.

4. Gøsta Esping-Andersen, *The Three Worlds of Welfare Capitalism* (Princeton, 1990).

5. Gunnar Myrdal, *An American Dilemma* (New York, 1944).

6. Lieberman, *Shifting the Color Line*; Jill S. Quadagno, *The Color of Welfare: How Racism Undermined the War on Poverty* (New York, 1994); Linda Faye Williams, *The Constraint of Race: Legacies of White Skin Privilege in America* (University Park, Pa., 2003); Gareth Davies and Martha Derthick, "Race and Social Welfare Policy: The Social Security Act of 1935," *Political Science Quarterly* 112, no. 2 (1997); Michael K. Brown, *Race, Money, and the American Welfare State* (Ithaca, 1999).

7. Brown, *Race, Money, and the American Welfare State*, 3.

8. Martin Gilens, *Why Americans Hate Welfare: Race, Media, and the Politics of Antipoverty Policy* (Chicago, 1999).

9. Davies and Derthick, "Race and Social Welfare Policy: The Social Security Act of 1935."

10. Lieberman, *Shifting the Color Line*.

11. Esping-Andersen, *The Three Worlds of Welfare Capitalism*.

12. See, for example, Gwendolyn Mink, *The Wages of Motherhood: Inequality in the Welfare State, 1917–1942* (Ithaca, 1995); Kessler-Harris, *In Pursuit of Equity*; Linda Gordon, *Pitied but Not Entitled: Single Mothers and the History of Welfare, 1890–1935* (New York, 1994); Skocpol, *Protecting Soldiers and Mothers*; Suzanne B. Mettler, *Dividing Citizens: Gender and Federalism in New Deal Public Policy* (Ithaca, 1998).

13. Skocpol, *Protecting Soldiers and Mothers*.

14. Linda Gordon, ed., *Women, the State, and Welfare* (Madison, 1990).

15. Kessler-Harris, *In Pursuit of Equity*; Mettler, *Dividing Citizens*; Mink, *The Wages of Motherhood*.

16. See Ann Shola Orloff, "Gender and the Social Rights Citizenship: The Comparative Analysis of Gender Relations and Welfare States," *American Sociological Review*

58 (1993); Dorothy McBride Stetson and Amy G. Mazur, eds., *Comparative State Feminism* (Thousand Oaks, Calif., 1995).

17. Joe Soss and Suzanne Mettler, "Beyond Representation: Policy Feedback and the Political Roots of Citizenship," paper presented at the Annual Meeting of the Midwest Political Science Association, Chicago, 2003.

18. See, in particular, Isabela Mares, *The Politics of Social Risk: Business and Welfare State Development* (New York, 2003); Colin Gordon, *New Deals: Business, Labor, and Politics in America, 1920–1935* (Cambridge, 1994); idem, *Dead on Arrival: The Politics of Health Care in Twentieth-Century America* (Princeton, 2003); Cathie Jo Martin, *Stuck in Neutral: Business and the Politics of Human Capital Investment Policy* (Princeton, 2000); Swenson, *Capitalists Against Markets;* Sanford M. Jacoby, *Modern Manors: Welfare Capitalism Since the New Deal* (Princeton, 1997). An important spur for much of this work is an emerging literature on "varieties of capitalism." This work argues that capitalism comes in at least two alternative forms: it may be oriented around the short-term, hyper-competitive, and based on arms-length contracts (the American, or "liberal market economy," model), or it may be long-term, consensual, and based on interlocking financial and social ties (the Continental European, "coordinated market economy," model). And while social welfare policies that strengthen workers' autonomy and power might interfere with the normal competitive market in the first model, they may be highly market-enhancing in the latter. For example, in an economy based on high skills and wages, protecting workers against the risk of occupational displacement encourages workers to invest in skills that are very specific to an industry or firm—skills they would otherwise fear investing in, because of their lack of transferability from job to job. Peter A. Hall and David Soskice, eds., *Varieties of Capitalism: The Institutional Foundation of Comparative Advantage* (New York, 2001); Torben Iversen and David Soskice, "An Asset Theory of Social Policy Preferences," *American Political Science Review* 95, no. 4 (2001).

19. The main exponent of this view is Peter Swenson, whose work I will discuss shortly.

20. Mares, *The Politics of Social Risk*; Gordon, *New Deals* and *Dead on Arrival*.

21. It might be supposed that this is the same as saying that social policies are economically beneficial; yet it is not. Many policies that are good for economic growth have no organized defenders. Moreover, the fact that certain policies benefit business leaves open the critical *historical* question of whether capitalists were behind their creation. The powerful, and controversial, claim of the new business-power literature is that capitalists have a first-choice preference for key social programs *before* they are enacted.

22. Swenson, *Capitalists Against Markets*, 194.

23. On the distinction between structural and instrumental power, see Charles E. Lindblom, "The Market as Prison," *Journal of Politics* 44, no. 2 (1982); Jacob S. Hacker and Paul Pierson, "Business Power and Social Policy: Employers and the Formation of the American Welfare State," *Politics and Society* 30, no. 2 (2002).

24. Swenson, *Capitalists Against Markets*, 191–220.

25. G. William Domhoff, *Who Rules America?* (Englewood Cliffs, N.J., 1967); Gabriel Kolko, *The Triumph of Conservatism* (New York, 1977).

26. On the limits of a historical "snapshot" rather than a "moving picture," see Paul Pierson, *Politics in Time* (Princeton, 2004).

27. On the power conferred on business by America's decentralized federalism before the New Deal, see David Brian Robertson, "The Bias of American Federalism: The Limits of Welfare State Development in the Progressive Era," *Journal of Policy History* 1, no. 3 (1989). The argument about the decline in business power during the New Deal is elaborated in Hacker and Pierson, "Business Power and Social Policy."

28. The term is from Jacob S. Hacker, *The Divided Welfare State: The Battle over Public and Private Social Benefits in the United States* (Cambridge, 2002).

29. Richard M. Titmuss, *Essays on "the Welfare State,"* 3d ed. (London, 1976).

30. Christopher Howard, *The Hidden Welfare State: Tax Expenditures and Social Policy in the United States* (Princeton, 1997).

31. Robert A. Kagan, *Adversarial Legalism: The American Way of Law* (Cambridge, Mass., 2001).

32. Ibid. See also Thomas F. Burke, *Lawyers, Lawsuits, and Legal Rights: The Battle over Litigation in American Society* (Berkeley and Los Angeles, 2002).
33. Katz, *The Price of Citizenship.*
34. Gordon, *Dead on Arrival;* Jacoby, *Modern Manors;* Jennifer L. Klein, *For All These Rights: Business, Labor, and the Shaping of America's Public-Private Welfare State* (Princeton, 2003). For the more traditional narrative, see Stuart D. Brandes, *American Welfare Capitalism, 1880–1940* (Chicago, 1970).
35. Michael K. Brown, "Bargaining for Social Rights: Unions and the Reemergence of Welfare Capitalism, 1945–1952," *Political Science Quarterly* 112, no. 4 (1997–98); Marie Gottschalk, *The Shadow Welfare State: Labor, Business, and the Politics of Welfare in the United States* (Ithaca, 2000); Hacker, *The Divided Welfare State;* Beth Stevens, "Labor Unions, Employee Benefits, and the Privatization of the American Welfare State," *Journal of Policy History* 2, no. 3 (1990).
36. Hacker, *The Divided Welfare State,* 7.
37. Christopher Howard, "Is the American Welfare State Unusually Small?" *PS: Political Science and Politics* 36, no. 3 (2003): 415.
38. Hacker, *The Divided Welfare State,* 36–38.
39. Jacob S. Hacker, "Privatizing Risk without Privatizing the Welfare State: The Hidden Politics of Social Policy Retrenchment in the United States," *American Political Science Review* 98, no. 2 (2004): 251.
40. On the obstacles to scholarly progress that conceptual disagreement creates, see Paul Pierson, "Coping with Permanent Austerity: Welfare State Restructuring in Affluent Democracies," in *New Politics of the Welfare State,* ed. Paul Pierson (New York, 2001), 421.
41. At the extreme, they simply assume that the effects *are* the motives, as summed up in the influential statement of the economist George Stigler that the "announced goals of a policy are sometimes unrelated or perversely related to its actual effects, and the *truly intended effects should be deduced from the actual effects.*" George J. Stigler, *The Citizen and the State* (Chicago, 1975), 140.
42. This argument is elaborated in Paul Pierson, "The Limits of Design: Explaining Institutional Origins and Change," *Governance: An International Journal of Policy and Administration* 13, no. 4 (2000). To be sure, political scientists have long recognized the "law of unintended consequences." But it is fair to say that they have shown little inclination to come up with systematic arguments about when and why we should expect unanticipated effects. Nonetheless, based on what we know about political action, it is possible to identify at least two critical factors that are likely to influence the probability of unforeseen consequences. First, unintended effects are most likely when policies are highly complex—interacting with many different dimensions of society simultaneously—for in these circumstances the limits of humans' ability to calculate multiple and interactive effects and the possibility of emergent "system effects" loom large. Robert Jervis, "Complexity and the Analysis of Political and Social Life," *Political Science Quarterly* 112, no. 4 (1997–98). Second, unintended effects are more likely to the extent that policymakers are focused on the near-term future (to use economics lingo, their "time horizons" are short), for in these circumstances actors are likely to pay little attention to the potential long-term or interactive elements of their policies. Needless to say, social welfare policies are often characterized by the first feature, and in many cases, especially when passed to respond to pressing social needs, the second as well.
43. One of the benefits of a substantial and intensively investigated archival record is that it makes it possible to trace the strategic behavior of actors over time. In many cases, one can actually document private acknowledgments that public positions represent a strategic accommodation to political realities.
44. John W. Kingdon, *Agendas, Alternatives, and Public Policies,* 2d ed. (New York, 1995); Frank R. Baumgartner and Bryan D. Jones, *Agendas and Instability in American Politics* (Chicago, 1993).
45. A case in point is Derthick's brilliant and highly influential study of the development of Social Security in the United States. Derthick's argument is that the advocacy

role of administrators and the closed circle of participation in the program's development are the prime reasons for its explosive growth. Yet she does not test her argument against the development of social insurance programs in other nations—which would show that the expansionary tendencies of the American system were scarcely unique and suggest that broader social forces were at least as powerful spurs to expansion as the specific characteristics of the American policymaking environment. Martha Derthick, *Policymaking for Social Security* (Washington, D.C., 1979).

46. Margaret Weir, Ann Shola Orloff, and Theda Skocpol, "Introduction: Understanding American Social Policies," in *The Politics of Social Policy in the United States* (Princeton, 1988), 9.

47. The logic of counterfactuals, and its relation to historical and cross-national comparison, is discussed further in Jacob S. Hacker, "Learning from Defeat? Political Analysis and the Failure of Health Care Reform in the United States," *British Journal of Political Science* 30 (2000). See also James D. Fearon, "Couterfactuals and Hypothesis Testing in Political Sciences," *World Politics* 43, no. 2 (1991).

48. Edwin Amenta, *Bold Relief: Institutional Politics and the Origins of Modern American Social Policy* (Princeton, 1998); Edwin Amenta, "Making the Most of a Case Study: Theories of the Welfare State and the American Experience," *International Journal of Comparative Sociology* 32, no. 1–2 (1991).

49. Hacker, *The Divided Welfare State.*

50. Skocpol, *Protecting Soldiers and Mothers;* Pierson, *Dismantling the Welfare State?;* Paul Pierson, "When Effect Becomes Cause: Policy Feedback and Political Change," *World Politics* 45, no. 4 (1993); idem, "Increasing Returns, Path Dependence, and the Study of Politics," *American Political Science Review* 94, no. 2 (2000).

51. Pierson, "When Effect Becomes Cause: Policy Feedback and Political Change"; idem, "Not Just What, but *When:* Timing and Sequence in Political Processes," *Studies in American Political Development* 14, no. 1 (2000).

52. Pierson, *Dismantling the Welfare State?*

53. Hacker, *The Divided Welfare State,* 52–58.

54. Andrea Louise Campbell, *How Policies Make Citizens: Senior Political Activism and the American Welfare State* (Princeton, 2003).

55. R. Kent Weaver, *Ending Welfare as We Know It* (Washington, D.C., 2000); Joe Soss, "Lessons of Welfare: Policy Design, Political Learning, and Political Action," *American Political Science Review* 93, no. 2 (1999).

56. Steven M. Teles, *Whose Welfare? AFDC and Elite Politics* (Lawrence, Kan., 1996).

57. Pierson, *Politics in Time.*

58. Kathleen Thelen, "Historical Institutionalism in Comparative Politics," *Annual Review of Political Science* 2 (1999); Eric Schickler, *Disjointed Pluralism: Institutional Innovation in the U.S. Congress* (Princeton, 2001).

59. Hacker, "Privatizing Risk without Privatizing the Welfare State."

60. Of course, drift can and does run in the opposite direction—that is, toward expansion. The proliferating use of disability insurance as a means of early retirement in Europe is a powerful contemporary example.

61. Jacob S. Hacker, *The Road to Nowhere: The Genesis of President Clinton's Plan for Health Security* (Princeton, 1997); Theda Skocpol, *Boomerang: Clinton's Health Security Effort and the Turn against Government in U.S. Politics* (New York, 1996).

62. As Derthick writes, in a statement as true today as when she penned it, "Much of the scholarly literature that analyzes policymaking focused on 'leading' or controversial cases—moments of crisis or innovation that are intrinsically interesting and undoubtedly important, but not in themselves typical. Policymaking is a compound of exciting innovative events . . . and not-so-exciting routines that are performed without much widespread mobilization, intense conflict, or much awareness of what is going on except among the involved few." Derthick, *Policymaking for Social Security,* 9.

Contributors

PETER BALDWIN is Professor of History at the University of California, Los Angeles. He is author of *The Politics of Social Solidarity: Class Bases of the European Welfare State, 1875–1975* (1990), *Contagion and the State in Europe, 1830–1930* (1999), and *Democracy and Disease: The State Faces AIDS in the West* (2005).

EILEEN BORIS is the Hull Professor of Women's Studies and Director of the Center for Research on Women and Social Justice at the University of California, Santa Barbara. She is working on a book, tentatively titled, *Citizens at Work, Bodies on the Job: Gender, Race, and Rights in Modern America*, and beginning a project on the politics of home care.

JACOB S. HACKER is Peter Strauss Family Assistant Professor of Political Science at Yale University. His articles have appeared in the *American Political Science Review; British Journal of Political Science; Politics and Society; Studies in American Political Development;* and the *Journal of Health Politics, Policy and Law.* He is also the author of two books: *The Divided Welfare State: The Battle over Public and Private Social Benefits in the United States* (2002) and *The Road to Nowhere: The Genesis of President Clinton's Plan for Health Security* (1997). He is currently writing a book, with Paul Pierson, on the Bush tax cuts, as well as a book on the politics of economic insecurity in the United States.

ROBERT J. MCMAHON is Professor of History at the University of Florida and past president of the Society for Historians of American Foreign Relations. His most recent books are *Limits of Empire: The United States and Southeast Asia Since World War II* (1999) and the *Cold War: A Very Short Introduction* (2003).

PAUL PIERSON is former Harold Hitchings Burbank Professor of Political Economy at Harvard University. He now teaches at the University of California at Berkeley. His main teaching and research interests are American politics, comparative public policy, and social theory. He is the author of *Dismantling the Welfare State? Reagan, Thatcher, and the Politics of Retrenchment and Politics in Time: History, Institutions, and Social Analysis.*

JILL QUADAGNO is Professor of Sociology at Florida State University, where she holds the Mildred and Claude Pepper Eminent Scholar Chair in Social Gerontology. She is past-president of the American Sociological Association and is the author of twelve books and more than fifty articles on aging and social policy issues. Her most recent book, *One Nation, Uninsured: Why the U.S. Has No National Health Insurance*, will be published in 2005 by Oxford University Press. She is also conducting research on long-term care in Florida.

REUEL SCHILLER teaches legal history and administrative law at the University of California, Hastings College of Law. He is currently completing a book-length study of the legal history of the administrative state in twentieth-century America.

DEBRA STREET is Assistant Professor of Sociology at the State University of New York at Buffalo. Her published work focuses on the politics of health and pension policies, including a book she co-edited with Jay Ginn and Sara Arber, *Women, Work, and Pensions: International Issues and Prospects*. Her current research focuses on long-term care policies and the intersection of private and public social welfare.

JULIAN E. ZELIZER is Professor of History at Boston University. Zelizer's works include *Taxing America: Wilbur D. Mills, Congress, and the State, 1945–1975* (1998; winner of the 1998 D. B. Hardeman Prize and the 2000 Ellis Hawley Prize), and *On Capitol Hill: The Struggle to Reform Congress and Its Consequences* (2004). He is the co-editor of *The Democratic Experiment: New Directions in American Political History* (2003) and *The American Congress: The Building of Democracy* (2004). Zelizer has also published pieces in the *New York Times*, the *Boston Globe*, the *Los Angeles Times*, and the *Albany Times Union*.